THAMES HAVEN
RAILWAY

Essex Branch Line and London Shipping Link 1835 - 1996

also covering the industries of Shell Haven

by
Peter Kay

To the memory of Henry Amsinck

INTRODUCTION & ACKNOWLEDGEMENTS

Now that the history of the LT&S line at large has been taken through to 1912 in *The London Tilbury & Southend Railway, A History of the Company and Line* Volumes 1 and 2, we can appropriately turn to consider in more detail the LT&SR's one and only 'constituent' company, the Thames Haven Dock and Railway Company, which was mentioned briefly in Vol. 1 but about which much more remains to be said. As the development and traffics of the Thames Haven branch have generally been very different throughout from those of the rest of the LT&S system, this volume is written as a full account of the branch's history from promotion through to the 1990s.

The Thames Haven line is perhaps the least-known public railway in the eastern counties. Probably regarded by many as a mere glorified oil siding of latterday growth, it actually goes back to the very dawn of railway promotion in the region, the company's Act being obtained in the same year (1836) as the Eastern Counties and the London & Blackwall. It was a 'first generation' railway in every way; the brainchild of a man who spent his career in the navy against Napoleon, it was wholly shipping-related in its intended purposes, meant to serve as London's fish and coal supply route and for taking passengers to Kent. The real perceptiveness of the THD&R Co's promoters was in noticing the site's suitability for deepwater wharfage if a rail link from London were provided. The line's eventual success came from a product, oil, that had yet to be discovered at the time of its promotion, and, perversely, from the fact that it was situated so far from any human habitation, the very type of site that the oilmen were looking for. Again, the real 'boom' enjoyed by the branch in the 1950s-1980s period was essentially the result of the rise of road transport which was having such negative impacts on the rest of the British railway system. In 1842 the THD&R Co was mocked for its claims that the line would produce a larger dividend 'than any other railway in the Kingdom'; if it had still been an independent company in the 1960s this seemingly-laughable prophecy could perhaps have been proved correct. In 1999 however the oil industry here is in decline, and it would be a rash gambler who placed any money on what the next century will hold for such a line!

The railway history of South Essex at large cannot be understood without knowledge of the THD&R Co and its politics in the 1830s-1850s period. It had much influence on what did eventually come to pass, and nearly succeeded in getting the railway map of the area laid out in a wholly different fashion. To many it was not so much odd that it took 20 years to build the line, as an amazing surprise that it (or part of it) ever actually got built at all - for the company had often been written off as one of those schemes destined never to come to pass. As with many companies long in the gestation, it has to be admitted that the events of those 20 years, including repeated failed politickings and reversions to the status quo, do not necessarily make easy or exciting food for the present day reader, so far as Chapters 1-3 are concerned. Indeed many felt at the time that the tale of the THD&R Co had become so repetitive and tedious that it would be better if it would just disappear altogether! The more arcane matters have been relegated to footnotes here.

The records of the THD&R Co do not survive (save for the prospectuses) and the account of the 1830s-1850s period is therefore mainly derived from the contemporary press, the ECR, L&BR, and LT&S minutes, and miscellaneous surviving documents. Although some points remain a little obscure, there are no major questions unexplained. It has to be noted, though, that many of the contemporary sources are very prejudiced (mostly against) and many a lie is mixed in with the facts.

'Acknowledgements' for the LT&S research generally have already been given at Vol. 1 page 3, but in relation to the research for this volume in particular thanks are due to :-
Randal Bingley (local historian of Thurrock and Fobbing)
Arthur Rees (Shell Pensioners Association)
Stephen Duffell (cattle importing)
Godfrey Croughton / Brian Pask / Ken Butcher (workmen's service)
Paul Armstrong / Steve Gwinnett (1990s developments)

Photographs of the branch are even more elusive than for the LT&S line generally; indeed, no pre-1920s photographs are known at all (hence there is nothing of the old piers at Thames Haven or the shipping activity there). It was effectively a place that no photographer had means of getting to. Even for the 1950s it has only proved possible to illustrate this work because of the visits made on several occasions by Frank Church. The photographs included here are what exists and any question of 'balance' is academic.

The work has been written in such a way that it can be understood by those who do not have copies of Vols 1 and 2, however to avoid annoyance to those who do, matters relating to the LT&SR at large (in particular re the 1846-1855 period) have been summarised as briefly as possible here, and reference should be made to Vols 1 and 2 as necessary for a fuller account.

Peter Kay   Teignmouth, January 1999

Shellhaven House and its farm remained undisturbed still in the interwar years, and this 1920s view, looking northwest up Shellhaven Creek at high tide, therefore provides an idea of what the whole vicinity looked like in the 1830s. The vulnerability of the old river walls is evident. Parts of the Cory's (ex Kynoch's) works are seen at left distance.
(Southend Museums Service, Padgett Collection)

CONTENTS

Shell No. 19 was new from John Fowler in 1949 and is seen here resting at Dock House level crossing in July 1952. It carries the then 'Shell Refining & Marketing Co. Ltd' name, and has the original exhaust. For a later view of this loco see Chapter 7.
(Frank Church)

THAMES HAVEN DOCK & RAILWAY.

FUMUM ET OPES.

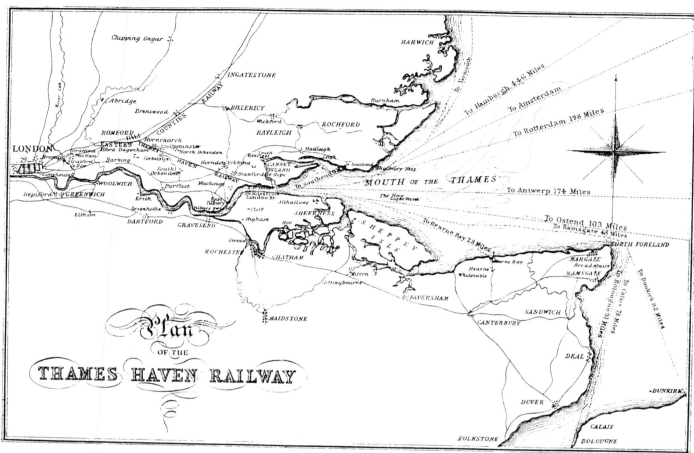

Plan OF THE THAMES HAVEN RAILWAY

To Hamburgh 446 Miles
To Amsterdam
To Rotterdam 178 Miles
To Antwerp 174 Miles
To Ostend 103 Miles
To Ramsgate 48 Miles
To Calais 76 Miles
To Boulogne 91 Miles
To Dunkirk 82 Miles

MOUTH OF THE THAMES

To Hearne Bay 28 Miles

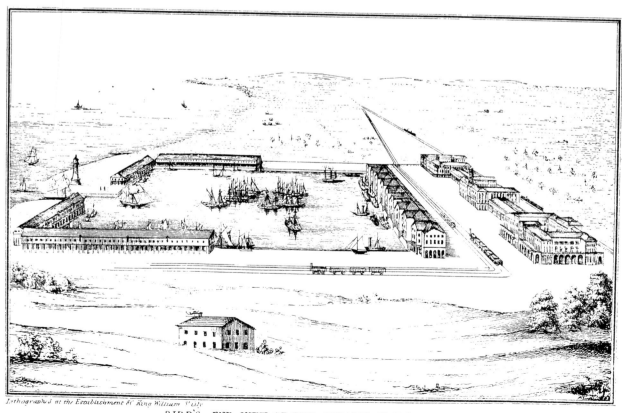

BIRD'S EYE VIEW OF THE THAMES HAVEN DOCK.

THE TIDE DOCK is proposed as a general Harbour but particularly for Steam boats & Fishing Vessels with 15 Feet Water Low Water Spring Tide

It will be one thousand feet long & eight hundred feet broad, or an area of eighteen Acres

CHAPTER ONE

BRIGHT THE VISION.........THE PROMOTION OF THE THAMES HAVEN DOCK AND RAILWAY COMPANY (1835-1839)

LIEUTENANT AMSINCK'S VISION

Although not opened until 1855, the Thames Haven Railway was very much a 'first generation' railway - a fact highlighted by the spelling 'Rail-Way' on the original prospectuses. It was a child of the 'Little Mania', conceived in 1835 and getting its Act in 1836 alongside the Eastern Counties and the London & Blackwall (with which two companies its history was to be inextricably linked). Unlike most 1830s schemes, however, it was not put together by any Committee of leading local trading interests wanting a railway link to London - there was nothing at 'Thames Haven' but empty marshes, and nowhere much intermediately on the line either, so 'local interests' hardly existed. The Thames Haven was rather the vision of one man, Henry Amsinck, a half-pay naval officer, and he seems to have evolved it, *ex nihilo*, in 1835 (1). In 1843 he was, not unreasonably, described as 'the Alpha and Omega of the project'. This in many ways was to be the weakness of the scheme, as there was never any solid group of supporters with a real interest in it to back up Amsinck. But in 1835 railway promotion was on the up, and anything seemed possible.

Amsinck - the name is of Dutch origins - was born in September 1799 in Chiswick, son of Thomas Amsinck. He entered the Navy, at the age of 12, in September 1811, as a 'First Class Volunteer', becoming Midshipman in 1812. He served on eight different ships 'on the home station', notably on the *Northumberland* 1816-1822; then in 1822-4 he was with the *Owen Glendower* and the *Bann* off the African coast (2). January 1824 saw promotion to Lieutenant but his active career came to an end (except for a couple of months on Coastguard duties in 1832/3) in May 1824 at the age of 24, whereupon he returned to England to join the ranks of 'half-pay' officers, who needed to find other posts to keep their minds occupied and their income satisfactory for a gentlemanly life. In 1827 he married Charlotte Elizabeth, daughter of the Rev. George Wilson of Kirby Hall, Norfolk; they seem to have lived in London (3) but what he devoted himself to in the 1824-1835 period is nowhere referred to. The Thames Haven scheme must then have taken up much of his time in 1835-8 in particular; he was Secretary of the company from the start until 1843.

Amsinck's dedication to the cause of the Thames Haven was to result in his being mocked as a wild dreamer by detractors, and indeed his own counsel in a libel case had to admit that he was 'no doubt a man of an extremely sanguine temperament'. But most of the attacks on him were very unreasonable, and the Thames Haven scheme (although defeated in part by circumstances, in the event) was perceptive and practical, if perhaps speculative. It has to be said per contra that Amsinck was himself largely responsible for the attacks on him, because of his talent for upsetting people and creating enemies in teacup storms (although this was all very characteristic of the period). Amsinck was however unfortunate in having to engage in prolonged dealings with the Eastern Counties, in circumstances which would have taxed the patience of any man.

The essence of the Thames Haven scheme was the building of a railway line from London (or from the ECR) to Shell Haven (to be renamed 'Thames Haven') on the Thames, where a dock would be built, by which means ships would be able to avoid the dangers and delays inherent in navigating the crowded upper reaches of the river. The traffics most particularly in mind are described below. At this time there was no existing 'London' port facility downstream of the East & West India Docks and Blackwall, so it was perhaps inevitable that those not yet attuned to the railway age should regard Amsinck's ideas as wild. Even two generations later, it was to prove difficult to persuade shipping to use Tilbury docks.

PROMOTION (1835/6)

After getting together some support (the personalities will be discussed later in this chapter), Amsinck had plans drawn up by Alfred and Francis Giles (4) and Bewicke Blackburn in the autumn of 1835. Blackburn and Alfred Giles are not otherwise known, but Francis Giles was a well-known figure in the railway world, having been in charge of the Newcastle & Carlisle from the start of work in 1829, and then of the London & Southampton from 1831 (until dismissed in 1837 because the Directors were unhappy with his way of arranging contracts). It is doubtful if the Thames Haven took up much of his time, as the railway at least was a simple job, and one suspects that Blackburn did most of the work on the ground anyway.

Parliamentary plans were deposited in good time on the 30th November 1835. A first Prospectus (5) was produced about this time, a simple 4-page sheet with a large map. This was quickly supplanted in December by a much lengthier 27-page version 'Thames Haven Rail-Way, with Observations on its Anticipated Advantages' (6) part of which is reproduced here. The first public meetings were also held in December 1835, but before referring to them it is appropriate to give more details of the plans, and the anticipated benefits as set out in the prospectuses.

The line of the railway is shown in detail on the one-inch map extract here. It had originally been intended to have a direct line from London independent of any other railway, but when the Eastern Counties Railway (which was conceived in 1834, but had not gone to parliament in the 1834/5 session) became seen as a definite thing, the Thames Haven line was altered to commence from the ECR at Romford, in order to save costs. The line in this form was 15 miles 43 chains long. It ran through flat countryside with no works of significance and a maximum gradient of 1/500. There was to be a triangular junction at Romford, but as this was west of the town (and the ECR station site) it would have meant that Thames Haven trains could not call at the ECR station there if running through from Shoreditch to Thames Haven. Such through running *was* intended; the prospectus states that 'no change of conveyance will be requisite between London and Shell Haven', and the Thames Haven considered that they had an agreed understanding with the ECR for the use of their line between Shoreditch and Romford (the ECR, as we shall see, did not agree!). The prospectus noted:-

'A direct line from Shell Haven to the city would perhaps be somewhat shorter [i.e. in the total railway mileage from London to Thames Haven] but then it would have been a line exclusively from Shell Haven to London. Romford is the principal market-town of the county - there are the Bankers and the men of business - and all classes of the South County residents are in the habit of meeting there almost weekly; it was therefore decided that the line taken should be to that town, and with as little interference with property as possible'.

The dock site at Shell Haven was chosen because it was the lowest point on the north bank of the river where there was deep

---

opposite This charming, pretentious, and very Amsinck-ian title piece comes from the 1842 prospectus. The 'view', however represents the original ideas of 1835/6, reverted to after the collapse of grander schemes. The artist is standing on a mountain of artistic convenience to the east of the Dock, but the majority of the surrounding area does at least possess a realistic flatness! The design of an appropriate track layout for a new rail-connected dock was very much in its infancy in the 1830s (London did not, in the event, have such a dock until the Victoria Dock in the 1850s) but it is doubtful if the THD&R Co ever got as far as thinking about such details at all. The arrangements seen here are probably only a counsel of desperation by the artist, obliged to depict the railway in some visible form. The 90 degree turn at the dock corner is particularly notable! - and one might ponder how the two trains in the foreground had just managed to pass each other. The dock buildings were described as 'Coal Stores, Warehouses, Hotel, Dock and Custom House, from designs of H. E. Kendall Architect'. The 'plan' here shows steamer routes to many continental destinations; the 1835/6 prospectuses had only shown services to Southend and Kent.

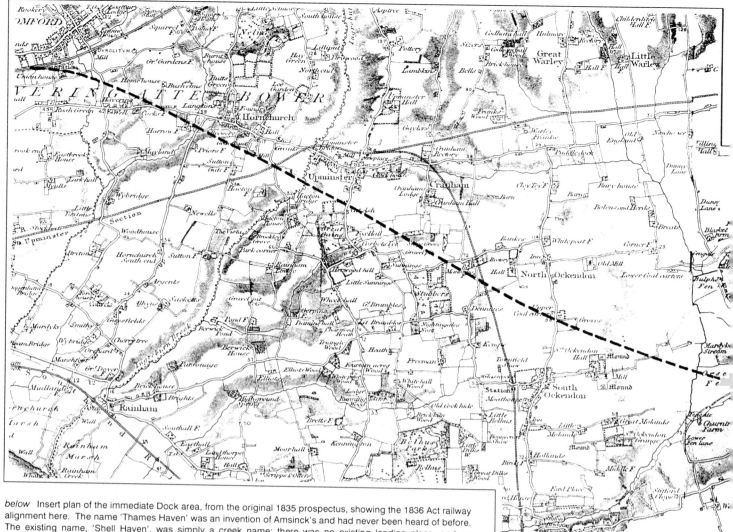

below Insert plan of the immediate Dock area, from the original 1835 prospectus, showing the 1836 Act railway alignment here. The name 'Thames Haven' was an invention of Amsinck's and had never been heard of before. The existing name, 'Shell Haven', was simply a creek name; there was no existing landing place, and no inhabitation in the vicinity, save for the scattered farms. In the decades after the railway opened the 'Thames Haven' name did catch on for general use, but in the 20th century the area has tended to become known as 'Shell Haven' again, not because of the creek (which is now partly filled in) but because of the complete coincidence of the Shell oil company having acquired most of it and having an obvious preference for that name!

This may be an appropriate place to note the pre-railway history of the Thames Haven site; refer to the 6" map at pp 36-37 and the lettered annotations there. The river walls had mostly been built on their present sites in the major reclamations of the sixteenth century. However the original wall ran from A to B, the promontory that later became the Thames Haven station area remaining as unreclaimed marsh at this stage. When this was reclaimed, c1700, it was as an 'island', with a wall from C to D and the small area between this and the original wall A-B still subject to tidal coverage. It acquired the name 'North Reedham Island'. Only in the late eighteenth century were the additional sections of wall A-C and B-D built, absorbing the 'island' into the mainland. All the 'island' belonged to Oil Mill Farm and was a 'detached' portion of the parish of Fobbing (as, therefore, was Thames Haven station when built) until 1887 when a tidying-up of boundaries saw it incorporated into Corringham parish.

right Extract from the December 1835 prospectus. By the 1836 prospectuses the 'Profit' had been enhanced to £94,354 per annum (mainly by adding £16,000 for 'Chalk & Lime' and reducing the expenses by £10,000). The 1841 and 1842 prospectuses managed to further enhance the claimed profit to £126,557 p.a.

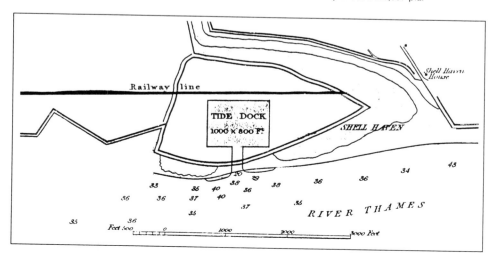

This First Edition OS 1in map is essentially an 1843/4 survey, with later railways, including the Thames Haven branch, added. It therefore gives a good picture of the area at the time when the Thames Haven Railway was being promoted - not that there were actually many changes afterwards, until the 1880s/90s. The never-built section of the 1836 Act route between Romford and Mucking has been superimposed as a dashed line. The railway passed through the parishes of Romford, Hornchurch, Upminster, Cranham, North Ockendon, South Ockendon, Orsett, Horndon, Mucking, Stanford-le-Hope, Corringham, and Fobbing. For two miles eastwards from Mucking the railway as built in 1855 was exactly on the 1836 Act line, but for the last 1½ miles at Thames Haven the railway as built was considerably different in its exact alignment from the straight line of the 1836 Act.

This map would have gladdened Henry Amsinck as the 'Dock' is shown on it as if it were a functional facility, when it was actually just a part-excavated hole.

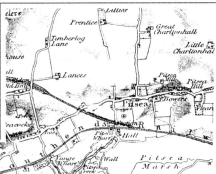

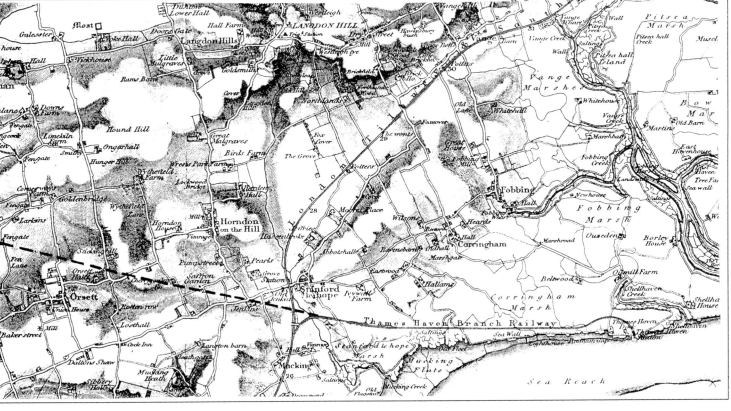

he Thames, near the mouth of the River, has long been considered a *desideratum ;* but until the introduction of loco-motive engine power, on the Railway, sufficient variety and extent of purpose could not be combined, to admit of the attainment of that object.

From a careful survey, it has been ascertained that at SHELL HAVEN (proposed to be called THAMES HAVEN) lying about Midway between TILBURY FORT and SOUTHEND, in Essex, a Tide-Dock, accessible at all times of tide, and well calculated for affording accommodation to shipping, may be constructed with facility. The embarkation and landing of Passengers is the principal object at present contemplated by making this dock; but the situation will admit of convenient adaptation to the Coal-Trade and other purposes.

It is proposed that the Company shall avail themselves of the Eastern Counties Railway as far as Romford; from thence the Thames Haven Railway will proceed through a rich and highly-cultivated country, within an easy distance of Southend and the fertile Hundred of Rochford, to its termination, but no change of conveyance will be requisite from London to Shell Haven.

Although the extent of the probable income cannot be stated with accuracy, the basis of the calculation is sufficient to justify the conclusion that it will be large and liberal, as will be seen by considering that the returns will be derived from the undermentioned sources; the sums placed under each head being the result of much consideration, and estimated on a very moderate view of the subject, but which must however be taken as matter of fair and reasonable expectation only, and not as admitting of demonstration;

1st, From the conveyance of Passengers to and from all parts of the Line, exclusive of Steam-boat Passengers £10,416
2nd, From the conveyance of Parcels . . . 2,000
3rd, From the conveyance of Agricultural Supplies, Meat, and generally, the produce of the country, in all the varieties required by the great market of London, and of the supplies required in return, including manure 33,781
4th, From the conveyance of Fish to the London market 20,000
5th, From the conveyance of Passengers to and from Steam-boats, a distance of 26 miles by land, in little more than one hour, the distance by water being 36 miles 60,000
6th, From the carriage of Coals . . . 41,375

167,572
Deduct for Expenses of Line, Carriage, Office, &c. 104,218

Profit . £63,354

In forming the above calculations, no credit has been taken for any increase of Passengers on the existing traffic to Southend and the immediate places on the line of Railway; nor for goods and traffic consequent upon Vessels laying in the Tide-dock; nor for the Pier and Harbour Dues; nor for Chalk and Lime: nor has any credit been taken for casual Passengers to and from Vessels in the River and Yachts:—less than one-third of the present Steam-boat traffic is given in the estimated ground of revenue; and Coals are taken at an eighth only of the importation into London—a very augmented scale of revenue may therefore be fairly calculated upon.

The Table of Rates is as follows :—Passengers, two-pence each per mile; Goods, Farming and Garden produce, two-pence per ton per mile; Coals, one penny halfpenny per ton per mile; Fish, sixpence per ton per mile.

The inclinations of the Railway are peculiarly favourable, not exceeding one in five hundred: at the lowest spring-tides the Tide-dock will have *twenty feet* water in it; and the depth, at the entrance in the River, from 37 to 40 feet.

The annual number of Passengers to and passing Gravesend by steam-vessels is calculated at 1,700,000, of whom about one-half proceed below Gravesend. As this calculation is entirely exclusive of the Scotch, Irish and Foreign Boats, it may be fairly considered that the advantages which this station will offer of perfect security under any weather and at any period of the tide, as well as the facilities of landing their Passengers and Goods, will be speedily appreciated, and consequently may reasonably be contemplated as a source of great probable revenue to the undertaking.

A Railway as projected from Herne Bay, by Canterbury, to Dover would complete the chain of communication by steam power between London and those places by a direct route, and when complete cannot but add materially to the use of the Thames Haven Railway.

It is intended to make application to Paliament for an Act of Incorporation in the ensuing session, the requisite notices having been given, and the Plan, Section, and Book of Reference lodged with the proper authorities.

A deposit of £2 10s. per Share, to be paid at the time of subscribing, and no further call will be made until the Act of Incorporation is obtained. No call to be made exceeding £5 per Share, nor at a less interval than three months between each call. The liability of a Proprietor to be limited to the amount of his subscription.

All measures deemed necessary, preparatory and previous to the passing of the Act, will be conducted by the Provisional Committee, who are to have the control and disposition of the fund constituted by the deposits.

Application for Shares to be made (if by letter, post paid) to Messrs. VAUX and FENNELL, *Solicitors,* 32, Bedford Row; or to the *Secretary,* at the Office, where Plans and Particulars may be obtained.

THAMES HAVEN RAILWAY OFFICE, 34, ABCHURCH-LANE, 1st *December,* 1835.

water, the mudflats beginning east of here. The 1000ft by 800ft dock was to be tidal, with no entrance lock, and would have had 20ft of water even at spring tide low tides.

The prospectuses claimed three primary benefits from the scheme. Firstly, for passengers to Southend and the Kent resorts, who could go by train to Thames Haven in an hour and join steamers there, so saving much time compared with the existing travelling by steamer all the way from London Bridge. (The London & Blackwall Railway had a similar aim but was aimed more at the Greenwich, Woolwich and Gravesend traffic, which of course the Thames Haven could not serve). As will be seen at page 19 of the prospectus extract here, it was claimed that some 850,000 passengers per annum travelled on steamers to destinations beyond Gravesend. This seems highly exaggerated given that even in 1850 there were only 183,000 passengers by steamer to Southend and the Kent resorts (7); it would seem that Amsinck was including certain other services as well, which might be less likely to transfer to Thames Haven. Another factor not stressed was that the Southend and Kent traffic was wholly seasonal, only lasting about 4 months in the summer. Despite stating that 'the embarkation and landing of passengers in the principle object contemplated', the prospectuses did not actually dilate very much on this theme, possibly because this aspect was seen as something that potential supporters would already be familiar with.

Secondly, the dock would be used by colliers from the north east, and the coal conveyed to London by rail, reducing its price by 5s or more per ton. This was a very topical subject. At things stood the colliers moored at 'tiers' in midriver below London Bridge, and were unloaded into lighters, with high handling costs. In 1835 7,980 colliers arrived with 2,298,812 tons of coal. Because of congestion upriver many had to wait further down until space became available at the tiers, and further delays were caused by the agreed system of permitting fewer ships at the tiers if the price of coal started to drop! All this was greatly resented by the colliery owners in the north east. It was also disliked by other river users, as the vessels at the tiers greatly reduced the available river channel, and the lighters went back and forth across the path of other shipping. The river byelaws were breached flagrantly. In 1836 a Parliamentary Committee on the Port of London was to consider all these points and confirm the need for collier docks in order to clear the river. (Another factor bringing dangerous river conditions was the heavy swamp from the increasing numbers of large and fast steamers overturning small craft - the Thames Haven played on this also, as the dock would keep many such steamers away from the upper river).

Thirdly, fish could be landed at Thames Haven and taken to London by rail, on a regular and reliable basis. At present much of the fish caught for the London market ended up being dumped at sea because contrary winds made it impossible for the fishing boats to get up river to Billingsgate. The market suffered from scarcity and glut, and the majority of the population of London could not afford fish at all. Amsinck does not seem to have thought of the 'fish' aspect until late in 1835 when it came to his attention that the Fish Association had in 1813 produced a report recommending a fishing dock at Hole Haven, just one mile east of Shell Haven. A road had been proposed then. The 1813 ideas had of course never came to fruition, but Amsinck was so struck by the coincidence that he added the whole of the 1813 report as an Appendix to the expanded prospectus of December 1835.

Further benefits claimed were
- Local passenger traffic in South Essex
- Transporting agricultural produce from the area to London, and manure in return
- Improved communication with the naval base at Sheerness
- Encouragement of gentlemanly yachting ('In one hour and a quarter a party may be at the entrance to the River, with an almost open sea, for the exercise of the vessels').

The first local meeting in the area was at the Court House, Romford, on 21st December 1835, but this was only seen as a 'preliminary meeting' and only 20 were present. Edward Ind (of the brewers Ind Coope) took the chair, and Amsinck and Blackburn attended. The predictable 'unanimous resolution in favour' of the line was secured. The anticipated further meeting followed on 19th January 1836, at the same venue. It is clear that Amsinck was making particular efforts to cultivate the Romford interests, who were attracted to the scheme because it was seen as drawing trade into the town. Messrs Johnson & Co were appointed as the Thames Haven's bankers in Romford, and Wasey Sterry as 'Agent'. From Amsinck's viewpoint, Romford was the only place in the area where

there was a business community who could be cultivated. (However the reality was that Amsinck had no real interest in Romford as such, and was always ready to ditch the Romford route for a 'direct line' from London. Conversely the Romford people would quickly lose their interest in the Thames Haven).

It seems to have been felt that these meetings had still not had sufficient impact, and a third meeting was arranged, this time with the local supporters more involved in the organising, at the Court House on 9th February 1836 (8). The press reported it as a 'Great Meeting at Romford' so it seems to have been a success. After 'considerable discussion', particularly about the reduced price of coals and the benefits in getting farm produce to London, and the passing of resolutions in favour, a 'Local Committee' was appointed to 'forward the undertaking', but also to protect the interest of landowners. There had been concern expressed about compensation at the January meeting, and the Thames Haven now undertook to abide by the views of the Local Committee on any property questions.

There was an opposition voice at the 9th February meeting, from Mr Stevens the trustee of the Ockendon Estate, an affected property. Stevens then organised an 'Opposition Meeting' at the Bell Inn, Upminster, on 27th February, where a motion against the Thames Haven was passed on grounds of damage to landowners (9). But nothing more is heard of opposition from this source, and the Thames Haven did not see fit to hold any further local meetings, so it seems that the affected landowners in this area were placated.

Opposition came also from Jane Baker (widow of Richard Baker) of Orsett Hall, where the railway passed through the grounds close to the Hall (something which could surely have been avoided). Parliamentary conflict seemed likely but in April terms were agreed, incorporated in an agreement of June 1836 under which the whole estate would be purchased for £15,000 (10).

THE SOUTHEND AND HOLE-HAVEN RAILWAY

Whilst the Thames Haven escaped lightly so far as property opposition was concerned, they did for several months have to face a rival scheme for the area, the Southend and Hole-Haven Railway (also referred to by its promoters as the 'Hole Haven and Southend Railway', and the 'Southend Railway') (11). This seems to have been evolved in 1835 at the same time as the Thames Haven, entirely independently and without any intention of hostility, but it was clear that the two schemes could not coexist. It was much more locally-based than the Thames Haven, and its route would probably have been of more use to the local interests. The promoters held a meeting in September 1835 but there was no publicity otherwise until late November when newspaper advertisements appeared:-
'Hole Haven and Southend Railway
with a view to adopting the line of the London & Blackwall Railway as an inlet to the metropolis, through Barking, Dagenham, Rainham, Purfleet, Grays to Hole Haven and Southend, with branches to Ilford, Romford, Tilbury Fort, Mucking, and Leigh, and other trading places on the line of the road.
Notice is hereby given that as soon as the survey and estimates are complete, a prospectus will be issued with all particulars ......'
Further advertisements in December concentrated on the benefits to Southend. These all appeared adjacent to Thames Haven Railway advertisements in the same editions, and clearly people would have started questioning the conflict. The Hole-Haven did not openly attack the Thames Haven, but their next advertisement in January
'The objects of this railway are not founded upon speculation but upon the intercourse that already exists between the trading towns on the line ....'
was clearly meant as a dig at the Thames Haven!

Amsinck had however noticed that the Hole-Haven promoters had failed to deposit any parliamentary plans before the 30th November 1835 deadline, and so could not proceed in the 1836 session. In February he put an advertisement in the newspapers pointing this out (the Hole-Haven promoters having covered up this fact until then), and this was really the undoing of the Hole-Haven, as they would have had to fight the Thames Haven in parliament without having any definite scheme of their own. They lost heart and their scheme was never heard of again after February 1836. Southend had to wait another twenty years for its railway. With its multifarious 'branches' the Hole-Haven was in many ways more of an 1810s/1820s tramway, although the basic route was a harbinger of the LT&S line as actually built in the 1850s.

THE 1836 ACT

With all landowners placated, the Thames Haven had an easy ride in Parliament. Although there was no opposition, evidence was given to the House of Commons Committee on 3rd May 1836. Francis Giles was the first witness but only spoke briefly. Amsinck then gave the main traffic evidence. This was based primarily on a survey carried out on the road between Romford and Hornchurch during one week in April 1836, which produced 1,637 people, 224 oxen, 650 sheep, 12 calves and 4 pigs. These figures were multiplied by 52! (Apart from the naivety of this, there is no evident reason why the traffic at that point would bear any relationship at all to the likely use of the Thames Haven Railway).

Additionally Amsinck foresaw

249,600 tons of goods from ships other than colliers at the dock
250,000 tons of coals from the dock (this was one eighth of the total London sea coal trade)
30,000 tons of fish
3,699 (sic) tons of market garden produce
13,500 tons of chalk and lime
8,000 tons of potatoes

plus the steamer passenger traffic.

This was supplemented by evidence from Edward Young Hancock, Occupier of the Tithes of the parish of Fobbing, who claimed *inter alia* that 'if this railway be formed there will be a vast quantity of Turnips Mangel Wurzel Sweed and such like grown [locally] for the use of cow keepers [in London] who feed their horses and cattle with that description of food'.

Finally Bewicke Blackburn appeared briefly. It was all over in the day. The House of Lords Committee did not bother to hear evidence at all and 'reported' the Bill directly.

The Thames Haven Dock and Railway Act 1836 received the Royal Assent on 4th July 1836 (12). It established the Thames Haven Dock and Railway Company, with a nominal capital of £450,000 in 9,000 £50 shares, plus borrowing powers of £150,000. Seven years were allowed for the works. The company were empowered to make a railway from Romford to a creek 'hitherto called Shell Haven, but which shall for the future be called "Thames Haven"...... and also to make .... a Tide Dock or Basin at the termination of the railway .... and also to construct .... such Pier or Piers, Lighthouses, Light-vessels, Breakwaters, Jetties, and other works or conveniences, for the safe and convenient entrance, egress, and navigation of ships into and from the said docks, and also to erect such Wharfs, Quays, Warehouses, Landing Places, Cranes, Weighing Machines, and other Works and Conveniences connected therewith ....' (s.7). There had been no piers (etc) shown in the Deposited Plans, and the company were obliged to obtain the consent of the Corporation of London before commencing works in or near the River Thames (s.16). The Corporation could also require removal of the works if they became a hazard (s.17) - this did actually happen in due course (see Chapter 6). The Limits of Deviation for the railway were to be 100 yards (s.10) (the Deposited Plans had not shown any Limits of Deviation at all). The junction with the ECR line was to made under the directions of the ECR Engineer (s.190) and the company might make agreements with the ECR or any other company for running powers over each other's lines (s.191). Occupiers of lands adjacent to the Thames Haven line might make their own branches to join it (s.92). Where the line crossed a public highway on the level, the company must erect gates which shall be kept shut except when 'carriages passing along the said railway shall have to cross such highway' (s.78). (There is no reference to keepers' lodges being required, as in many Acts; nor are the level crossings, of which there would have been several, listed).

There was no mention in the Act of gauge, which could not be decided yet as it was dependent on the ECR's gauge. The ECR were still considering the 7ft gauge at this time, and it was only in the spring of 1838 that they made a definite decision to go for the 5ft gauge. The THD&R Co do not seem to have worried much about all this - by the time that work began in 1838 they knew definitely that they must adopt the 5ft gauge, and in any case they never got anywhere near track laying in the event. (The London & Blackwall was also 5ft gauge, so if the THD&R Co had instead adopted a 'direct line' to London joining the Blackwall line, the 5ft gauge would still have been necessary).

As usual there was also nothing in the Act about station sites, nor was anything said in Parliament about this. The 'obvious' station sites were Hornchurch, Upminster, Ockendon, Orsett, and Horndon/Stanford-le-Hope, and it might be noted that these are the places specifically named at the start of the prospectuses. An independent station at Romford on the Thames Haven line might also have been needed, but there are no references. There was however undoubtedly some thought given to station sites, as the Orsett Hall agreement specifically mentions that it is intended to erect a 'Station House and Depot' at that point.

It was intended, at this time, to build the Thames Haven line as a double track line.

DIRECTORS AND SHAREHOLDERS

Shares had been offered in February 1836 with a closure date for applications of 31st March. The 'deposit' on the £50 shares was £2.10s.

The original subscription list survives with the Deposited Plans and shows that 7,925 of the 9,000 shares had been subscribed for (but see below!). As with most East Anglian schemes of this period, including the ECR, the majority of the shares had been taken by Manchester and Liverpool business men, with 20 - 70 shares each. Shareholdings in London were much smaller, though William Price, 'Merchant in the City', took 500, and J. B. Hodgson and J. R. Gomme, Surgeon and Estate Agent in Chesham, took 250 each; and holdings in Essex were minimal. (This 'Manchester versus London' situation always caused difficulties in due course, though the THD&R Co suffered less than some other companies from this). In August 1836 Amsinck went to Manchester for a meeting with the Manchester shareholders, held on the 25th. They seem to have been fretting already, as the resolution passed was 'this meeting is perfectly satisfied with the explanation given by the Secretary'. On return Amsinck reported that the Manchester meeting had been 'attended with the best effects'.

At the first half-yearly meeting of the company on 28th September 1836 (marked, as was usual at first meetings, by congratulation and contentment), the Directors elected were:-

⋆Horace Twiss MP
+⋆Donald MacLean MP
+⋆James Saumarez Jephson
+⋆Ernest Vaux (13)
+⋆Charles Henry Clay
⋆Francis Graham Moon
⋆James Esdaile
  Lieutenant-Col Sir J.M.F. Smith
  Richard Baker Wingfield
  Joseph Ablett Jesse   (a Manchester man)
  James Richmond   (a Manchester man)
  William Archer Price (the London merchant with 500 shares)
+ indicates the survivors of those named in the 1835 prospectuses as Provisional Directors, and
⋆of those named in the Act as Directors. It will be seen that only four of the ten named in the prospectus had 'survived', and two of the nine named in the Act had also disappeared, probably because it was necessary to allow two of the Manchester shareholders on to the Board in lieu. Most of these 1836 Directors had precious little influence on the company in the event and need not concern us; all except Vaux, Esdaile, and Wingfield left the scene in the first years, prior to 1842. The more significant people were :-

Horace Twiss (1787-1849). Barrister, MP, and a great wit and leading figure in the London literary and social scene. He was thus a good establishment 'catch' for the company, and became the first Chairman. However he severed all connections in 1837 and was reported as having 'feelings of disgust' for the company.

Donald MacLean MP. He became Chairman briefly after Twiss but is not heard of after 1838.

Thus it is unlikely that either of these two establishment figures had any great influence on the company.

Sir J. M. Frederic Smith (1790-1874). At this time he had not really gone outside of his career in the Royal Engineers, but soon afterwards he became much more involved in the railway scene. In 1839-41 he was appointed, with Professor Barlow, to report for the government on railway communication between London and Dublin and London and Scotland. Amsinck became Secretary to this commission. In December 1840 Smith was also appointed as Inspector General of Railways in the then-new Board of Trade Railway Department (but he resigned in 1841). However he had ceased to be a THD&R Co director prior to this.

James Esdaile the owner of Saw Mills in the City Road, London, also owned property at Upminster, which seems to have been the cause of his involvement with the Thames Haven. He lived at Upper Bedford Place, Russell Square. He was a Director from 1836 until 1856, after the line had opened, he (and Wingfield) far outlasting the other original Directors. In 1838 he became Chairman and remained so until the 'Chadwick takeover' in 1847 (see Chapter 2), when he became Deputy Chairman, but he is not heard of actively in the 1850s and resigned from the Board in 1857. Along with Amsinck, Esdaile must be regarded as one of the most important influences in the company pre-1847; but his motivations and impact are almost impossible to analyse owing to lack of evidence.

Richard Baker Wingfield 'son of the Master in Chancery, Brother-in-law of Lord Cottenham, nephew to Lord Digby, lives in Lowndes Square, has property in Essex on the line' (1842 notes). His property was at Orsett and he was also trustee of the will of Richard Baker of Orsett Hall (referred to earlier). The Wingfields, the Bakers, and the Barrett Lennards of Belhus, were all interrelated. Wingfield almost certainly began his involvement as a property-owner concerned by the line, but then, as so often happened, took an interest in it. He remained a Director until the 1850s.

At the first shareholders' meeting in September 1836 it was stated that 8,200 shares had now been taken. £15,105 had been received from payments of the deposit; expenditure had been £6,383 (plus unpaid liabilities of £2,837). It would not have taken much mathematical ability to work out that £15,105 represented the payment of the £2.10s deposit on only 6,042 shares rather than 8,200, and this was indeed the case. A few others paid their deposits after this, to the eventual total of 6,163 shares which was, therefore, the highest number of paid-up-to-date shares that the company ever actually had.

A 'First Call' of a further £2.10s was made in January 1837. The response was very slow and in May the Board decided to allow an extension of time. Only 2,850 shares were ever paid up on, however (some of them not until 1838). This was a great disappointment and a poor omen given that a further £45 was still due on each share. The THD&R Co therefore laboured under financial problems from the very start. There were of course many people who had taken shares in all railway companies in the 'Little Mania' of 1836 and then found it impossible to pay the calls, especially as the money market became generally very bad in the years after 1836. But the Thames Haven probably suffered particularly because it was a 'speculative' scheme whereas most of the other railways of 1836 were for routes between major cities which seemed a 'sure bet' in their likely financial return. Most of the THD&R Co shareholders also had shares in other companies, and when things started to go wrong it was the Thames Haven that they ditched. The THD&R Co then started to *look* like a lost cause, so the process was self-reinforcing. No (or almost no) further shares were taken after 1836, and the number of shareholders therefore went down and down in the years that followed, as more and more shares were 'forfeited' because the calls had not been paid, until in time there were hardly any shareholders left except the people running the 'company'.

At the second shareholders' meeting in February 1837 it was announced that work would be started on the dock first, before the railway. 'This looks like business' commented the *Railway Magazine*. But at the third meeting in August 1837 it was reported that the commencement of work had been prevented by financial problems. As a result the dissatisfied Manchester shareholders proposed a resolution that the company be dissolved. A special meeting was fixed for 31st October to confirm this. On 23rd October a notice was put in the *Times* that this meeting was being postponed, but it was in fact held, attended only by Amsinck and one Director, who did pass the resolution to dissolve. Afterwards, however, they had second thoughts, and the matter was suppressed (14).

1837 was therefore a very disappointing year for the company. But 1838 was in many ways to prove its finest hour.

THE COMMERCIAL AND COLLIER DOCKS SCHEME

In the high days of summer 1836, a grandiose plan was evolved for making a 3000ft by 400ft 'Commercial Dock' to the west of the tidal dock, and a corresponding 3000ft by 400ft 'Collier Dock' to the east. A tasteful engraving of this enlarged scheme was commissioned and copies sent to the press (15).

This was all forgotten when things turned bad in 1837, but was republicised in the next active period in summer 1838. The *Railway Magazine* in June 1838 included a long feature on Thames Haven (clearly all supplied by the company) and a plan and view of the three docks. However it was noted that 'at present the undertaking is limited to the centre, or Tide-dock'.

After 1838 these grand ideas were never mentioned again.

THE LONDON TILBURY & GRAVESEND RAILWAY (1836)

In the late 1830s the Gravesend traffic was growing very quickly. The Thames Haven scheme as it stood was unable to serve Gravesend and the THD&R Co therefore decided to promote a branch from Ockendon to Tilbury. Notices were placed in the *London Gazette* in October 1836 for this line , under the name 'London Tilbury and Gravesend Railway'; powers would also be sought to run a ferry at Tilbury. The Solicitor for the Bill was Wasey Sterry, the Thames Haven's 'Agent' in Romford.

However no plans were ever deposited (16), and the idea died as the company's financial problems became evident. But it was to be revived in 1842 (Chapter 2).

PROBLEMS WITH THE EASTERN COUNTIES (1836-8)

In Amsinck's view, the ECR Provisional Committee had promised in 1835 that if the Thames Haven gave up their ideas of an independent route to London, the ECR would grant especially favourable rates for the running of the Thames Haven's trains between Romford and Shoreditch.

When the companies gained their Acts in the summer of 1836, Amsinck lost no time in pushing to get the details of this agreed. The very first ECR Board meeting on 14th July 1836 had before it a letter from Amsinck asking for a meeting between Directors. No doubt feeling that they had more important things to consider, the

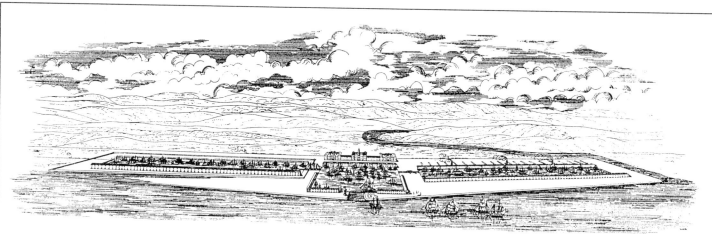

BIRDS EYE VIEW
of the present intended
THAMES HAVEN TIDE DOCK,
1000 FEET BY 800
also of two projected closed docks for Colliers and Merchandize.

The 'view' from the June 1838 *Railway Magazine* feature on Thames Haven, showing the expanded 3-dock proposals. The Collier Dock (right) and Commercial Dock (left) would have had to be built largely on mudflats below high water level. Shell Haven Creek winds off into a background of romantic hills decidedly unrelated to reality.

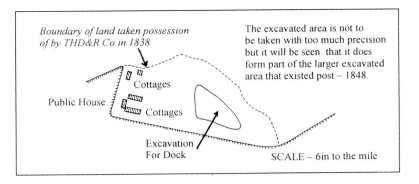

This sketch map is included to show conveniently the extent of the work done in the 1838/9 period. For further details of the Thames Haven station site see the 1863 OS map at p. 30.

The 1839 Fobbing Tithe Map confirms the THD&R Co as 'occupiers' of these fields of Oil Mill Farm (pieces 20,21,22 and 23 on the 1863 OS). They are (correctly) not shown as 'owners' because they had not made full payment even for this small part of the farm that they had begun work in. The Tithe Map also confirms that all these buildings do date from 1838. The map was prepared by Henry Crawter of Southampton Buildings, who was also the THD&R Co's land surveyor at this period.

ECR Board resolved that their Secretary J. C. Robertson should ask for more details, but Amsinck was not to be fobbed off, and three weeks later the ECR had to agree to meet a delegation of THD&R Co directors. In fact Amsinck himself attended the ECR Board on 29th August.

Nothing came of this initial flurry. In February 1837 the ECR Board had another Amsinck letter before them, asking what tolls the ECR proposed to charge. Robertson replied that it was as yet too soon to say whether the THD&R Co could be offered any reduction on the normal charges as set out in the ECR's Act.

After this Amsinck went quiet for several months, no doubt as a result of the THD&R Co's financial problems.

At this point the THD&R Co had the misfortune to become embroiled in the personality warfare surrounding the ECR, which was being run in an appallingly corrupt fashion, not least due to Robertson. In December 1837 Robertson started a new journal the *Railway Times* (keeping his ECR job as well) mainly in order to defend himself and the ECR from the attacks being made by the *Railway Magazine* (whose editor, John Herapath, had been previously involved with the ECR and thus had both inside knowledge and a personal dislike of Robertson). All this was nothing to do with the THD&R Co but, having established his journal, Robertson was also able to use it to attack others, and in December 1837 he launched an attack on Amsinck who he seems to have regarded as a bumptious little nuisance. For the next seven years all 'news' reporting of the THD&R Co's affairs was destined to be wholly prejudiced pro or anti; Herapath began putting propaganda for the THD&R Co in the *Railway Magazine* in 1838 merely to annoy Robertson, but the majority of what the public saw would be hostile (17).

After the initial Robertson attacks Amsinck had a paid piece put in the *Times* on 2nd January 1838, accusing the ECR of being 'so faithless to engagements, bonded and verbal ..... The Thames Haven dock has the advantage of deep water, open space, good holding ground, and a neighbourhood of plenty of ballast. It labours under but one disadvantage, having trusted in the faith of the Eastern Counties'.

The ECR seem not to have noticed this at first; in February they allowed a THD&R Co delegation to attend an ECR Board meeting to discuss the tolls question, and had a lengthy discussion, ending with the Thames Haven being asked to furnish a statement of how much they would be willing to pay. But immediately after this they got on to a very high horse over Amsinck's piece, and informed the THD&R Co that they would not speak to them at all unless this 'most groundless charge of breach of engagement' was retracted.

The THD&R Co Board (who apparently had not been consulted by Amsinck in January) were anxious to sort out the tolls question, now that they were moving to a start of work on the dock (see below), and caved in to the ECR's demands, placing another piece in the *Times* on 14th March 1838, disassociating themselves from Amsinck :-

'...... this Court of Directors do hereby totally and fully disavow that the same was in any manner authorised by them, and that they have not sanctioned, nor would they sanction, that or any other statement reflecting on the Eastern Counties Railway Company or its Directors'.

A further deputation of THD&R Co directors was then permitted to attend the ECR Board in April. However they were told by the ECR that whilst they would be spoken to, Amsinck himself would not be until he personally apologised for his words! This he never did and the ECR seem to have carried on for another year or so refusing to speak to him. This again was all typical 1830s behaviour, but the ECR nevertheless seem to have been in a constructive mood in 1838. After advice from the Attorney-General that it would be illegal under their Act for them to allow the THD&R Co to 'carry' on their line for a lesser toll than others - this of course was at a time when railway Acts were still being worded on the assumption that private carriers would be able to run trains on a company's line - a section was inserted in the 1838 ECR Act empowering them to make agreements with the THD&R Co at such annual payment 'as may seem expedient'. In August the ECR appointed a Committee of Directors to negotiate with the Thames Haven, but despite the apparently genuine desire of both parties to reach agreement, there was no progress. They were, it appears, trying to agree on an annual lump sum payment, even though (obviously) nobody had any real idea how much traffic there would be. The later inter-company practice of payment *per train mile* had yet to become accepted.

By the end of 1838 the THD&R Co had given up on the ECR and were turning back to the 'independent line' idea, (see below.)

START OF WORK ON THE DOCK (1838)

The shareholders' meeting in March 1838 was presented with a very optimistic report and held in high spirits. 'The prospects of the company were never more bright' said the new Chairman James Esdaile. Amsinck stated that he had had better offers of employment but was so 'wholly devoted to the company' that he had turned them down. The Board were given a vote of thanks by acclamation and even the *Railway Times* gave a non-critical report.

Quite why the company's depression of 1837 had lifted is not clear, but it is known that certain large shareholders were pushing the idea that as the company did have some money in the bank (the exact position is clouded by contradictory figures) it would be beneficial to make a start on the works, which would then encourage shareholders to pay their calls and generally give the company a more credible image as an investment. The decision to make a start made everybody more positive. Many shareholders had still not paid the £2.10s 'First Call' of 14 months previously, and they were told it must be paid by 14th April or the shares would be considered forfeited. This seems to have produced another £3,000 or so.

The friendly *Railway Magazine* reported in April that 'the officers are now preparing for the vigorous prosecution of the undertaking'; in May 'the engineer is preparing for active operations, the line is being staked out for purchase and the contracts being got ready for the dock'; and in June that tenders for the dock had been sought.

It is very doubtful if any part of the railway was actually 'staked out' as claimed here; certainly no land for the *railway* was ever actually purchased, or taken occupation of, prior to 1847 (18), although arrangements had been come to for purchase with some landowners, and Amsinck did send out notices (dated 14th May 1838) to most (or all?) landowners on the line (19). Amsinck's statement to the March meeting that 204 acres of land 'had been purchased' was not true. However the company did in 1838 make a part payment for, and take possession of, 14 acres of land at the dock site, part of Oil Mill Farm.

The contract for the tidal dock (now to be 900ft by 1000ft instead of 800ft by 1000ft) was let in June for £209,000 (this figure excluded warehouses etc). The name of the contractor is not given. The contract provided for work to start immediately and be completed by November 1840. Work did begin in July 1838 and the *Railway Magazine* noted in August that 100 men were on site.

The next shareholders' meeting was held on 29th August 1838 and was 'well attended'. At the end of the meeting (at the London Tavern, Bishopsgate) the shareholders were given a trip down to Thames Haven in the steamer *Victoria*, and were able to watch the labourers at work. 'A very handsome dejeuner was provided on board. In the course of the evening several appropriate toasts were given in reference to the prosperity of the undertaking'. In retrospect this day was probably the high spot of the company's life.

As there was a lack of accommodation locally, two rows of cottages were built at the dock site for the contractor's men.

In December it was noted that 'excavation is as deep as 6-7 feet', and the report for the March 1839 shareholders' meeting stated that work had been done 'to the extent of 400,000ft of excavation' but that further progress was being delayed due to land possession problems. This is the last reference to work being in progress. It appears that the contractor (who was paid £1,662 by the company for the work done) ceased work in the spring of 1839 because it became evident that the company was not getting in the extra money needed to keep things going.

As the owners of Oil Mill Farm put it, the company 'having obtained possession, commenced excavating for their tide dock, and after filling about 14 acres of land with holes and earth heaps and building some cottages, gave up their works for want of money, and declined to complete their purchases' (20).

The excavation done was but the southwest corner of the proposed dock. The waterfilled hole remained as it was until 1847 when some further excavation was done (Chapter 2).

THAMES HAVEN FOR THE CONTINENT: THE BELGIAN EPISODE (1838)

In 1835/6 the company had spoken only of steamboat traffic to the Kent resorts, with no mention of any continental traffic. However in the summer of 1838 Fauche, the British Consul at Ostend, was cultivated and became very enthusiastic about Thames Haven. He had been negotiating with the Belgian government about making Ostend (which had its rail link opened at this time) the continental port for the British mails to Europe, Egypt, and India (via Germany and Trieste). He had been intending to use Faversham as the English port but now decided on Thames Haven and offered to use his influence to sell shares in Belgium.

In December 1838 the press reported that Amsinck had been to Belgium and laid matters personally before King Leopold, who had recommended the scheme to the head of the principal bank in Brussels 'who will, there is little doubt, take the remaining shares'. A copy of the THD&R Co's prospectus was placed in the hands of every Deputy and Member of the Senate.

Unfortunately there was then a serious political crisis in Belgium, which prevented any progress, and the idea died.

REVERSION TO THE 'INDEPENDENT LINE' (1838)

By the autumn of 1838 the THD&R Co had turned back to the original 1835 idea of a 'direct line' to London, and this was made publicly known. Notices of parliamentary application for a line from Minories were served in February 1839 and Francis Giles surveyed the $25\frac{1}{2}$ mile route (21). The THD&R Co Directors' report for the March 1839 shareholders' meeting cited as justification the ECR's intransigence plus the fact that the ECR might not have capacity on their line for heavy coal trains in any case.

It was proposed to have a 4-track line in order to keep fast passenger trains and coal trains separate (22). This was a very advanced idea for the 1830s, although not unprecedented; the Leeds & Selby had taken land for four tracks (although they had only laid double track).

It had been hoped to get the shareholders' approval for the 'independent line' at the March 1839 meeting, but this was not possible owing to the meeting not taking place (see below), and the parliamentary application could not be proceeded with.

However the idea was to be revived again in 1842 (Chapter 2).

COLLAPSE (1839)

All the high ideas of a vastly-expanded dock, continental packets, and a four-track railway, came to an end in the spring of 1839 with the cessation of work at Thames Haven.

The March 1839 shareholders' meeting was postponed till May but even then did not take place. The *Railway Times* reporter found nobody in the room at the London Tavern; eventually a waiter arrived with a message that it was cancelled.

The August 1839 meeting did not take place either. As the *Railway Times* put it,

'It seemed to be the intention of all concerned to let the concern 'rest', as Mr. Amsinck termed it, in consequence of the state of the money market'.

(1) The idea of a railway to link London and the Essex coast to convey shipping traffic had been floated previously in the 1811 scheme for an 'Iron Railway from a point near London to Wallasea Island with a collateral branch to Mucking' (Deposited Plans at Essex CRO Q/RUM 1/19), and a (rival?) scheme in the same year for a 'Inclined Plane or Railway' from London to Foulness with branches (*London Gazette* September 1811 p.1836). These stillborn tramway proposals, however, had no impact on the actual railway development in South Essex a full generation later, and Amsinck was probably not aware of them. The idea of a dock near Shell Haven had also been previously conceived, in 1813, as a non-railway-related proposal (see later in this chapter; again Amsinck had not been aware of this initially).
(2) The details of Amsinck's naval career are derived from PRO ADM 23/36, ADM 107/50, and ADM 196/3; also the Navy List and W. R. O'Bryan's 'A Naval Dictionary of All Living Naval Officers' (1847). Amsinck is not to be confused with the 1850s GNR Director Major W. Amsinck.
(3) Amsinck's correspondence is generally from office addresses and the only known private address is 25 Notting Hill Terrace in 1847.
(4) The plans deposited on 30.11.1835 are preserved at Essex CRO Q/RUM 1/55, and give *Alfred* Giles, and are indeed signed by him. Alfred Giles is also named as Engineer in the first prospectuses (vide the pages reproduced here). The House of Lords Deposited Plans are dated 1.6.1836 and give *Francis* Giles, and indeed it was Francis Giles who gave evidence in Parliament, and remained the company's Engineer subsequently. Alfred Giles was perhaps a relative of Francis called in to do the work because of a scarcity of labour in the profession in this 'Little Mania' autumn. Francis Giles is still listed as Engineer in the 1841 prospectus but is otherwise not heard of after 1838/9 and probably had no actual involvement after then.
(5) Copy at PRO RAIL 1075/435. Not in Ottley. It is simply dated '1835'.
(6) Ottley 6864, first item. Copies at BM and Dartford Library. A very similar revised version, 26 pages, followed in 1836 (Ottley 6864, second item), and a longer 44-page version was produced after the 1836 Act was passed (Ottley 6864, third item), thus making four consecutive prospectuses in 1835/6. Still further prospectuses followed in 1841 and 1842 (see Chapter 2).
(7) See table at p.12 of *The London, Tilbury & Southend Railway* Volume One.
(8) For reports of the three meetings see *Essex & Herts Mercury* 29.12.1835, 26.1.1836, 16.2.1836. There are also Thames Haven Railway advertisements, 1.12.1835, 8.12.1835, 9.2.1836, 23.2.1836.
(9) *Essex & Herts Mercury* 1.3.1836.
(10) Copy of the agreement at Reading University Library, ESS 17/9/60. See also Essex CRO D/Dwt E3 (correspondence).
(11) For the Southend & Hole-Haven Railway see *Railway Magazine* September 1835, and the advertisements in *Essex & Herts Mercury* 24.11.1835, 1.12.1835, 15.12.1835, 5.1.1836, 9.2.1836. In the absence of plans, the precise route is not known, and the verbal descriptions suggest several versions in detail. The Hole-Haven Counsel Charles Barrett Lennard (of the Belhus family) was a relative of Jane Baker of Orsett Hall and involved in opposition to the Thames Haven in that context. The Engineer is stated to be George Kennett (perhaps a printing error for George Hennet, who was involved in

London schemes at this period).
(12) 6&7 William IV Cap. 108. Although the dock had of course been intended from the start, the publicity prior to the Act had always been under the name 'Thames Haven Railway', but the Act now established the company as the 'Thames Haven Dock and Railway Company'.
(13) Named as *Edward* Vaux in the 1835 prospectuses, elsewhere Ernest. Probably a relative of the company's first Solicitor F. Vaux.
(14) These events of August-October 1837 are only known of from 'Verax', whose account may of course not be entirely the whole truth! (see Chapter 2).
(15) Reported in the *Morning Herald* 3.9.1836 and the *Public Ledger* 2.8.1836, but neither reproduced the illustration. The undated engraving at Essex CRO D/DU 576/30 is probably this 1836 view.
(16) Plans were deposited in November 1836 for a 'London Rochester & Chatham Railway' on a similar route from Ockendon to Tilbury, plus an additional section from Gravesend to Frindsbury opposite Rochester (Essex CRO Q/RUM 1/61). The advertisement in the *London Gazette* 18.11.1836 does not admit to any relationship with the THD&R Co, but (whilst it is clear that only one of the schemes could go ahead) one suspects that there was collaboration rather than hostility. This was a very prolific autumn for schemes; rival 'collier docks' upriver were also being proposed.
(17) A full account of Robertson, Herapath, the ECR, and the 1830s railway press is given in an article by the late J. E. C. Palmer 'Authority, Idiosyncrasy, and Corruption in the Early Railway Press, 1823-1844', *Journal of the Railway and Canal Historical Society* No. 161, July 1995. Robertson was sacked by the ECR in 1839 and in 1839-41 he devoted himself primarily to attacking the ECR, a complete turn-round, leaving the THD&R Co alone. However in 1841 Robertson lost control of the *Railway Times* to the ECR figure J. T. Norris who carried out an even more sarcastic attack on the THD&R Co in 1842/3 (see Chapter 2).
(18) Cf the Tithe Maps for Corringham (1839), Stanford-le-Hope (1840), and Mucking (1845) which show no land in those parishes as owned or occupied by the company.
(19) Plans deposited 1.3.1839, 'Thames Haven Railway', Essex CRO Q/RUM 1/68, with Francis Giles' name as Engineer.
(20) The THD&R Co had agreed to purchase the whole of Oil Mill Farm in 1836, but this did not happen until 1847. When the THD&R Co eventually served notice for acquiring the whole farm in December 1846, they were taken to court by the owners Messrs Long, who were holding out for the £5,000 that had been agreed in 1836. The case went to arbitration before William Tite, who awarded £3,633. (Long v. Thames Haven Dock & Railway Co, Sheriff's Court Romford, 18 May 1847 - Essex CRO D/DW T278/4, from which this quotation comes).
(21) Plans deposited 1.3.1839, 'Thames Haven Railway', Essex CRO Q/RUM 1/68, with Francis Giles' name as Engineer.
(22) *Railway Magazine* December 1838. However the 4-track idea had actually evolved prior to the reversion to the 'independent route', the *Railway Magazine* June 1838 noting 'Mr. Giles is prudently taking land for four sets of rails' for the line to Romford. It no doubt occurred to the THD&R Co, though, that there was little benefit in four lines to Romford if the ECR remained double track only, and this may itself have been a factor in reviving the 'independent route'.

CHAPTER TWO

AN UNLIKELY SURVIVOR: THE THAMES HAVEN DOCK AND RAILWAY COMPANY 1839-1850

KEEPING ALIVE (1839-45)

After 1839 the THD&R Co became seen increasingly as a failed organisation, and many people in Essex started to assume that the railway and dock would never actually be completed. But the project still received favourable comment in the general press from time to time. One factor in its survival was Sir George Stephen, who became the company's solicitor in 1840. Stephen (1794-1879) was a solicitor with a taste for politics, admired by many for his ability and upright outspokenness, but hot-tempered and prone to get involved in disputes to the detriment of his career. (He eventually emigrated in 1855 after losing most of his practice). Why he became involved in the THD&R Co is not known. He might have been considered far from ideal as a partner for Amsinck! - nevertheless he threw himself into the company's affairs with enthusiasm, revived spirits after the 'torpor' of 1839/40, and took the leading role, with Amsinck, in promoting the company in 1840-1843.

Amsinck himself was, as noted earlier, heavily involved in 1839-41 in the post of Secretary to Sir Frederic Smith's Commission, but continued to be active on the Thames Haven front as well. He came to see himself as something of an 'expert' on railway matters, as a result of his experience with the Commission, and in 1842 he wrote an (anonymous) work *Railways, Their Uses and Management* (1) to give people the benefit of his views. This naturally had much to say about the Thames Haven (it also referred to the Eastern Counties as 'an abortion of a deviation worthy only of the contempt of all right-minded men'!). The Commission's investigations also resulted in Amsinck becoming still further convinced that the Thames Haven would be one of the most profitable lines in the country.

Whilst the company did keep alive, nothing that was done in the 1839-45 period really brought any benefit in the event.

In 1840/1 the disagreements between the 'Manchester' and 'London' shareholders came to a head. A half-yearly meeting was held in August 1840 (one of only three held in the period between August 1838 and August 1846 - the others were March 1841 and February 1842). Attendances having diminished, it was held in the company's offices at Moorgate Street. Esdaile as Chairman stated that the Directors had no report to submit in the circumstances. Two of the 'Manchester' men, Mr Bury and Mr Scott, then moved for the dissolution of the company. This provoked a discussion 'of a stormy character'. Amsinck, who had been under the impression that the six Manchester men now on the Board (2) were intending to resign and let the company carry on without them, made a speech in defence of his child, 'as a shareholder, not as Secretary'. The Manchester shareholders' objection was most likely to 'throwing good money after bad' and when the Board promised that no further calls would be made until the whole of the 9,000 shares were taken, they were placated and Bury withdrew the motion. A vote of thanks was then given to the Chairman, and to Stephen who had 'exerted himself most strenuously to revive the undertaking'. Soon after this, however, four of the Manchester Directors did resign. Two 'London' men were appointed as Directors in lieu, Robert Ewart Norman and Benjamin Ifill; and a deliberate point was made at the March 1841 meeting of stressing that this had been done 'to secure a good London Board'. The Manchester influence seems to have faded altogether after this, most of their shares being forfeited. The next available full list of Directors is for May 1841 and the Board then comprised only seven: Esdaile, Wingfield, and Vaux as the remaining 1836 survivors; Norman and Ifill; and two new men, J. Barclay and J. R. Thomson, who were also both London businessmen. There were no Manchester men left at all.

The 'independent line' having been given up for the moment, intermittent discussions with the ECR were held again in 1840-1842. In October 1840 a specific proposal was formulated but rejected by the THD&R Co. By 1842 the ECR had become positively friendly and Amsinck sought to encourage this further by going to Liverpool and organising a meeting of *ECR* shareholders to persuade them to push the ECR Board into a favourable agreement with the THD&R Co.

Attempts to provoke public interest continued. New prospectuses were produced in May 1841 and January 1842 (3), but the money market was still slow at this time. In February 1841 Amsinck and other supporters attended at the Mansion House to discuss the coal trade with the Corporation. Later in 1841 the Margate local authorities and business interests were being cultivated in the hope of shares being taken up there. But none of these efforts produced hard support.

In 1841 it was decided that the railway should be built first and the dock afterwards (4), reversing the previous policy, probably because the railway was the cheaper and quicker task and its opening would have given a little income and enhanced credibility.

DEALING WITH DEFAULTERS (1841-3)

Ever since 1837, the Board had allowed any shareholders who wished to withdraw from the company to sell their shares back to the company (provided that they were paid up to date), and a good number had taken advantage of this.

At a Board meeting held on 21st October 1841 it was resolved to take action against non-payers. All shares in the hands of dead, untraceable, or bankrupt persons (some shareholders had purposely transferred their shares to such persons in order to get rid of them), or on which calls had not been paid, were declared forfeited, as a result of which the number of 'good' shares was reduced to 1,571 (see the account here). Legal proceedings were to be taken against some shareholders, 'more with a view to determining the proprietorship of the shares for their future sale, than under the hope of receiving payment of the arrears'.

The Board was especially keen to deal with the former Director William Archer Price (5), who had taken the largest holding of all (500 shares), been particularly influential in pushing for work to start in 1838, but had then failed to pay up on the calls. This was alluded to at the February 1842 shareholders' meeting although Price was not actually named.

The *Railway Times* editorial after the February meeting was very mocking of the Thames Haven, and this marked the start of a year and a half of attacks on the company in that paper. In the 2nd April 1842 edition there appeared a long pseudonymous letter from 'Verax' castigating the THD&R Co, outlining its affairs to date, and insinuating corruption. Amsinck suspected that 'Verax', who was clearly someone with past inside knowledge, was none other than Price. Sir George Stephen immediately wrote to the paper threatening a libel action, which was proceeded with, thus giving the paper encouragement to find more 'dirt' on the company. Fiction was also resorted to, the Christmas 1842 numbers carrying a spoof report of a supposed THD&R Co meeting at the dock site in August, and an 'advertisement' 'Preparing for Publication - The History and Mystery of the Thames Haven Dock and Railway Company .... containing a full, true, and particular account of this very extraordinary Undertaking, and of the Parties who have from time to time honoured it with their sanction and support .... Any communication on the subject, of an authoritive character, will be gratefully received ...'.

The first of the defaulters' cases came to court in January 1843, against Henry Wait Hall, a Bristol lawyer. The court initially ruled that proceedings should be stayed on the grounds that the company was extinct! The Price case was set down for February, and then for July, 1843, but the THD&R Co backed off at the last moment and it was not heard. It seems doubtful that any money was ever recovered from defaulters.

The libel case, *Amsinck v. Norris*, was heard before Lord Chief Justice Denman and a special jury on 1st July 1843. ('Verax' not being definitely identifiable, the case was brought against J. T. Norris the owner of the *Railway Times*). Amsinck sought damages

General Statement of the Receipts and Expenditure of the THAMES HAVEN DOCK AND RAILWAY COMPANY, *from September, 1835, to December, 1841.*

DR. To amount received for—	£	s.	d.	CR. By amount paid for—	£	s.	d.
Deposit on 6,163 Shares, at £2 10s	15,407	10	0	Preliminary Expenses	895	1	7
1st Call on 2,850 Shares at £2 10s	7,125	0	0	Parliamentary ditto ..	1,078	8	2
2d Call on 1,025 Shares at £2 10s	2,687	10	0	Law ditto	3,057	0	8
Call in advance......	25	0	0	Commission & Agency	887	6	2
Re-sale of 10 Shares ..	10	0	0	Office Furniture	179	18	6
Sale of Field of Oats..	80	0	0	Advertising, Printing, and Stationery; including Maps, Plans, Views, and Lithographing	2,839	8	2
Rent of Land & Offices	583	2	3	Engineering	1,429	6	6
Interest and Premium	995	0	3	Surveying, &c.	88	19	0
				Common Seal of Company	38	9	6
				Travelling Expenses ..	276	6	11
				Incidental Expenses ..	240	11	8
				Office Expenses	34	12	6
				Rent of Offices	520	14	0
				Salaries	3,796	17	3
				Shares re-purchased ..	1,864	17	9
				Petty Expenses	327	6	11
				Purchase of Land, &c.	4,833	17	0
				Excavation, & Expenses of Contractors......	1,662	14	10
				Repairing Sea-wall....	147	10	6
				Boring for water at Dock	50	0	0
				Interest on land, & purchase of Exchequerbills	817	4	6
				Cash in hand	1,846	10	5
	£26,913	2	6		£26,913	2	6

Assets and Liabilities at the present date.

DR. ASSETS.	£	s.	d.	CR. LIABILITIES.	£	s.	d.
To Oil-Mill Farm	5,000	0	0	By Out-standing Bills ..	2,949	5	6
Rent...............	203	15	0	Land	2,936	17	9
Cash at Bankers:				Interest	73	8	6
Glyn & Co. 1,450 6 3				Secretary's Salary	1,620	0	0
Marylebone Bank.... 351 6 10				Clerk's Salary........	12	10	0
	1,801	13	1	Rent of Offices	81	5	0
Calls due	1,902	10	0	Contingencies	300	0	0
Furniture	50	0	0	Balance carried down..	984	11	4
	£8,957	18	1		£8,957	18	1

To Balance brought down £984 11 4

Available Cash Assets.

		£	s.	d.
Rent		£203	15	0
Cash at Bankers		1,801	13	1
Calls due, being good		1,902	10	0
		£3,907	18	1

Statement of Shares.

Original Shares sold		6,163
Forfeited for non-Registration...	541	
Re-purchased	1,382	
Transferred to the Company.....................	855	
On Books	3,385	
		6,163

		£	s.	d.
On Books......................	3,385			
Forfeited	1,874			
Remaining	1,571			
Calls due on Shares................................		£12,147	10	0
Good Debts	£1,902	10	0	
Doubtful	762	10	0	
Bad	9,482	10	0	
	£12,147	10	0	

HENRY AMSINCK, *Secretary.*

This combined account for the whole period to December 1841 was included in the 1842 prospectus, and is the best surviving record of the company's financial situation in the first years. Even so it must of course be taken with pinches of salt, and the whole truth is never going to be established.

Dealing firstly with the shares, the 'second call' of £2.10s had been made in September 1839, but it will be seen that only 1,025 shares had responded (not surprisingly, given the company's inactive state). A 'third call' of £2.10s had been made in September 1841 (contrary to the pledge given in August 1840) but no income is listed as having come in from this as of December 31st. It is not clear on what basis the figures (at the end) of £12,147 'due' in calls, of which £1,902 (only) is considered 'good', are calculated. What is clear is that the number of 'good' shares is down to 1,571 at best, nowhere near enough to pay for any useful works even in the (highly unlikely) event of all 1,571 being able and willing to pay up the full £50 in due course. Only 10 of the shares repurchased by the company had actually been resold (Amsinck had claimed in 1838 that 970 shares sold back to the company had been resold at a profit of £2,381).

Turning to the Balance Sheet, the company did not actually own Oil Mill Farm as they had only paid an initial sum. The liabilities therefore really exceeded the assets, although the 'Secretary's Salary' and 'Land' payments would not need to be paid in practice, so the position was by no means hopeless.

Whilst the THD&R Co suffered from an inability to raise money, there were no major scandals in its finances, by the standards of the day (and certainly not by the standards of the ECR!). The original solicitors Vaux & Fennell had been avaricious (like so many of their brethren operating in the railway field) and had sent in a bill for £3,400 for legal charges in 1835-7, which was admitted to include over £2,000 profit, but the company had picked up on this and the solicitors resigned. All this came out in the wash in the *Railway Times* in 1842 when Vaux was sued by a former partner; the paper sought to imply this was a 'Thames Haven scandal', but if anything it surely showed that Amsinck had been on the ball?

opposite Sketch map showing the route of the THD&R Co's proposed 'independent line' and the Tilbury branch. The main route was almost identical on each occasion but the terminal arrangements varied; the 1839 scheme was from Sion Square (no L&BR link, and no Tilbury branch); the 1843 session 'Thames Haven Railway Extension' was from both Jubilee Street and the L&BR, with a Tilbury branch; the 1844 session 'Tilbury & Blackwall Junction Railway' was from the L&BR only, with a Tilbury branch. No plans were actually deposited in 1847 but Chadwick's references to the 'Green Line' and 'Yellow Line' in the 1847 Committee hearings indicate ideas the same as in 1844.

of £1,000 but the jury, after retiring for two hours, awarded him one farthing, and the judge made him pay his own costs. The *Railway Times* (8th July) gave a ten-page report of the case and probably considered it worthwhile for the amusement value. We should be grateful too, for the 'Verax' letter and the court case are important sources for the history of the company.

THE 1842 ACT

The 1836 Act powers were due to expire in July 1843. Any company whose powers were allowed to lapse was liable to become seen as an even less likely investment, and the Thames Haven were alive to this. Initially they intended a Bill for the 1841 session (two years earlier than was necessary) but this was not proceeded with. In 1842 a Bill was proceeded with and, passing through Parliament without opposition, received the Royal Assent as **The Thames Haven Dock and Railway Act 1842** (6) on 30th June 1842. The land purchase powers were extended to July 1844 and the construction powers to July 1846. Additionally s.7 of this Act empowered the making of agreements with the ECR for the ECR to run trains over the Thames Haven line. This possibility had not been heard of previously, and was seemingly not discussed as such now, but it would not have been any surprise if the ECR had ended up working the line, as it did of course for other small companies.

THE 'INDEPENDENT LINE' AND THE TILBURY BRANCH REVIVED (1842-4)

The passing of the 1842 Act, reviving the Romford line powers, affirmed how the THD&R Co felt pushed back into the arms of the ECR again in the 1840-42 period. However by the autumn of 1842 they had given up on the ECR for the second time and, just as in 1838, the 'independent line' idea came back to the fore. The general financial situation was now beginning to pick up after the country's post-1836 depression, and the THD&R Co was inspired to new promotions again.

In November 1842 plans were deposited for a 'Thames Haven Railway Extension', on the same route as proposed in 1839, from an independent terminus at Jubilee Street, Stepney, to join the existing alignment near Orsett, plus a branch at Stepney to link with the London & Blackwall. (The Blackwall was not actively involved in this scheme; the Thames Haven were just sensibly 'playing it both ways'). The existing line between Romford and Orsett was to be abandoned. A branch was also now proposed to Tilbury with a ferry to Gravesend (reviving the 1836 ideas, although the detailed alignment of the branch was different). However no Bill was proceeded with in the 1843 session, in the event.

From this time on the THD&R Co's affairs were to become increasingly influenced by proposals for rail links to Tilbury (promoted for the most part by other parties).

After getting cold feet on this Bill, the THD&R Co attempted further talks with the ECR in summer 1843, Sir George Stephen

attending the ECR Board in June. However in August the ECR informed the THD&R Co that they would not lower the proposed tolls, which had been fixed 'after mature deliberation', and in the context of 'the many inconveniences of a slightly remunerative coal traffic coming upon an important passenger line'. (This anti-goods view was a pet notion of the ECR's at this period, and no doubt one of the reasons why they were not really enthusiastic about the Thames Haven).

Accordingly the THD&R Co went 'independent' again, depositing in November 1843 plans for a 'Tilbury & Blackwall Junction Railway' which was identical to the previous year's scheme except that the Jubilee Street branch was omitted, thereby making it wholly dependent on L&B support. The L&B had again not been consulted in advance. In November Sir George Stephen attended the L&B Board and they 'expressed themselves willing to receive any additional traffic'. But after Amsinck saw them in February 1844 in order to secure a definite agreement, they responded that 'the Board did not see reasons cogent for furthering the project'. In the circumstances the THD&R Co decided not to proceed with their 1844 Bill. They were back at square one.

AMSINCK RESIGNS (1843)

For reasons which are nowhere stated, Amsinck resigned as Secretary in March 1843. It does not seem that he was 'pushed', as he continued to be active on the company's behalf in 1844 (vide above). After that, however, he is no longer heard of, except as an 'opposition' voice at the time of the Chadwick takeover in 1847 (in his capacity as a shareholder). He was only 44 in 1844, and was to live until December 1878, but nothing is known about his later years, save for the naval lists recording his promotion from Lieutenant to Commander in 1864.

Lieut. Col J. H. Humfrey, formerly Secretary of the Glasgow & Ayr Railway, was appointed as Secretary in lieu of Amsinck He did not last long; Frederick Edgell had replaced him by late 1844.

The *Railway Times* commented in August 1843
'We believe the old crew have been entirely swept away ...... ';
but this seems not to have been the case.

However Sir George Stephen did disappear from the scene some time in 1844. The simultaneous loss of Amsinck and Stephen must have left the company somewhat leaderless. With the money market quickly improving and no rival schemes as yet for the area, this time might otherwise have been the best chance the Thames Haven ever had to get things moving. Instead the leaderless company seems to have 'slept' for over a year after the Blackwall's rebuff in February 1844, and thereby 'blown' the opportunity.

THE 1846 SESSION

Up to 1845, thanks to the general depression in railway promotion after 1836, the often-dormant THD&R Co had not been

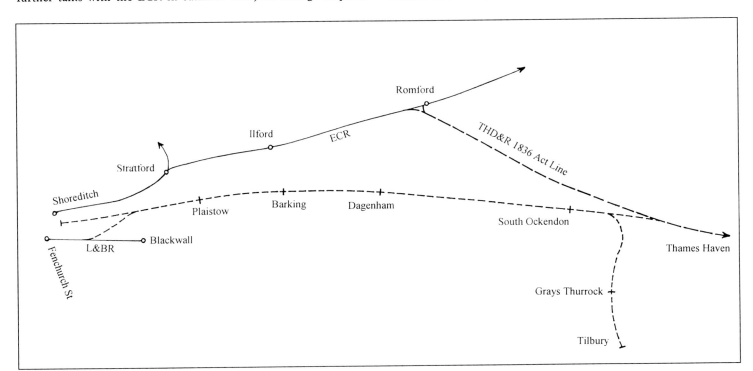

troubled by any rival schemes for the area. However as the 'mania' heightened in 1845 it was inevitable that other schemes would now be put forward, and the remainder of the THD&R Co's independent life as a railway company (1845-52) was largely a tale of having to react to the schemes of others, 'playing it by ear' and seeking alliances with the ECR or the Blackwall as the politics of the moment dictated, for the most part in relation to ideas of a short branch to Thames Haven being grafted on to one of the other schemes. However whenever nothing seemed forthcoming this way, the THD&R Co would revert to 'going it alone' again!

No less than four rival schemes for the area were put forward in the 1846 session. These have already been described (with map) at pp 9-10 of Volume 1, and it is therefore only necessary here to elaborate on the THD&R Co's perception of the situation. The London & Blackwall-backed 'London & South Essex Railway', which became public in May 1845, was clearly incompatible with the full Thames Haven line, and the THD&R Co immediately sought a meeting between Directors regarding 'amalgamation of their schemes'. In June it was agreed that the L&SER would 'purchase the interest' of the THD&R Co. Secondly there was the independently-promoted 'Eastern Counties Junction and Southend Railway' whose line directly paralleled the Thames Haven's between Romford and Orsett, its promoters probably regarding the THD&R Co as defunct. In May 1845 both the THD&R Co and the ECJ&SR approached the ECR seeking support. The ECR responded favourably to both, telling the THD&R Co that 'in the event of their determining to construct their line, the undertaking will receive every facility from this company', and the ECJ&SR that they would be 'happy to afford it every facility'. The other two schemes, the 'North Gravesend Railway' and the 'London & Southend Railway', were not so directly in conflict with the Thames Haven line. The ECR themselves had no Bill for the area in this session.

In the event none of these four schemes were successful. However the THD&R Co had also promoted a Bill in the 1846 session, for another extension of time for the 1836 Act powers, and this was passed, receiving the Royal Assent on 3rd July 1846 as **The Thames Haven Dock and Railway Act** 1846 (7). The land purchase powers were extended until July 1847, and the construction powers until July 1851.

Thus by the summer of 1846 everybody was back to exactly the same position as they had been in the spring of 1845! But it was clear that there was 'more to come'. Indeed the THD&R Co Board themselves made it known (at their half-yearly meeting in August 1846 - the first one actually held since 1842) that they intended to apply to Parliament for a Tilbury line again 'so soon as the circumstances of the company allow'. It also became known that the ECR were intending a Tilbury and Southend scheme for the 1847 session.

In July 1846 Geary, the THD&R Co's new Engineer (8) attended the ECR Board to 'give an explanation' of the THD&R Co's intentions. Everybody was hedging their bets.

THE CHADWICK TAKEOVER (1847)

At this point the THD&R Co underwent a change of ownership. In the autumn of 1846 the six remaining Directors (Esdaile, Wingfield, Thomson, Barclay, Norman and Ifill) entered, apparently unanimously, into negotiations with William Chadwick, who had recently successfully promoted the Richmond Railway, with a view to his taking control of the THD&R Co and introducing new money into it via his associates. This was all agreed in December 1846/January 1847, and then implemented in February/March 1847.

Chadwick had started as a contractor, building part of the GWR main line (including Maidenhead Bridge) in the 1830s, and then the Didcot-Oxford line, and other contracts. He did well out of these and, as many contractors were to do, then started getting involved in railway promotion. At this date he was best known as promoter of the Richmond Railway (he was 'Surveyor' to the company initially, but soon became Chairman) which got its Act in 1845 and opened in July 1846. This company was sold to the LSWR in January 1847. Chadwick pushed for extensions to Staines and Windsor, and also became involved in the North Wales Railway (Bangor-Caernarvon) and was made its Chairman in 1846. In 1847 he launched the 'North & South Western Junction Railway' for a line from Harrow to Brentford; this was thrown out at that time but was the origin of the Willesden-Brentford line as built.

Despite these existing commitments, Chadwick was clearly still on the look-out for other schemes to get involved with. He was introduced to the Thames Haven scheme by a Mr Cowan (9) who had acquired a number of shares with the intention of becoming actively involved, but needed further backing. Under the deal arranged with the old Board, Chadwick purchased 5,600 shares (all 'forfeited' shares) at 1s each, on the basis of their being regarded as having £12.10s already paid up on them, and agreed to pay £5 on each for a new 'call' that was made as part of the arrangements (10). In fact he registered only 1,000 shares in his own name and disposed of the remainder to his associates, 'chiefly amongst those who were shareholders in the Richmond Railway', at 30s each, thereby making a nice immediate profit for himself on the deal. (The others were not told at the time he was making 29s profit on each share, but it was not unreasonable for him to make some profit as he had 'gone to a very considerable expense in surveying the line'). Chadwick's associates in turn quickly disposed of many of their shares to others in order to reduce the amount they had to pay for the £5 call. However it appears that the new call was actually paid by all the new shareholders.

A half-yearly meeting was held on 26th February 1847, but no substantive business was transacted as Esdaile in the Chair proposed adjournment for four weeks as 'certain negotiations are pending with gentlemen of property and high standing, with a view to enabling them to carry out the undertaking'. It was only in the first week of March that the new share distribution was effected. The resumed meeting on 26th March 1847 was told that 'the Directors have been successful in their exertions for resuscitating the company', and that negotiations were already under way for land purchase and for a contract to complete the dock. Three 'Chadwick men' were elected to the Board at this meeting (in place of Barclay, Norman, and Ifill), and another six 'Chadwick men' (including Chadwick himself) were also appointed as Directors around this time. Chadwick was elected Chairman in April, Esdaile the previous Chairman becoming Deputy Chairman. The new Board therefore comprised three 'survivors' (Esdaile, Wingfield and Thomson) and nine 'Chadwick men', being (apart from Chadwick himself) :-

Henry Broadwood   (MP for Bridgwater)

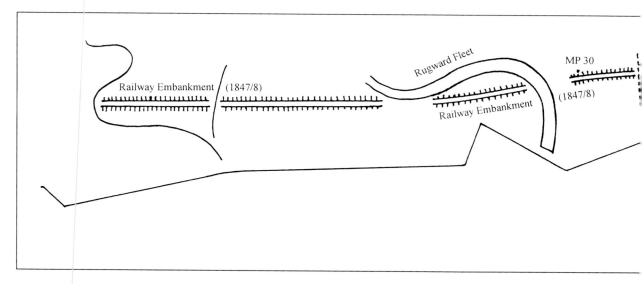

Benjamin Edgington (The Southwark Sail- and Tent-maker; also Auditor to the Richmond Railway)
Andrew Inderwick
John Dawson Lowden (Retired businessman, Director of Richmond Railway, also of Wimbledon and Croydon)
Lewis Pocock (Colliery owner in Wales, residing in London)
Thomas Bridge Simpson (of Brixton)
J. W. West (Corn Factor, Datchet)
Charles Fenton Whiting (Printer, The Strand)

none of whom appear to have had any local interests in Essex.

The 'old' shareholders were now a hopeless rump with no say in the company's affairs. There were only about twenty of them, and their holdings now represented only 10% of the total (11). Amongst them was Amsinck who had not paid the new £5 call and was deemed to owe £2,000 in unpaid calls in consequence.. He attended the 26th March meeting and objected to it as illegally constituted, also claiming that the Board had acted improperly in 'forfeiting' certain shares on which the new £5 had not been paid, without the authority of a shareholders' meeting. He announced that he intended to take legal action, and did initiate a case, but seems to have dropped it in August after negotiation.

Nevertheless there were certain indelicacies in what had been done, some of which came out in the wash when Chadwick gave evidence against the Eastern Counties' Bill (see next section) in the House of Commons in June 1847, and was grilled by hostile Counsel. In order to authorise (retrospectively) the new forfeiting of shares, a Special General Meeting was held on 25th June. There was only one dissentient, Geary the company's (ex-) Engineer, who was also a shareholder and had not paid the call. Another Special General Meeting on 16th July authorised (again retrospectively) the Board to resell the forfeited shares.

THE EASTERN COUNTIES' 1847 BILL

At the same time as the Chadwick takeover was being implemented, the THD&R Co had to turn its thoughts to opposing the ECR's 1847 Bill for a line from Forest Gate to Tilbury and Southend. This again, has already been described at Volume 1 pp 9/10. The London & Blackwall (London & South Essex) had intended to return with a rival Bill in the 1847 session, and the THD&R Co themselves had announced their intention to promote a Tilbury branch, but both backed out, leaving the ECR as the sole contender in the 1847 session, and therefore likely to succeed.

The THD&R Co petitioned against the ECR Bill. The ECR considered that the THD&R Co's opposition was angled with the intention of forcing the ECR to buy them off, and indeed the ECR Vice-Chairman David Waddington had been approached in May by 'a gentleman from Birmingham' suggesting that the THD&R Co were willing to sell out if the ECR wished - clearly an agent of Chadwick's, although Chadwick denied in parliament that he had bought the Thames Haven with a deliberate intention of selling out to the ECR at a profit.

G. P. Bidder, who was Engineer for the ECR scheme and also heavily involved in its promotion, pushed the idea of making a junction on the ECR line at Stanford-le-Hope and only building the easternmost $1/4$ of the Thames Haven line, between there and Thames Haven. [This, of course, is what eventually happened in the 1850s]. Waddington confirmed in parliament that the ECR would be willing to do this. Chadwick however was wholly opposed to it, claiming that 'we should be deceiving the whole country' (i.e. the area between Romford and Orsett, which had been promised railway communication).

The Commons Committee hearings took place on 18th-22nd June 1847. Chadwick, introduced by his Counsel as 'the Chairman of that much abused concern the Thames Haven Dock and Railway Company', was able to cut a credible figure despite the THD&R Co having no Bill themselves, and was allowed to elaborate on the THD&R Co's own ideas for serving the area better, producing a plan showing 'Yellow lines' to Tilbury and Southend, and a 'Green line' direct from London to be built if the ECR would not come to agreement (i.e. the old 'independent line' again). The fact that construction work was now under way again (see next section) also helped the THD&R Co's credibility. However their opposition was not successful and the Commons Committee passed the Bill. Unfortunately for the ECR, it then became one of a number of Bills 'suspended' until the 1848 session for time reasons.

This gave the chance for more negotiation. In June 1847 Chadwick saw the London & Blackwall directors regarding the 'South Essex' line, and was told they were still keen to carry it out (but they did not, in the event, promote any Bill in 1848 either). Continuing the (sensible) bet-hedging policy, discussions also began with the ECR, with Bidder as the main driving force. Bidder was an easier and more persuasive negotiator than the ECR Directors, and by November Chadwick had agreed to the Stanford-le-Hope junction concept, giving up the Romford - Stanford-le-Hope section. Chadwick and Bidder met the ECR Board about this on 27th January 1848, and it began to seem likely that things would go ahead on this basis. Bit in February the ECR's Bill was rejected by the House of Lords owing to technical irregularities.

Everything was now back into the melting pot yet again. At the 29th February 1848 THD&R Co half-yearly meeting, Chadwick said that they should congratulate themselves on the way things had turned out, as the ECR had been 'kept out' of the area. The proposed agreement was now regarded as void owing to the failure of the ECR Bill. The THD&R Co had really had a charmed life in the 1846 and 1847/8 sessions, with rival proposals that seemed likely to suceed falling by the wayside for unlikely reasons.

RESUMPTION OF WORK (1847)

Thanks to the new 'Chadwick' money, 1847 was to prove the THD&R Co's most dynamic year since 1838. For some months it must have seemed that success was indeed round the corner. 'The trains will be running to Thames Haven within $1^1/_2$ years', said Chadwick in June 1847.

With the 'new', and some of the 'old', shareholders paying the £5 call, £28,760 was raised from this source in the first half of 1847. A further call was planned for the autumn (but this never actually happened).

A new set of Chadwick appointees took over the company's work :-

James John Greer	Secretary
Walter Charles Venning	Solicitor
Thomas Hay	Engineer

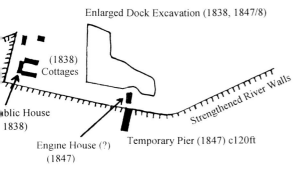

obbing Parish boundary

Enlarged Dock Excavation (1838, 1847/8)

(1838) Cottages

Strengthened River Walls

blic House 1838)

Engine House (?) (1847)

Temporary Pier (1847) c120ft

SITUATION AT CESSATION OF WORK IN SPRING 1848
Scale 6 in to the mile

Based on November 1851 LT&SER Deposited Plans: there is no evidence that anything happened 1848-51.

The 1851 Plans simply describe the whole station/dock area en bloc as 'Pasture Land, Engine House, Storehouse, Part of Proposed Dock and Landing, Cowhouse, and Premises'. The Engine House was probably the building by the temporary pier (this building lasted until c1860). The temporary pier itself was gone by 1855; it is not clear whether it had survived to be used by Peto Brassey & Betts in 1854-5. The railway embankment built in 1847-8 ran from 29m 15ch to 30m 12ch (in the later mileages) (grid refs 722- to 735-). As at 1848 the THD&R Co still owned no land on the next stretch, between Mucking and 29m 15ch.

None of these had any previous association with the company. Henry Crawter remained as Land Surveyor.

The purchase of land was set in motion very actively by Crawter in the spring of 1847. In June it was stated that 411 acres had been 'agreed for' and only 20 acres not yet agreed for; then in August that all land had been agreed. This included all the land for the railway from Romford. Some landowners were paid in full, notably the Dean & Chapter of St Paul's (Mucking), C. T. Montgomerie (Horndon), and Messrs Long of Oil Mill Farm (see Chapter 1) which was needed to enable the dock works to be continued. Most, however, were only paid a 10% deposit. Something in the region of £12,000 was spent on land at this time.

Contracts were let in April 1847, for the whole of the railway from Romford to Thames Haven, and for the dock (although not for the full 1000ft by 800ft of the 1836 plans - it was said by Chadwick in June that only £60,000 was to be spent initially on the works at the dock, the remainder (to a total of £150,000) being left until the traffic grew). The railway was to be built double track. There were two contractors, named as Stevens, and Stoval(?) & Taylor, 'one for the masonry and one for the earthwork' according to Hay, who however also says that the railway and the dock are being built by different parties, which seems a more likely division.

Work began, on both the railway and dock, some time in May/June 1847 (12). Possession had been taken of Oil Mill Farm in May (the company having seemingly had no access, even to the field on which the 1838 excavations had been done, prior to this). A 'pier' was being built at Thames Haven to enable materials to be brought in by water. The railway was to be started at the Thames Haven end, and initially no work was to be done west of Stanford-le-Hope. This, one suspects, was partly in case the company did end up only building that section if a deal was done with the ECR, although it may have been for the contractor's benefit as this section through the marshes was all on low embankment for which material could be obtained from the dock excavation, working westwards.

The August 1847 shareholders' meeting heard a confident report :-

'the construction of the railway is in active operation. The cottages necessary for affording shelter and protection to the mechanics and labourers engaged on the works of the Dock [i.e. those built in 1838, and no doubt left to nature since then] have been put in a state of substantial repair at a very moderate outlay, affording accommodation for 150 men'.

Work continued after this, but at the next meeting in February 1848 it was openly stated that only the Stanford-le-Hope to Thames Haven section of the line had been worked on, because of the likely agreement with the ECR (which, however, had just collapsed, as noted above).

Had things still been healthy financially, one would have expected the THD&R Co to have begun work on the full line from Romford, after all, at this point. But in fact silence starts to descend again after this. The national climate was turning bad in the post-mania collapse and it was clear that many people (including Chadwick himself) would not be able to pay another call. The

August 1848 meeting was told that 'the Directors have very little to report' and that work of late had been 'limited to the excavation required for the tidal dock'. Nobody asked any questions.

It is to be deduced, therefore, that work had in fact ceased in the spring of 1848, after about 10 months activity. What had done in this period?

The railway embankment had been made for one mile near Thames Haven (see map) albeit with gaps at 'difficult' points by watercourses. This embankment of 1847/8 was used for the laying of the railway in 1854/5, so the THD&R Co could claim to have 'built' this small part of the railway prior to the arrangement with the LT&S. Nothing was done at the Thames Haven station site, and indeed it is not clear from the available references whether it was still intended in 1847/8 to run the railway due east along the north side of the dock, or whether the idea of a steamer pier had already emerged (13).

The dock excavations had been roughly doubled in size (but were still just a useless hole, which quickly became waterfilled again).

An 'Engine House' had been built (presumably primarily for pumping?).

The river walls at Thames Haven had been rebuilt (in situ) in a stronger form. There were river walls before, but these were insufficient and the THD&R Co had been in trouble with the Fobbing Commissioners for not keeping them in good repair.

COLLAPSE AGAIN (1848-50)

The 'Chadwick' THD&R Co had been defeated by the same circumstances - a national economic slump following a boom - that had defeated the company in 1838. Chadwick and his allies had a proven record of getting things done in good times, but when things turned bad they ran out of 'real' money.

After the August 1848 meeting there are two years of almost total silence. No further meetings are known until August 1852. The Secretary was dismissed, on the grounds that he was 'doing nothing at all for £200 a year'.

Herapath's commented in September 1848 :-

' This magnificent line is in status quo. The public will not bite. They have no cash .... There has, time after time, been a little coquetting with the Eastern Counties; but it is no go. Mr Hudson would not be so unwise as to touch the line. The Eastern Counties company have quite enough, indeed too much, dead weight on their hands without adding that hopeful concern, the Thames Haven, to it'.

In the spring of 1850 Chadwick himself pulled out of the company. He had lost most of his money and became seen as a 'bubble' man, so that the news of his going was seen as having a favourable impact. However his allies remained in control of the company, John Dawson Lowden being made Chairman.

Thanks to the national slump, there were no rival schemes for the area in 1848-50, so the Thames Haven was not defeated because of its dormant state. It was to rise again, this time, thankfully, bringing matters to a conclusion.

---

(1) Copy at BM 1936.g.13.

(2) Names unknown. There had been only two 'Manchester men' on the Board in 1836 but clearly others had come on since in place of other Directors who had resigned.

(3) 1841 Prospectus - Ottley 6864, fourth item. Copy seen in private collection. This is basically as the December 1835 prospectus but the four page 'Prospectus' section is largely rewritten, and 51 pages were added of correspondence and articles relating to the project in the railway press in the years since 1835.

1842 Prospectus - Ottley 6864, fifth item. Copy in LSE Library. Basically as 1841 but in a rearranged order and with further addition of the February 1842 Half-yearly Report and Accounts.

(4) Amsinck letter, *Railway Times* 11.9.1841. The 1842 Prospectus also speaks in these terms.

(5) Referred to as John Archer Price in the *Railway Times* in 1843, but it is made clear that it is the former Director who is being described.

(6) 5 & 6 Vic cap. 89.

(7) 9 & 10 Vic cap. 144.

(8) In the 1842 Prospectus Sir John Rennie had been named as Engineer (Francis Giles having ceased to be involved). It is doubtful if Rennie was ever called upon to do anything. Geary was brought in when the THD&R Co reawoke in 1846; little is known of him and his involvement ceased on the Chadwick takeover in 1847.

(9) Not identifiable (none of the Cowans in contemporary Bradshaw's Manuals seem likely). Cowan is only known through Chadwick's 1847 parliamentary evidence, and his presence at the August 1847 meeting where he stated that he was involved in the negotiations with the ECR.

(10) The exact details of the THD&R Co's share capital are lost in a welter of absent or confused 'facts', but the December 1841 accounts show that 3,797 shares had been

repurchased or forfeited by then (541 + 1,382 + 1,874). After that there seems to have been no further forfeiting until 23.2.1847 when (as described in the text) the Board resolved to declare forfeit all shares on which the new £5 call was not paid. *Herapath's* 26.6.1847 reported that 1,791 further shares were forfeited as a result. It may be fallacious reasoning but 3,797 + 1,791 comes to 5,588 which seems to equate to Chadwick's 'about 5,600' purchase (although it is not clear how 1,791 shares could be forfeited in 1847 when only 1,571 had been regarded as 'good' in 1842!). In June 1847 Chadwick stated that at the time of his purchase 600 shares were still 'live' with 'old' shareholders. The total number of shares is given as 6,200 in June 1847 (i.e. 5,600 plus 600).

All sources from 1847 on agree that £12.10s had been 'called' on the shares prior to the £5 call in 1847. Only £10 (Deposit, 1st, 2nd, and 3rd calls) had been called up to 1842 so it seems that an unknown 4th call had been made between 1842 and 1847.

For subsequent developments see Chapter 3 note 5.

(11) There is a complete list of the 68 current shareholders in Chadwick's 21.6.1847 evidence to the House of Commons Committee on the ECR Bill.

(12) In the House of Commons Committee evidence, Chadwick says on 21.6.1847 'they have commenced the line in the marshes ..... They have been at work upon the line for the last two weeks'; and Hay says on 22.6.1847 that he had visited the site 'nine days since' and there was then work in progress on both railway and dock, the men having been at work for two weeks already at the time of his visit.

(13) The *Railway Times* 4.3.1848 reports Chadwick as having said at that week's THD&R Co half-yearly meeting that 'the engineering arrangements for constructing the pier' had been completed. This can hardly refer to the 1847-built contractor's temporary pier (which Hay observed being built already in June 1847) and is therefore suggestive of work being about to start on another pier. That there is no sign of such a pier on the 1851 plans is not surprising; Chadwick was speaking just before all work ceased.

CHAPTER THREE

AN UNLIKELY SUCCESS - THE BUILDING OF THE THAMES HAVEN BRANCH AND SALE OF THE LINE TO THE 'LT&S' (1850-1861)

THE LONDON & BLACKWALL 1851 TILBURY BILL AND THE THD&R Co 1851 ACT

The start of another chapter in the Thames Haven saga in 1850/1 provoked a groan from *Herapath's* (24.5.1851) :-

'We thought this concern had years ago sunk into the grave never to rise again, but it seems it has more lives than a cat ....'

Indeed it did. The THD&R Co needed to reawaken in the autumn of 1850 (a) because the London & Blackwall were promoting a Tilbury line for the 1851 session, which would clearly influence the whole fate of South Essex railway development, and (b) because the THD&R Co's own powers would expire in July 1851 unless a Bill for extension was promoted.

And with the national economic situation just starting to improve a little after the post-mania slump, this necessary reawakening became possible.

As in 1847 with the ECR Tilbury & Southend scheme, the THD&R Co decided in 1850 to take an aggressive approach towards the L&BR scheme, no doubt primarily in hopes of getting a good price for withdrawing their opposition after negotiations. On 13th November 1850 they gave notice of a THD&R Co Bill for

- Another extension of time for their 1836 Act line.
- A branch from South Ockendon Hall Farm on the 1836 line to Tilbury Fort (the fifth time that the THD&R Co had given notice for a Tilbury branch - the previous occasions being, as mentioned earlier, for the 1837, 1843, 1844, and 1847 sessions - but no Bill was ever proceeded with in any of these sessions).
- Changes in the THD&R Co's share capital structure.

The L&BR scheme has been dealt with previously in full detail at pp 10-12 of Volume 1, and here we need only recap on it from a more THD&R Co-centric viewpoint. Essentially it was the publishing of the L&BR's intentions in November 1850 that began the sequence of events that led directly to the construction of part of the Thames Haven line in 1854/5 and the abandonment of the rest.

The predictable negotiations with the L&BR quickly produced results, Tyerman the L&BR Solicitor telling his Board on 21st January 1851 that the THD&R Co

'were disposed to agree to the following proposition, viz. that they should abandon their line to Romford, with the exception of that portion between the site of the proposed dock and Stanford-le-Hope a distance of about three miles, which they should at once construct, and that an Act should be applied for in a future session to make a connection with the Tilbury line at the joint expense of the two companies'.

i.e. exactly the same as the THD&R Co had agreed with the ECR in 1847/8, save that with the L&BR promoting a line as far as Tilbury only, there was this time the little difficulty of a 4$\frac{1}{2}$-mile 'gap' between Tilbury and Stanford-le-Hope which would have to be left until the next session. On 28th January the L&BR Board were told that a formal agreement had been made with the THD&R Co. All this had also been agreed by Bidder, Peto, and Brassey, who were the real influences behind the L&BR scheme.

Although an (unnamed-probably Wingfield ?) THD&R Co director had petitioned against the L&BR Bill, in his capacity as a landowner but really to give the THD&R Co another lever if the negotiations went sour, this was not pursued and in the House of Commons Committee on 9th April 1851 a letter from the THD&R Co Chairman J. D. Lowden was read out stating that there was no opposition to the L&BR Bill, which was accordingly passed in the Commons. But on 2nd June it was unexpectedly thrown out by the Lords on technical grounds.

Hedging their bets again, the THD&R Co had also been dealing with the ECR in winter 1850/1. A THD&R Co 'deputation' of 'Mr Chapman' (W. Chapman an active shareholder) and the new company Solicitor Henry Toogood (1) attended the ECR Board on 3rd December 1850, and were asked to forward a detailed written statement. However on 2nd January 1851 the ECR resolved not to give any assistance to the THD&R Co (2).

The THD&R Co's own 1851 Bill was proceeding in the meantime (without the Tilbury branch, which never had plans deposited, owing to agreement with the L&BR having become likely). It was unopposed in the Commons, but in the Lords there was a petition from the North Ockendon landowner Sir Benyon de Beauvoir, as a result of which Lowden had to appear to give evidence on 17th July 1851. This gave de Beauvoir's counsel a chance to engage in some sneering about the THD&R Co's finances, claiming that one Mr Poynting, a £1-a-week office clerk, had 250 shares to his name, and that William Gun with 1,250 shares had left his address and disappeared without trace - the relevance of all this being, of course, that with over £30 still to be called on each THD&R Co share, the company was not likely to get far if a large number of shares were held by such characters. However the Lords Committee decided in favour of the Bill, provided the THD&R Co agreed to a deviation of the line through de Beauvoir's property (not specified in the Act, but to be negotiated).

The Thames Haven Dock and Railway Act 1851 (3) was therefore passed on 1st August 1851. It extended the company's land powers until 4th July 1852, and construction powers to 3rd July 1854; reduced the number of Directors from 12 to 7 (4); and authorised a reduction in the nominal value of the shares.

A 'financial reconstruction' was then effected in 1852. £50 shares had been common in the 1830s but were now disliked. A Special General Meeting in May 1852 approved the nominal value of the existing 6,063 shares (5) being reduced to £25 so that there was now only £7 still to be called on each share instead of £32, no doubt to the relief of those who did not actually have cash readily available to pay further calls!

THE 'LONDON, TILBURY & SOUTHEND EXTENSION RAILWAY' AND THE 1852 AGREEMENT

The failure of the L&BR's 1851 Bill meant, in principle, that the THD&R Co was (just as it had been at the end of the 1846 and 1847/8 sessions) now back at square one as the only company with an authorised line for South Essex. The political reality was, however, now very different. After years of fighting over the territory, the ECR and L&BR were now, under Bidder's persuasive influence, coming together to promote jointly a line from Forest Gate to Tilbury and Southend in the 1852 session. There was no longer any chance for the THD&R Co to survive by playing off the ECR and L&BR against each other; and there was every sign that this joint promotion would be successful in parliament.

The THD&R Co therefore had to get a deal arranged - but they were not powerless beggars, as their possession of an Act for a 'rival' line could have made them a powerful opposition force in parliament if the ECR and L&BR could not 'buy them off'.

The 'London Tilbury & Southend Extension Railway' plans deposited jointly by the ECR and L&BR in November 1851 in fact included a rival Thames Haven branch of their own, directly alongside the THD&R Co's line from Mucking to Thames Haven. But this was purely a negotiating ploy on their part. The THD&R Co had already proposed to the L&BR in October 1851 that there should be a deal on the same basis as had been agreed in 1847/8 and 1850/1, i.e. that they should abandon the Romford-Mucking section and build only the Mucking to Thames Haven section, with a junction with the LT&SER at Mucking. The ECR and L&BR were happy enough with the THD&R Co's attitude and withdrew their rival Thames Haven scheme before promoting their Bill. However it took some months to come to a firm agreement. The THD&R Co's special meeting in May 1852 was told that the company proposed to proceed at once with the full line from Romford (now to be single track (6)), and the THD&R Co began by opposing the LT&SER Bill in the Commons. But agreement was reached in the last days of May, and there would never be any further reference to

Romford.

A formal agreement, signed by Lowden, Waddington, and Daniell the L&BR Chairman, was dated 3rd June 1852, the day before the Lords Committee hearings ended (and, therefore, only just in time). The provisions of the agreement (7) were as in the 1853 and 1854 Acts discussed below, i.e. the THD&R Co, having built the Mucking to Thames Haven section of their line (only), plus wharves at Thames Haven, would then sell the railway and wharves to the ECR and the L&BR, to form an additional part of the 'LT&S' joint line.

The LT&SER Act was passed on 17th June 1852, and the THD&R Co Agreement was approved by an LT&SER shareholders' meeting on 14th September 1852 and a THD&R Co meeting similarly on 15th September.

THE THD&R Co 1853 ACT AND THE ABANDONMENT OF THE LINE FROM ROMFORD

The Thames Haven Dock and Railway Act 1853 (8), passed on 28th June 1853 without any parliamentary opposition, authorised (and *required*) the THD&R Co to abandon the section of the 1836 Act line between Romford and the point of intersection with the LT&SER line at Mucking.

As a result the company's nominal capital was reduced from £450,000 in shares and £150,000 borrowing, to £300,000 in shares and £100,000 borrowing (9).

Nothing was said about the dock, and the THD&R Co were effectively left free either to build or not build a dock at a later stage. But whereas in 1847/8 the THD&R Co had started work on building a pier *and* (part of) the dock, the agreement in 1852/3 was that only wharves (alias a pier) (10) were to be built in the immediate term and the dock was to be left for another day if at all.

Once the agreement was reached in summer 1852, the THD&R Co land agent Crawter immediately commenced dealings with the landowners on the Romford-Mucking section in order to sell back the land that had been taken. Most of these landowners had only been paid a 10% deposit, and the THD&R Co made itself unpopular by trying to get the landowners to take the land back at the same price as they had been paid, without any interest, even though the THD&R Co had been pocketing the agricultural rents for several years. Although there is no specific record, it would seem that all this land was sold back quickly.

There was need for a 'curve' at Mucking to join the THD&R Co line to the LT&SER line (see Vol. 1, p. 19, Map 8) but no specific parliamentary authority was ever sought for this. The alignment of the railway at Thames Haven itself was also, thanks to the pier, quite different from that authorised by the 1836 Act; but the land in question was all owned by the THD&R Co and again no parliamentary authority was sought for the changes.

CONSTRUCTION AND OPENING OF THE RAILWAY AND PIER (1854/5)

The special THD&R Co shareholders' meeting in September 1852 appointed a Committee of three shareholders (D.W. Harvey, C. Hills, and Whetham) to confer with the directors as to the best way of carrying out the works; effectively whether to do the work themselves or 'hand it over' to Peto Brassey & Betts who were building and leasing the LT&SER line. The THD&R Co may well have been as confused as many others as to the exact legal relationship between the ECR, L&BR, and Peto Brassey & Betts!

It was decided to get Peto Brassey & Betts to build the Thames Haven line and pier, but as contractors to the THD&R Co and under an entirely separate contract from their building of the LT&SER line. Given that Peto Brassey & Betts were already to be active in the area on the LT&SER line, it was of course sensible, in practical terms, for them to do the THD&R Co's works as well. It took some time to arrange the details with Peto Brassey & Betts, but an agreement with them was signed on 31st August 1853 for the single-track line, and 'wharves', to be built for £49,500.

This money had to be found by the THD&R Co (albeit with the understanding that they would effectively get it all back again when the line and pier were sold to the ECR/L&BR on completion). In September 1852 the THD&R Co had £6,413 in the bank with £3,580 due in arrears of previous calls but £1,400 old debts still unpaid, all the company's other debts from the past having been paid (or, one suspects, forgotten!). There are no detailed accounts for the post-1851 period but it appears that the various new 'calls' made in 1853-5 totalled £4 per share, which should have brought in a further £22,000 or so (11). In addition several thousand pounds

would have come in from resale of the land on the Romford-Mucking section. This does not quite explain how £49,500 was raised, but it does bring us within range of it!

George Berkley was appointed by the THD&R Co as their Engineer to supervise the works. He had actually been working for them since early 1851 (Hay, the previous THD&R Co Engineer, having not been heard of again after works ceased in 1848) when he had been approached by the solicitors of Richard Baker Wingfield to look over the scheme with a view to possible resumption, along with John Hawkshaw. Trained under Robert Stephenson, Berkley was also acting as the L&BR's Engineer by this date and was thus no doubt very much 'in' on everything (although he had no direct role with the LT&S line which was entirely Bidder's responsibility, assisted by Fowler). Berkley (and Hawkshaw) had given evidence to the July 1851 Lords Committee on the then THD&R Co Bill, expressing the view that it had been 'an ill-judged scheme and ill-managed'. He considered that the railway should have been built first and the dock later; in any case there would be 16ft depth of water at low tide at a Thames Haven wharf so it was not clear to him why a dock was necessary at all. Berkley's 1851 views on this front no doubt had some influence on what happened subsequently.

Work seems to have begun around March 1854 (12). The 27th February 1854 THD&R Co shareholders' meeting was told by Lowden that when the contract with Peto had been signed in August 1853, it had been understood that work would not begin 'until such time as the progress of the Southend line should render it advisable', with the intention that the two lines should open together. 'That time has now arrived', said Lowden. However there is a lack of credibility here; Peto had reported in January 1854 that the LT&SER works (which had been commenced back in the autumn of 1852) were nearly complete from Forest Gate Junction to Muckingford (three miles beyond Tilbury, and only a flat and easy 1½ miles short of 'Thames Haven Junction'). Far from there being any danger of the Thames Haven line being completed too soon, it must have been clear that even if work had begun on it immediately after the August 1853 agreement, it was still unlikely to be ready by the time the LT&SER line was complete to the junction. In the event the 'LT&S' was opened as far as Tilbury in April 1854 and on to Stanford-le-Hope in August 1854, with the Thames Haven works still less than half-done. There are no detailed reports on the building of the Thames Haven line but Peto Brassey & Betts were able to bring in construction materials by rail on the newly-laid 'LT&S' from an early stage in the branch works; it would be surprising if they did not bring in material by sea at Thames Haven also.

The THD&R Co's statutory powers actually expired in July 1854 shortly after work began, but this did not affect things, it being common enough for lines to still be under construction when the powers expired.

Eleven months after work began, the 28th February 1855 THD&R Co meeting heard that 'the line and wharfage are so near to completion as to be ready for opening for the start of the spring weather'. A week later on 7th March the THD&R Co directors, their solicitors, Berkley, and Wightman the LT&S line Manager (who would be in charge of working the line after opening), made a visit to the Thames Haven line to inspect the works. *Herapath's* reported

'Arrangements are making for the early establishment of an important traffic from Thames Haven to our own coast watering places, as well as to France, Holland, Denmark, etc; and the place will probably ere long become the great depot of the London fish market, as well as the principle landing place for foreign cattle. Houses are already being erected for the officials and public accommodation, and there is little doubt that a spot once the most cheerless and desolate will in a few years exhibit a large and thriving population'.

This was no doubt all 'fed' by the company and gives our only real clue if what they thought they were building the line for, by this date. The fish aspect (which never actually materialised) is still prominent; the cattle importing, which soon became important, had in contrast hardly been mentioned as a traffic target prior to 1855. (The importing of live animals had been banned until 1842 - hence the absence of any reference to such traffic in 1836 - but was now a growing business). These traffics could however hardly be facilitated by the decision to build a pier only capable of taking one vessel at a time. Coal is no longer mentioned at all.

The line was inspected by Major Wynne for the Board of Trade on 27th April 1855. In the way of the time his report, dated 28th, is very short and undetailed. Initially he refused to sanction opening owing to a dislike of the proposed working arrangements (see Chapter 11), but he was placated by Wightman and gave permission on the 30th. The line is therefore to be regarded as having been completed and available for traffic from that date, but there was no traffic on the goods front, and it was only on 7th June, when the Thames passenger steamer services to Margate began for the season, that public traffic (passenger only) began on the branch. This passenger traffic is described in full in Chapter 4, and the start of the slow-to-materialise goods (livestock) traffic in Chapter 5.

Wynne's only specific reference is to 'two timber viaducts of piles and timbers, each of three 12ft openings'. He must have been referring to the bridges over Mucking Creek (27m 0ch in the later mileages) and the creek near Mucking Lighthouse (29m 12ch); both of these are decidedly lengthier than that but they were and are the only 'structures' of any significance on the branch (13).

The 3 miles 67 chains long branch (14) was single throughout except for the first 16 chains at the Junction which were double in accordance with the then Board of Trade expectations of a 'double junction', but which were within the Junction signalman's direct control. As with most single track lines, the earthworks were built for double track in case that should become necessary in future (15). The description of the branch which follows should be read in conjunction with the OS 6in map at pp36-37.

From Thames Haven Junction the branch curved away in cutting, on a 1/116 downhill grade, then quickly on to embankment either side of the bridge over Mucking Creek, where the '1836 Act' alignment was joined. The relatively steep gradient here (which was to cause trouble later - Chapter 11) arose from the need to link the 1852 Act LT&S line, originally planned to *pass over* the THD&R Co line, with the 1836 Act line. From the level crossing at Wharf Road (27¼ miles), only an 'occupation crossing' in status but in reality quite busy with 'public' traffic to Stanford-le-Hope Wharf, the line ran through near-flat fields for nearly a mile, at ground level save for a short cutting at 27¾ miles. Near MP28 it passed onto the marshes and from this point on is mostly on low embankment with drainage ditches either side, quite straight as far as 29½ miles, then curving away northwards past the blocked-off Rugward Creek to the Manor Way (alias Dock House) occupation level crossing, and finally turning southeast to the riverbank. There were several other occupation or accommodation crossings besides the two just referred to, but these others were of no significance.

SALE OF THE LINE AND PIER TO THE 'LT&S'.

The sale needed parliamentary approval, and the **London Tilbury & Southend Railway Deviation and Amendment Act 1854** (3rd August 1854) effected this.

s.28 provided that when the railway was complete with a single line of rails, and £10,000 had been expended on the wharves, the THD&R Co might sell the railway and wharves to the ECR and L&BR.

s.31 that 'from and after the completion of such purchase, the Thames Haven Branch, Wharfs, and Lands shall form part of the Undertaking of the London Tilbury and Southend Extension Railway, and shall vest in the Eastern Counties and London & Blackwall Railway companies jointly, and shall be forever held and enjoyed by them ..... the branch and works shall ... be deemed to be amalgamated with the Extension Railway in the same manner as if it had formed part of the works authorised by the [1852] Act'.

s.33 empowered the raising of (£52,000) extra 'LT&ESR' shares to pay for the purchase, and s.35 authorised the THD&R Co to take payment in LT&SER shares instead of cash, if they wished.

When the line opened it was still the THD&R Co's property, and remained so for the first three months, although it was in practice worked from the start as part of the 'LT&S' system, within the terms of the Peto Brassey & Betts lease and under Wightman as manager (16), and with the trains provided by the ECR under contract to Peto Brassey & Betts.

It must be emphasised that the THD&R Co merely *sold the railway and pier* to the ECR and the L&BR, and continued to exist as a company (see next section). As a result there was the question of what land exactly was to be transferred, to be sorted out, as well as the need for formal agreement that the works were 'complete'. On 12th June 1855 Bidder told the LT&S Joint Committee that he was 'approving the works of the Thames Haven Railway so far as they have been executed, and also the area of land to be appropriated to the use of the company'. However there was disagreement between him and Berkley as to the cost of works remaining to be completed, £1,700.12s.0d per Bidder and £1,015.10s.4d per Berkley (17). The

Joint Committee naturally supported Bidder's figure but resolved privately to 'split the difference' if the THD&R Co would not agree. The THD&R Co, however, did accept Bidder's figure and this enabled the holding of Special Meetings of LT&SER and THD&R Co shareholders, on 2nd and 3rd July 1855 respectively, to approve the purchase/sale of the line and wharves. The transfer was made by a deed dated 8th September 1855. In addition to the land deemed to be part of the railway and wharves, the ECR and L&BR took extra land for future expansion at Thames Haven station (18).

The THD&R Co had opted to take the payment in LT&SER shares. The raising of these shares (£52,000, under the 1854 Act, as noted above) was approved by the July 1855 LT&SER shareholders' meeting, and after their successful raising the THD&R Co were paid quickly - an initial payment of £43,360 in shares in early October 1855 and, after the chasing of some Chancery documents relating to proof of title of the Oil Mill Farm land (Thames Haven station), a further payment of £6,000 in shares in January 1856. These figures total to £49,360 which more or less equates to the £49,500 quoted in the press as the agreed purchase price (19). These shares were then redistributed by the THD&R Co amongst individual THD&R Co shareholders in proportion, effectively reimbursing them for the money they had paid in 'calls' in 1847 and 1853-5. Quite how much each shareholder got is a little obscure from the press reports (20), but there is no doubt that they were happy - THD&R Co stock had been unsaleable at most periods in the past, but the 'LT&SER' stock paid a guaranteed 6%. To demonstrate their satisfaction, a Committee of Shareholders was appointed, by a resolution at the February 1855 shareholders' meeting , to arrange for the presentation of a piece of plate to the Chairman J. D. Lowden 'for the zealous manner in which he has upheld the undertaking'.

In 1862 the branch passed, along with the rest of the 'LT&S' line, from ECR/L&BR joint ownership, into the ownership of the newly-constituted London Tilbury & Southend Railway Company (see Volume 1 p. 30). This had no real impact on day-to-day operation which remained under the Peto Brassey & Betts lease until 1875.

THE THAMES HAVEN DOCK & RAILWAY COMPANY AFTER 1855

At the July 1855 shareholders' meeting, Lowden referred to 'a project set on foot by some of the shareholders for making a dock on the land', on which the directors would issue a circular in a few days time. The Board were in favour of going ahead with the dock, but there was opposition from many shareholders, and a 'long and stormy' discussion ensued at the half-yearly meeting on 29th August 1855, a rival motion being put in favour of selling the land and abandoning the company. The meeting had to be adjourned for a week until 5th September, when a vote was taken, revealing 143 in favour of the dock and 83 against, and in consequence a formal resolution was passed in favour of the dock project.

It might be deduced, from the absence of any move on their part to take over the THD&R company in toto, that the ECR and L&BR had been unwilling to take over the dock project themselves. In this context it might be noted that Bidder, Peto, Brassey, and Betts, who pulled the strings behind everything connected with the 'LT&S', were at this very time engaged in building the Victoria Dock (authorised in 1850, and opened in November 1855) and were hardly likely to want to encourage a rival project! However there is no trace of any public comment on these aspects. Not everybody in the ECR and L&BR was irrevocably in bed with Bidder and Peto. The THD&R Co shareholders were told at the abovementioned September 1855 meeting that Daniell the L&BR Chairman had agreed to join the THD&R Co Board if the dock scheme were to be proceeded with, and he was duly elected in February 1856 (Esdaile resigning) (21). The L&BR, it might be noted, did not stand to gain as much from the Victoria Dock as the ECR did, but would have a full share in any dock traffic from the Thames Haven via its 'LT&S' involvement. Nevertheless Daniell's presence was not, in the event, to result in the L&BR offering any support to the dock project.

Following the September 1855 resolution, a Bill was promoted which was passed as **The Thames Haven Dock Company's Act 1856** on 21st July 1856 (22). This

- gave renewed powers, for 5 years, for building a dock (now on a different plan, to the 'southwest' of the railway at Thames Haven station, as the line ran through the middle of the 1836 dock site to reach the pier).

- changed the company's name to the 'Thames Haven Dock Company' (so that it no longer had any railway powers).

- repealed all previous THD&R Co Acts.
- reduced the nominal capital to £51,000 in shares and £10,000 borrowing (the £51,000 being the existing 12,000 authorised shares reduced in value to £4.5s.0d each, each existing shareholder to get one of the 'new' shares for each old share held).
- authorised the use of lands at Thames Haven as cattle lairs (this was not something for which parliamentary sanction was compulsory, but was a good precaution in case of opposition to such use from any source).
- reduced the number of directors from 7 to 6.

In May 1856 it was stated that the dock would be tidal (as intended since 1836) but when George Berkley reported to the half-yearly meeting in August 1856 ideas had changed, probably under his influence. It was now intended to build a 1100ft-1200ft river wharf frontage plus an *enclosed* dock with 50ft wide lock gates. Berkley estimated the costs to be £40,000 and the Board recommended an immediate start, which was approved by the meeting. 'Calls' would of course be needed to finance the work, but none was proposed immediately.

After this, silence descends again. The next we hear of the company is at the August 1859 meetings (the meetings of 1857 and 1858 had probably not been held through inquoracy) where Mr Hickson, the head of a Committee of Shareholders which had been investigating the company's situation, noted

'the company possessed at Thames Haven a site for dock purposes unequalled at any other point of the river, but from the irruption of the sea on the dock (sic) wall, the Committee had come to the conclusion that, unaided by any other resources, they had no alternative but to realise their assets and wind up the company'.

The problem was that as owners of the river frontage land the company was obliged to maintain the river defence walls which could impose very serious costs if storm damage occurred. Lowden the Chairman agreed with the Committee, stating that

'he lived in fear of the sea wall falling in and invading the country. All their money had been spent on this wall'.

The August 1859 meeting approved the Committee's report, and all enthusiasm having now waned, asked the directors and the Committee members to meet to discuss whether the company should be wound up. They confirmed this policy, and a circular was sent out to all shareholders in October. This was the last nail in the coffin. Lowden told the February 1860 meeting that the company had now had to borrow from the bank to pay for further wall repair works, and that

'nothing had occurred to offer any prospect to the Directors of a successful prosecution of the scheme'.

A Bill would be proceeded with in the 1861 session (it was too late now for the 1860 session) for abandonment, as counsel's advice was that it would be improper to dispose of the assets without a winding up Act. **The Thames Haven Dock (Abandonment) Act 1861** (23), passed on 11th July 1861, repealed the powers to build the dock and abolished the company. The 'lands and effects' were to be sold off within twelve months and any balance after the payment of debts was to be distributed amongst shareholders.

The company's assets were £3,600 in LT&SER stock (part of the 1855/6 payment - see footnote 17) and 130 acres of land (24) at Thames Haven, worth about £3,000, and mostly let, at £85 per annum. This land was the parts of Oil Mill Farm not used for the works; it had remained in agricultural use throughout, with the former owners Messrs Long as tenants. The THD&R Co now sold it to Samuel Sharp(e) and for the moment it passes from our interest, but not for good, for much was to be resold to the LNWR, the London & Thames Haven Oil Wharves, and Shell.

So ended, with a whimper, the not entirely glorious 25-year life of the company. It was perhaps the more remarkable that a significant part of the project had come to fruition, than that much of it had not! Although the company had long had a bad name, it was never, so far as can be established, guilty of anything very scandalous, by the standards of the day. All the landowners and creditors were paid in the end; the pre-Chadwick directors do not seem to have made anything out of it; and (whilst seven Acts had been necessary) the proportion of the company's money going into the pockets of grasping lawyers rather than on constructive work seems to have much less than with many small impoverished companies. The original 1830s shareholders had certainly lost money, but the post-1847 shareholders were left with worthwhile 'LT&S' stock which would bring good dividends to their heirs and successors until LMS days.

Unfortunately the tide of change had, by the time the line opened in 1855, wiped out many of the purposes originally foreseen by Amsinck for building it. In most respects it was actually the spread of the national railway system that had done this. The Kent resorts now had direct rail links from London (although a worthwhile steamboat traffic remained, and the branch took part in this, as described in the next chapter). The Barking fishing fleet, which had supplied London, decamped to Yarmouth and Lowestoft from the 1850s, as these ports were much nearer the north sea fishing grounds and fish could be taken to London quickly by railway, so there was no longer any significant 'London' fishing business. The coal business underwent more complex changes and it would require a more in depth study of the London coal trade than is possible here to demonstrate exactly why no collier was ever seen at Thames Haven in the event; but one reason was that an increasing proportion of London coal started to come south by rail (on the GN, Eastern Counties, and then the Midland) from the 1850s/60s.

Essentially, therefore, the line opened as a white elephant, the creation of a political deal to buy off the THD&R Co's opposition to the 'LT&S' and resolve the sixteen years' fighting over South Essex from 1835 to 1852. For the first years after 1855 the branch was almost wholly pointless, as the few Margate boat trains could just as well have used Tilbury. Of the worthwhile traffics that did eventually use the line, cattle importing had hardly been mentioned until the line was already nearing completion and so can hardly be regarded as having been a significant 'reason' for building it; and oil, which after many decades actually made it a useful piece of railway, had not even become known as a product at the time the line was conceived. Such is the faith to be put in traffic witnesses.

THAMES HAVEN DOCK & RAILWAY COMPANY
(THAMES HAVEN DOCK COMPANY FROM 1856).

Chairman	Horace Twiss	1836-1837	Engineer	Alfred Giles	1835-1836
	Donald MacLean	c1837		Francis Giles	1836-c1841
	James Esdaile	c1838-1847		Bewicke Blackburn (assistant)	1835-c1838
	William Chadwick	1847-1850		Sir John Rennie	c1842
	James Dawson Lowden	1850-1861		.... Geary ('Surveyor')	c1846-1847
Secretary	Henry Amsinck	1835-1843		Thomas Hay	1847-1848
	J. H. Humfrey	1843-1844		George Berkley	1851-1856
	Frederick Edgell	1844-c1846	Office Address	34 Abchurch Lane	1835-1838
	James John Greer	1847-1849		28 Moorgate Street	1838-c1840
	Arthur Graham	c1849-1851+		2 St Mildred's Court, Poultry	c1840-c1843
Solicitors	Vaux & Fennell	1836-1837		72 Lombard Street	c1844-c1846
	Lyon Barnes & Co	1837-c1841		no office address given in any later documents	
	Sir George Stephen	1840-c1844			
	Walter Charles Venning	1847-1851			
	Henry Toogood	1851-			

(1) Toogood had been appointed THD&R Co Solicitor early in 1851. According to the previous solicitor Venning, who was now replaced save for a few residual matters, this was because 'new parties' had come into the company to 'infuse new blood', and they were friends of Toogood. However there is no other reference to new people at this date and Toogood himself stated that it was Wingfield, Lowden, and West who had offered him the job. Henry and his brother William Toogood were to become notorious for their frequent involvement with small, impecunious, and dubious railway companies, see e.g. P. Kay, *The Teign Valley Line*, p.6.

(2) It is most likely that the THD&R Co were approaching the ECR re the possibility of reviving their Romford line, in case the deal with the L&BR collapsed. The ECR were *opposed* to the L&BR Tilbury scheme in winter 1850/1 so it was not unreasonable to think that they might have supported the THD&R Co on this. However after Waddington came back as ECR Chairman in March 1851, the ECR became *pro* the L&BR Tilbury scheme, which was essentially a promotion by Waddington's allies Bidder and Peto.

(3) 14 & 15 Vic cap. 123.

(4) There were actually only six active Directors at this time; Lowden, Esdaile, Wingfield, Pocock, West, and Whiting. The others had faded out during the 1848-50 collapse period.

(5) 6,063 shares always quoted in 1851 documents (there is no explanation of the reduction from 6,163 (*alias* 6,200) quoted in 1847, but this is hardly significant). Again in 1851 it is stated that £32 was still uncalled whereas the last figure given in 1847/8 was that £32.10s was uncalled. The 1851 Act authorised a doubling of the nominal number of shares from 9,000 to 18,000, as the total nominal capital remained at £450,000; but this had no impact in practice as there was no chance of such large numbers of new shareholders being attracted! See also footnote (9) re the 1853 Act, and footnote (11).

(6) The idea of building the line single track had been pushed by George Berkley who became the THD&R Co's Engineer in 1851.

(7) No copy of the Agreement itself is known but it is described, probably with the exact wording being cited, in the report of the 3.7.1855 LT&SER shareholders' meeting (*Herapath's* 1855 p. 668).

(8) 16 & 17 Vic cap. 70.

(9) The £300,000 being 12,000 £25 shares. The 1853 Act explains this by saying that 6,000 of the formerly-authorised 18,000 shares 'shall not be issued'.

(10) The word 'wharf' (or 'wharves') is always used in the 1852-5 period, but what was actually built was a steamer pier. The site was well suited to building a lengthy river wharf and Lowden had spoken at the May 1852 meeting of a possible 1800ft wharf with 15-20ft of water. Possibly the June 1852 ECR/L&BR/THD&R Co Agreement mentioned more specifically what was to be built, but it may not have done; the 1854 Act only refers to 'wharfs' and the fact that £10,000 is to be spent. (Lengthy continuous wharves were built at a later date).

(11) At the 2.1853 meeting it was stated that a £1 call had been made. At the 5.1853 meeting it was said that all debts had been cleared and there was £11,000 in the bank; this fits with £6,000 or so having been raised (from this call) since late 1852. At the 8.1853 meeting a call of £1.12s.6d was said to be needed; at the 8.1854 meeting one of about 15s; and at the 2.1855 meeting a call of 5s plus another of 2s 9d (2s 6d?) for river wall repairs. These total to £3.15s.0d which, when added to the £18 already called at 1847, gives £21.15s.0d called (and this tallies with a statement at the August 1855 meeting that £3.5s.0d was still uncalled). Finally in 2.1856 it was reported that another 5s call had been made, bringing the total called to £22, which is the figure given in the share tables in *Herapath's* in 1856.

(12) The only evidence is Lowden's comment in February 1854 that the time had come to start work; the remark in the LT&SER 1854 Act (written by June-July 1854 at the latest) that work on the Thames Haven line is now under way; and the report at the 30.8.1854 meeting that 'considerable progress had been made with the works'.

(13) It is not known how long the original pile bridges lasted - most of Peto's 1850s timber bridges did not last very long! The bridge at 27m 0ch was replaced (again ?) in concrete in 1943, probably because of the much increased number of heavy trains then.

(14) The mileages were originally from Bishopsgate via Forest Gate Junction, 26m 41ch at Thames Haven Junction to 30m 28ch at the terminus stops. Around 1900 the whole LT&S system was remileaged from Fenchurch Street via Plaistow, and the branch mileages became 26m 57ch to 30m 44ch. These later mileages are used throughout this work irrespective of date (except insofar as pre-1900 OS map extracts naturally show the original mileages). In 1955 the sidings were cut back 28 yards at the terminus and the line has therefore ended at 30m 43ch since then. In 1973 the remodelling of Thames Haven Junction resulted in the branch points being moved to 26m 41ch. The branch is therefore now 4m 2ch in length.

(15) This is not specifically mentioned in any contemporary 1852-5 period source, but can be seen in the later 2 chain survey maps. Also the eastern end of the line had been built as an embankment in 1847, when it was still intended to have double track. Ideas of doubling were floated in the 1916-18 period - the April 1916 plan for the Miners Safety siding and the 1918 plan for the LATHOL Reedham sidings both show a provision for doubling (on the north side) noted as 'possible' in the first case and 'proposed' in the second - but nothing ever came of it.

(16) Subsequently an additional agreement of 30.6.1856 was made between the ECR/L&BR and Peto Brassey & Betts under which the Thames Haven line and pier were deemed to be comprised within the main LT&SER 'lease', but this only formalised the situation which had applied since opening in 1855.

(17) It seems likely that what this all meant was not that any extra work of substance was still to be done, but rather that the cost of building the 'wharves' had turned out to be that much less than the £10,000 specified in the 1854 Act. The figures are taken from the LT&S Joint Committee minutes (PRO RAIL 437/1). Bidder's figure must actually have been £1,700.12s.10d as Berkley's 'certificate' formally given on 7.12.1855 stated his agreement that only £8,299.7s.2d had been spent on the 'wharves' (i.e. £10,000 - £1,700.12s.10d). Between 1855 and 1857 Peto Brassey & Betts carried out an extra £1,792 of work on the branch (full details not known) for which they presented an account to the LT&S Joint Committee in November 1857, but these were all matters that had come up since the summer 1855 expenditure reconciliation and therefore a separate issue.

(18) The only contemporary reference to this is the LT&S Joint Committee minutes (RAIL 437/1). The 3.7.1855 Special General Meeting approved purchase of the 'railway, with wharfage and works thereto, and 20 acres of land'. This 20 acres, which had been agreed in 1852, was in addition to the land occupied by the then railway layout at Thames Haven station. The extra land purchased for the LT&SER was all 'north-east' of the station (see 25in maps); the LT&SR never owned any land 'south-west' of the station. In the 2nd and 3rd editions of the 25in map, the LT&SR land at Thames Haven (east of the Dock House level crossing) totals about 23 acres. About 6 acres of riverbed were owned in addition.

(19) The price agreed in 1852 (per the report in *Herapath's* 1855, p. 668) was £48,000, with interest to be paid on £12,000 of this at 4% immediately from June 1852, and on the remainder from such times as the THD&R Co had actually expended money, pro rata. In 1855 it was agreed that the interest shuld be taken as £1,500, hence the figure of £49,500 quoted in most reports in 1855. The £49,500 figure must also relate directly to the sum of £49,500 paid by the THD&R Co to Peto Brassey & Betts for building the line, but owing to the complexity of all the relationships between the ECR and L&BR and Peto Brassey & Betts, it is doubtful if most of the 'players' had a full understanding of exactly how the two sums related at the time, and (with the 1853 Peto contract also not surviving) one cannot hope to resolve the greyness now.

(20) The THD&R Co's nominal capital by this date was, as noted above, 12,000 x £25 shares. The press reports of the July 1855 shareholders' meeting quote Lowden as having stated that the THD&R Co were to get one £10 'LT&SER' share for every 2½ THD&R Co shares, which agrees with this, if one takes the £48,000 figure (4,800 £10 shares x 2½ = 12,000). The THD&R Co *shareholders* were offered the option of either cash from the company or shares, but it seems that they chose the shares for the most part. The number of actual *issued* THD&R Co shares was now about 5,700 (6,063 less 360 further shares 'forfeited' in July 1855 for non-payment of calls). It therefore appears that the THD&R Co shareholders actually got LT&SER stock at about £8 per THD&R Co share from the initial distribution of £43,360 in October 1855 (the residual £6,000 in January 1856 appears, per LT&SER Committee minutes 29.12.1855, to have gone to paying debts (£1,660) (?) or been registered in Lowden's name pro the THD&R Company itself (£4,340), rather than being for distribution to THD&R Co shareholders). Most of the THD&R Co shareholders had bought their shares in 1847 for about 30s and paid calls of £9-£10 since purchase, total expenditure therefore about £11 per share; they were now left with about £8 in LT&SER stock but also retained their THD&R Co shares with a reduced nominal value of £4.5s.0d each (see text), and a sale value of something less. In essence therefore they had survived their involvement with a decidedly dubious scheme, which they had latched on to in the 'mania' height, without financial loss - a much better fate than many at this period! (However it should be understood that this analysis is a jigsaw picture with missing pieces).

(21) According to the Times 3.7.1855 all but 2 of the THD&R Co directors were now 'LT&SER' men. But this seems unlikely. There are no full listings of the THD&R Co directors after this date. Lowden stated in August 1855 that the Board was to be strengthened by 'new and influential names'.

(22) 19 & 20 Vic cap. 119.

(23) 24 & 25 Vic cap. 125.

(24) So stated in 1859, but this seems a large figure; the 1851 Fobbing Commissioners' Survey shows the THD&R Co owning 108 acres of Oil Mill Farm, which fits with the ground; and they had since sold about 30 acres to the LT&SR in toto.

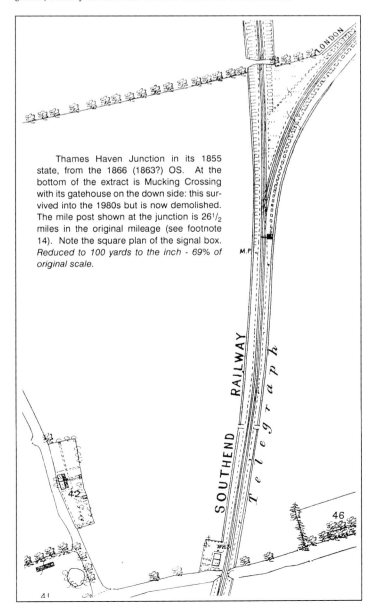

Thames Haven Junction in its 1855 state, from the 1866 (1863?) OS. At the bottom of the extract is Mucking Crossing with its gatehouse on the down side: this survived into the 1980s but is now demolished. The mile post shown at the junction is 26½ miles in the original mileage (see footnote 14). Note the square plan of the signal box. *Reduced to 100 yards to the inch - 69% of original scale.*

23

THAMES HAVEN FOR MARGATE : PASSENGER SERVICES 1855-1880

This was the only one of the THD&R Co's originally intended traffics that actually came to pass.

THE ECR TILBURY - MARGATE SERVICE (1854)

When the LT&S line opened to Tilbury in 1854, the ECR and Peto decided to run a Tilbury - Herne Bay - Margate steamer service, with train connections from London, in competition with the General Steam Navigation Company who were always the leading (and sometimes the only) operator on the London Bridge - Margate/Ramsgate route in the 1820s - 1880s period. No attempt seems to have been made to collaborate with the GSNCo in 1854; the fact was that the ECR had just 'inherited' some steamers from the Eastern Union in January 1854 when it took over the working of that company. The Eastern Union had been using these steamers to run an Ipswich - London boat service in competition with the ECR trains, which was obviously unnecessary once the ECR took over the EUR, so a new job had to be found for them, and the Tilbury - Margate service suggested itself. The ECR Traffic Committee approved this on 17th May, and it began on 16th June and continued until 30th September 1854, in accordance with the established pattern of the other operators on the Margate/Ramsgate route, which was always summer season only, usually beginning about the start of June and ending in September. The boats used were (probably) the *Orwell* and *Prince Albert* (1).

The ECR service attracted a reasonable number of passengers away from the GSNCo, but the running of the boats seems to have been managed somewhat inefficiently and the passengers had not been over-impressed. As a result the LT&S Committee made approaches to the GSNCo after the end of the season to see if a joint operation, with through ticketing, could be agreed for the 1855 season in lieu.

START OF THE THAMES HAVEN SERVICE (1855)

These talks proved successful and the GSNCo was already able to announce in its February 1855 half-yearly report that 'the Directors have undertaken to perform the service between Holy Haven (sic), a convenient landing place to which the railway is now completed, and Margate and Herne Bay', in connection with the LT&S. Thus it had become known by February that there would at least be this Margate 'boat train' traffic on the Thames Haven line after its completion. *Herapath's* noted in March that arrangements were being made for services from Thames Haven to 'our watering places' (and also, it was said, to France, Holland, and Denmark; which did not come to pass in 1855). The new LT&S - Thames Haven - Margate service began on 7th June 1855 (2). It is possible that in 1855 the GSNCo ran special boats from Thames Haven, rather than just making calls there by the London Bridge boats (as happened in later years), but the available information is not sufficiently precise (3).

The boat trains, like the regular LT&S line trains at this period, were formed of ECR locos and stock and ran in two portions, from/to both termini, joining at Stratford in the down direction and splitting there in the up direction.

The down train timings, as given in *Bradshaw* July 1855, were

	Mon - Sat	Mon - Sat	Sun
Fenchurch St/Bishopsgate d.	10.22am	4.7pm	10.7am
Thames Haven a.	11.18am	5.0pm	11.0am

the Fenchurch Street portion calling at Stepney also.

The 'down' boat times are not given. In the 'up' direction it is noted that the boats leave Margate at 9.20 am and 4 pm on weekdays, and 4.30 pm on Sundays (but the train times are not given).

The steamer run from Thames Haven to Margate was 38 miles and was done in 2 hr 30 mins on average.

Thames Haven had only a marginal advantage over Tilbury for the purpose. Had the LT&S wanted, they could have run special boat trains fast to Tilbury in 40 - 45 minutes for passengers to join the steamers there rather than at Thames Haven; the extra sailing time from Tilbury was about half an hour, so twenty minutes at most was saved by using Thames Haven, and that in a situation where

passengers were not overconcerned about time anyway. The suspicion must be that Thames Haven was being used in part for the sake of 'creating a traffic' for the new line.

The harmony intended for this summer 1855 service was spoilt when the rival 'Commercial' steamboat company, who had planned to abandon their Margate/Ramsgate service and sell their ships, found themselves without a buyer and so decided to run an 1855 service after all. This began in July, with very low fares, using the *Eagle*, Tilbury to Margate/Ramsgate/Boulogne. The LT&S collaborated with this, to the annoyance of the GSNCo, who had to respond by reducing their fares and asked the LT&S to accept a reduction in their portion accordingly, which however was refused.

The services ended in the last week of September, and the LT&S had carried 86,400 passengers for Margate in total (4). The competition had been good for the LT&S but the GSNCo thought otherwise and in April 1856, when the time came to finalise the 1856 season's services, they told the LT&S that they would only agree to a joint service if the LT&S collaborated with them exclusively, or would accept a reduction in the LT&S cut. The LT&S refused.

THE 1856 SERVICE

The GSNCo therefore decided to run from London Bridge only in 1856, and abandon Thames Haven. The LT&S seem to have already been making alternative arrangements; Wightman the LT&S line manager stated in May that the Margate service would run again and that 'I also contemplate vessels to Calais and Dunkirk this year, from Thames Haven'. Exactly what did happen is not clear, although *Herapath's* in June refers to the low LT&S fares to Margate, Ramsgate, and France, and the GSNCo reported in August that the LT&S were running a Thanet service in conjunction with (unnamed) 'other parties'. Certainly the LT&S Thames Haven/Margate boat trains did run in 1856 (5).

THE MARGATE SERVICE 1857 - 1880

The GSNCo having (predictably) taken retaliatory measures to ensure that they kept the bulk of the traffic, the 'other parties' found themselves operating at a loss, and told the LT&S at the end of the 1856 season that they would have to withdraw. At this point the LT&S seem to have realised that there was no great benefit to be gained by taking an over-aggressive attitude towards the GSNCo, and in the spring of 1857 they were obliged to go back to them to seek an alliance again for the 1857 season. This was soon sorted out and was to prove the start of a happy relationship and a stable service via Thames Haven for 24 years. As it happened, there were no rival steamboat operators on the Kent service at all in 1857. *Herapath's* commented in July, on a recent trip to Margate via the LT&S, that it 'enables us to speak with pleasure of the manner in which the line is worked and the efficiency of the General Steam Navigation Company's steamboats'. And in their February 1858 half-yearly report the GSNCo Board felt sufficiently confident of the relationship to state that 'similar arrangements will no doubt be carried out during the ensuing season'.

The LT&S/GSNCo through ticketing via Thames Haven, and the LT&S boat trains to Thames Haven, ran every summer from 1857 to 1880 (except in 1876 - see below). The LT&SR always referred to the service as its 'Margate service' with little or no reference to other destinations, but in fact the GSNCo steamers generally called at Herne Bay and continued on to Ramsgate, and sometimes to Deal and Dover. At certain times at least there was through ticketing available to Herne Bay and Ramsgate (6). So far as can be established the GSNCo in this period did not at any time run special sailings from Thames Haven, but merely called there in the course of the passage from London Bridge to Kent. The LT&S service appealed to those who appreciated the reduced overall trip time, and the shorter time on the steamer, but there were many who preferred the full steamer trip from London Bridge (and all the steamer companies continued to run from London Bridge, even in later decades when the joint rail/steamer facilities via the LT&S at Tilbury were much more extensive and more heavily advertised). One is left to wonder how things were handled on the busiest days when the steamer might be already at or nearing its carrying capacity on leaving London Bridge; there was no way of knowing how many people had booked via the LT&SR until after the steamer was on its way.

It is probable that much the same level of service operated throughout, but there are no surviving timetables pre-1875 (7). Certainly in 1875 - 80 there was a consistent pattern, as exemplified by the 1877 timetable :-

	Mon - Sat	Sats	Suns
Fenchurch St	10.40am	3.7pm	9.7am
Stepney	10.46	3.13	9.13
Plaistow	10.55	3.21	9.21
Barking	11.03	3.29	9.29
Thames Haven a.	11.43	4.7	10.7
Margate	c2.15pm	c6.45pm	c12.45pm

	Mons	Daily incl Suns
Margate	7.0am	3.30pm
Thames Haven d.	10.0am	6.15pm
Barking	10.38	6.53
Plaistow	10.46	7.1
Stepney	10.55	7.10
Fenchurch St	11.0	7.15

(but see comments below re intermediate stops).

The Sunday morning down train always left earlier in order to encourage day trips to Margate, for which there was a bigger market on Sundays (although even then there was only $2^1/_2$ hours available in Margate). Some people would also do a day trip on weekdays but that was not the main usage. The Saturday afternoon down service and Monday morning up service were known as 'the husbands' boat' and were primarily for business men whose families were 'residing' in Thanet 'for the season' but who had to continue working in London during the week themselves. The fares (1877) Fenchurch Street (and intermediately) to Margate were :-
-Single 5s 1st, 4s 2nd, 2s 6d child. (The fares by boat throughout from London Bridge were the same)
-Return 6s 1st, 5s 2nd, 3s child, available for return on the following day also. (By boat throughout there was a slightly cheaper Sunday excursion return at 5s 6d / 4s 6d / 2s 6d).

After the 1856 season, there were no Bishopsgate portions (8), which had proved under-used. However there was still through ticketing from Bishopsgate in 1857/8/9, after which the ECR decided to withdraw it owing to low demand.

From 1858 the trains would have run via Plaistow and no longer served Stratford. By the 1870s at least they were calling at Plaistow and Barking in addition to the established Stepney call. In 1875 a stop was made at Low Street in order to pick up passengers from the Southend direction, but this does not seem to have been repeated. The 1880 service shows Grays stops.

In the 1869 - 80 period through NLR coaches were run in the boat trains, running from Chalk Farm and stations to Plaistow where they joined with the Fenchurch Street portion (Vol. 1, p. 41).

The pier at Margate was under repair in the summer of 1876 and no steamers were able to call there. The GSNCo continued its Thanet service, calling at Herne Bay and Ramsgate only, but the LT&SR did not run any trains in this season, another indication of the Margate-centric view that they have seem to have taken (yet the overall Ramsgate steamer traffic was not much below the Margate traffic).

The exact start and finish dates of the steamer services (and, thereby, the boat trains) varied from season to season, but were always June to September. This meant that the Thames Haven branch, which had no other regular traffic in the first years, was to all intents out of use for 8 - 9 months each year (9) initially.

In adverse weather, or against a strong tide, the steamers could take much longer than usual on the passage, and the up boat trains were accordingly often late in leaving Thames Haven. This is brought out by two accidents which occurred to them in the 1850s. On 21st August 1854 the up train was 30 minutes late when it came to a stand at Bow Junction owing to a locomotive defect, and was run into by the following train. Five years later, on 17th August 1859, the train left Thames Haven late at 7.10 pm because the boat 'had made a long passage', and the locomotive (2-2-2 No. 54) then suffered an axle failure on the Tilbury north curve. There were eight carriages and a van; the first was 'broken to pieces', the next ended on its side badly damaged, the third was derailed but remained upright, and the rest were unharmed. Eight passengers were injured, one of whom died afterwards, with claims of £1,552.

THE END OF THAMES HAVEN CALLS (1880)

On 3rd September 1878 there occurred the *Princess Alice* steamer disaster when 700 people were drowned after a collision on the Thames. This had a bad impact on the steamer traffic initially (but opinions are divided on whether it had any permanent impact on patronage of the Thames steamer services). At the next LT&SR half-yearly meeting the Chairman noted that the boat train traffic had 'fallen off entirely' in September after the disaster.

Whether this was a factor or not, Stride the LT&SR General Manager got very negative about the Margate service in 1881 and presented a report in May on the results of the service since 1874 (he probably had no earlier information). He stated that traffic was 'not increasing' and that the service was 'not very creditable'. The LT&SR Executive Committee accepted Stride's arguments and agreed to discontinue the service. The GSNCo had not sought to end their Thames Haven calls or the joint arrangements; it was entirely an LT&SR decision.

As a result the Thames Haven branch (and Thames Haven station) was effectively 'closed' to passenger traffic in September 1880 (10). It would not of course have been conceived of as a closure at the time, but in the event there was never any public service run.

The LT&SR did not advertise any Margate service at all in the 1881 season. The GSNCo, however, who continued their service from London Bridge to Margate (etc) as before save for the fact that no call was now made at Thames Haven, added a note to their 1881 timetable to the effect that the steamers would call at Tilbury pier 'if there is room on board'.

There must have been a 'reaction' to the LT&SR's ending of the facility, as Stride told the directors in March 1882 that he was negotiating with the GSNCo for an 1882 season service. On 25th May he stated that a service would run, from Thames Haven to Margate. But this was changed at the last minute to through bookings via Tilbury (11). This seems to have proved satisfactory to all, and the LT&SR then ran 'Margate' boat trains to Tilbury for the GSNCo service every summer from 1882 until 1914. All of which only proved the point, made earlier, that Thames Haven was not really necessary at all for this traffic!

OTHER PASSENGER SERVICES VIA THAMES HAVEN

An Ipswich to Thames Haven steamer service was initiated in summer 1858, using the *Orwell* (which had been sold by the ECR in 1857). The ECR were not amused, especially as Wightman the LT&S line manager had arranged for Fenchurch Street train connections, and was advertising the service. Wightman was 'spoken to' and the advertisements ceased. The *Orwell* ceased running for the winter in October, but in summer 1859 a Mr Marriott was noted to be running an Ipswich - Thames Haven steamer, and this was probably the *Orwell* again. But in July the *Orwell* was sold off.

Any steamer that called at Thames Haven had to have a special boat train, as there was no other way in which the boat passengers could get to/from Thames Haven pier.

However the only other definite reference to Thames Haven boat passenger traffic is in 1867 when it was reported that a tidal service between Thames Haven and Boulogne had begun on 24th April 'in connection with the Paris exhibition'. This was no doubt shortlived, in the circumstances. Possibly there were other short-lived services not recorded in the minute books, or odd calls, but there is no evidence of anything else.

PRIZE-FIGHT SPECIALS

Prize-fighting (bare-fist boxing-cum-wrestling) was illegal, but in practice was supported primarily by the upper echelons of society, and allowed to continue until the late 1860s when it was finally suppressed after long efforts by the forces of 'morality'. Local police forces often sought to break up the fights, and it therefore became the practice for the organisers to decide on the venue only at the last minute. The supporters were primarily 'London', and the decision was spread by word of mouth. From 1840 a special train was usually run from London to the venue; not all companies would participate, and the LSWR, SER, and the disreputable ECR were most often involved (although the GWR actually ran trains on two occasions) (12). The venues were generally chosen for their remoteness, and if possible on a county boundary so that the fight could move over from one county to the other depending on which constabulary appeared first. The Thames Estuary marshes were the most favoured area of all in later years, steamers being used instead of (or as well as) trains on some occasions, which gave a splendid ability to move between Essex and Kent or between one island and another in a few minutes.

So far as can be ascertained only one fight, Tom King versus Jem Mace on Wednesday 26th November 1862, was held at Thames Haven station itself. At 5am that morning Fenchurch Street station bustled with unwonted activity as cabs drew up bringing those in the know to the 17-coach special train. After some delays the train reached Thames Haven where the stakes were pitched beside the station. Two steamers were ready at the pier in case a 'move' should be needed. The fight began at 9.15am, King beating Mace the favourite. Another fight, Hicks v. Gallagher, began at 10.20, but the Rainham and Grays police intervened at 10.48 (it is not clear how they managed to get there!) whereupon the contestants and the whole crowd packed up and went over to Kent in one of the steamers, and resumed the fight there. This day came to be regarded as one of the great days of prize fighting, which was soon to end.

PASSENGER USAGE OF THE BRANCH AFTER 1880

There is no record of any public passenger traffic on the branch after the Margate boat trains ceased in 1880, nor of any passenger boat calling at Thames Haven pier (13).

The only known passenger trains in this period were non-public and not in connection with steamers. In January 1881 there was a breach in the sea wall at Thames Haven and special trains were run daily to bring in labourers from East London (14). Later, occasional specials were run for the managers of the London & Thames Haven Oil Wharves company when they needed to visit the site. On 17th February 1910 they went to Tilbury in an ordinary train and then had a special, formed of one 1st class carriage and two brakes, to Thames Haven and back. Similar arrangements were made in April 1910 and July 1912.

However by the 1900s the increasing industrial activity in the area was creating a new demand for a regular passenger service to bring in workmen. This eventually began in 1923 (Chapter 9).

---

(1) No times are known for the 1854 ECR service. The GSNCo August 1854 and February 1855 half-yearly reports state that the ECR were running from Tilbury to Herne Bay and Margate; and the November 1855 ECR Shareholders' Investigatory Committee's report also says Tilbury to Herne Bay and Margate. ECR Traffic Committee 17.5.1854 resolved to put on 'two of the Ipswich boats' between Tilbury and Margate; on 31.5.1854 asked for a table of fares to be prepared for the packets 'from Tilbury to Southend, Margate, and other places'; and on 28.6.1854 noted the fares which are only quoted for Margate. On balance it would seem that the ECR boats ran Tilbury - Herne Bay - Margate. The *Orwell* had been built in 1839 for the Ipswich Steam Navigation Co. and sold to the EUR in May 1853. The *Prince Albert* (built 1842) had also been bought by the EUR in 1853. The *Orwell* was formally registered under ECR ownership in June 1854 and the *Prince Albert* in July 1854.
(2) This date is quoted in a statement at the 3.7.1855 LT&SER Special Meeting and reported in the *Times* 4.7.1855 and *Herapath's* 7.7.1855. Additionally the August 1855 London & Blackwall half-yearly report states that 'the route to Margate and Ramsgate by way of Thames Haven' was opened at 'the beginning of June'. Most probably 7th June was the date when the GSNCo's Kent operations began for the season. The date of 1st July quoted in some previous works is an error deriving from the fact that *Bradshaw* only includes the service as from the July edition, but that is what one would expect in the circumstances.
(3) The GSNCo February 1855 report says 'the direct service from London to these places will be continued as heretofore by this company and both the routes will be so conducted, as to afford full satisfaction to the public'.
(4) Per Wightman, the LT&S line Manager, evidence to Commons Committee May 1856. Wightman says 'from Tilbury and Thames Haven' and is therefore presumably combining figures for both the rival services.
(5) See the 1.9.1856 ECR Staff Timetables, which include several Thames Haven boat trains, but not in a fashion that enables one to determine what the full service was. *Herapath's* 26.7.1856 refers to 'two trains per day from Fenchurch Street for Tilbury or Thames Haven'; thence by boat to Margate or Ramsgate.
(6) ECR Traffic Committee 8.7.1857 (Herne Bay and Ramsgate) and 9.5.1860 (Ramsgate). Cf also note (9) infra, and the ticket illustrated above.
(7) There are no LT&SR working timetables surviving for this period, and only one LT&SR public timetable (for 1879). The GER working timetables do not include the LT&S line at all. The GER public timetables included LT&S line services (until 1885) but the Thames Haven boat trains do not appear in them until 1875; similarly *Bradshaw*

(apart from 1855) does not show the boat trains until 1875. It is therefore evident that until Stride took over the management of the LT&SR in 1875, little effort was made to publicise the service through the normal timetable channels. In the General Steam Navigation Co.'s records (at the National Maritime Museum) the only timetables are those of 1877, 1878, 1881 and 1882.
(8) In the absence of known timetables from 1856 on, it cannot be regarded as proven that Bishopsgate portions on the boat trains ended after the 1856 season, but it is exceedingly unlikely that they continued after Bishopsgate portions on the regular LT&S trains, which were definitely abandoned at this time.
(9) The Board report to the LT&SR half-yearly meeting in February 1865 notes that the branch had 'hitherto been used almost exclusively for the Margate and Ramsgate traffic during the summer'. At another meeting on 27.12.1865 Eley the chairman stated 'up to within a comparatively recent period the Thames Haven branch has only been open during the summer and autumn months'.
(10) The exact date of the end of the 1880 season service is not known. The boat trains are, as one would expect, in the September 1880 *Bradshaw*, but not in in October 1880. Hence no precise 'closure' date can be given.
(11) The GSNCo timetables for summer 1882, and *Bradshaw* (July and August), both show the service via Tilbury.
(12) For the role of railway companies in prize-fighting generally see G. Guilcher, *The Involvement of Railway Companies in Victorian Prize-Fighting*, Journal of the Railway & Canal Historical Society 1986, pp 339 - 348.
(13) Borley states that 'occasional passenger trains (ran) until 1909', apparently choosing this 1909 date because of the pier being rendered unusable then. Clinker states 'trains as required in connection with steamer sailings continued to the second half of 1909, probably advertised locally', which one suspects is merely a piece of unjustified embroidery on Borley, the last three words meaning in effect 'no actual reference is known'. In recent years others have embroidered further by stating that such trains *were* advertised locally! Whilst one cannot say for certain that no boat ever called and no boat train ever ran post-1880, there is no sign that Borley and Clinker really had any hard evidence for such trains.
(14) Accommodation for LT&SR (or LT&SR contractors') workmen was no doubt also provided on other occasions, e.g. the Midland notices for November 1916 note that a 4-wheel carriage is to be attached daily to morning down and afternoon up light engines, to convey Engineer's men working at Thames Haven.

This view from LMS days is the only known photograph of the 1855 Thames Haven station building's main frontage in its active days. Passengers (pre-1880) passed through the centre archway en route from platforms to pier. Note the unusual windows with (it would appear) the centre panes fixed and only the bottom left and bottom right being moveable sashes.

CHAPTER FIVE

CATTLE AND SHEEP (1864 - 1895)

The first references to a possible livestock traffic, in 1855, were mentioned in Chapter 3. As far as can be established, however, there was no actual livestock traffic in the first years. In 1863 the General Steam Navigation Co with whom the LT&SR were already working on the summer passenger traffic, and who had been into the continental livestock importing trade in a big way since the 1840s, applied to the LT&SR to use Thames Haven for a continental goods traffic also. However they do not seem to have done anything at Thames Haven, in the event; they had a big livestock trade at their own London wharves.

THE THAMES HAVEN COMPANY

The real beginning of the cattle traffic at Thames Haven was in 1864 (1), the importers being Messrs Phillips Graves & Phillips. In November 1864 they asked the LT&SR if they might lease Thames Haven pier and adjoining land 'with a view to improve the foreign trade in passengers and cattle and to create a trade in goods'. It appears that the Chairman Charles Eley, who often criticised Peto Brassey & Betts for not developing traffics, was the chief protagonist of this on the LT&SR side. However Peto Brassey & Betts still had to give their agreement. It was also necessary for Phillips Graves & Phillips to approach the GER, who would run the necessary cattle trains from Thames Haven to Maiden Lane (for the New Metropolitan Cattle Market at Caledonian Road): not so much because of the 'LT&S' section of the route (where the GER were merely acting as 'contractors' providing trains to Peto Brassey & Betts) but because of the purely-GER section west of Forest Gate Junction. Phillips' told the GER that they would spend £15,000 improving the facilities at Thames Haven if the railway would reduce the rate for oxen (sic) from 3s to 2s 5d throughout, meaning a cut from 5d to 4d in the GER share. This was refused - the GER, as ever, had a vested interest in conflict!, in this case its efforts to encourage cattle importing via Harwich, with much greater 'mileage' on GER tracks. However in January 1865 Phillips' were placated with a GER promise not to increase their portion beyond 5d (2).

Phillips' negotiations with all the parties took a year to sort out, but all turned out well and on 27th December 1865 a special LT&SR proprietors' meeting was held to approve the proposed agreement with them. Formally dated 22nd March 1866 (3), this provided for the building, partly by the LT&SR, and partly by Phillips', of a 'new pier or landing stage, dolphin, steam cranes, cattle pens, slaughter house [never built], and other buildings and works at Thames Haven'. These, plus the existing 1855 pier, were to be leased to Phillips' for 21 years, but others were still to be allowed to use the piers also.

As soon as this was sorted out, Phillips Graves & Phillips set up a separate limited company, The Thames Haven Company Ltd, to take responsibility for their operations at Thames Haven (but not for their main shipping and sales activities). The new company was wholly owned and controlled by themselves, the subscribers being the Ship Brokers George Christopher Graves, Richard Phillips, and John Phillips Charles Graves; and the Sheep Salesmen John Honck, James Brewster, and William George Guernier, all of London (4).

Work began quickly once the agreements had been formalised. In August 1866 it was reported that 'the works at Thames Haven to provide for increased cattle traffic are in a forward state'; and on 27th October that 'the works being completed, a party of leading Tilbury directors and others interested in the success of Thames Haven, proceeded yesterday (26th?) by special train to view them, and we believe were much gratified'.

The 1866 works comprised essentially the building of another pier, and cattle lairs: for details see Chapter 6.

Unfortunately the period since Phillips' had first approached the LT&SR had been an uncertain one for the cattle importing business generally: the 'great cattle plague' of 1865 had been followed by government restrictions on importing, imposed in a vacillatory fashion. Cattle traffic at Thames Haven sank to lower levels in 1866, and in February 1867 the LT&SR shareholders heard that the new facilities at Thames Haven were ready for traffic 'as soon as the government decide their policy', implying that they had not yet been used at all. However these problems evaporated in 1867

bringing the start of a boom period, as described in the next section.

In October 1866 the Thames Haven Co told the LT&SR that they wished to build a Hotel at Thames Haven in connection with their ideas of a regular continental passenger traffic which were clearly still very live at this date; but as the passenger services did not materialise, the Hotel remained on the drawing board as well.

With business good the Thames Haven Co found the facilities under pressure and in 1874/5 they approached the LT&SR as to further enlargements of the lairage. However they considered that their 21-year lease (ending in 1887) had too short a period remaining, and therefore asked the LT&SR to extend it for a further 21 years (i.e. to 1908). A new agreement seems to have been made in 1875/6 and the further works (for details of which, again, see Chapter 6) went ahead in 1876/7.

However this was immediately followed by a bad decline in the traffic and in 1883, with no sign of better days returning, the Thames Haven Co sought to give up their lease of the Thames Haven facilities. This was agreed in October on the basis of a £16,300 payment(s) by the LT&SR (5), and LT&SR took formal repossession of the property as from 1st November 1883, thereafter running everything at Thames Haven directly, as a normal part of the railway's operations. The 'Thames Haven Company' was now pointless and it was wound up in that same month by Phillips'.

LIVESTOCK TRAFFIC AT THAMES HAVEN 1864 - 1895

After the problems of 1865/6, 1867-76 proved a very solid period for the livestock trade generally, and for Thames Haven in particular. At the end of the cattle plague period in 1867, the government introduced restrictions under which only specified ports were authorised for cattle importing, and all imported cattle for the New Metropolitan Cattle Market were to be sent by rail; both of these benefited Thames Haven. Whilst the cattle tended to steal the limelight owing to the more frequent disease problems, sheep were also imported in a big way at Thames Haven and elsewhere, plus a smaller number of pigs.

In these years about a third of the total UK livestock imports came through Thames Haven. The other 'Port of London' locations were the main rivals but Southampton, Harwich, Hull, Newcastle, and other ports provided competition for the main continental traffic, and Birkenhead became important as the American trade grew. Most of the Thames Haven traffic in the first years after 1867 was Phillips Graves & Phillips' own trade with Tonning in Denmark. There were of course little problems from time to time even in these good years; the Continental War in 1870, blocking of the German ports by ice for many weeks in 1871, etc.

In 1877, unfortunately, the tide turned against Thames Haven as a livestock port. There was another outbreak of cattle plague which was introduced into the UK by imported cattle. This was soon eradicated, and cattle plague itself (rinderpest) was not to trouble the UK again, though foot-and-mouth and other diseases were to be a recurring trouble. The real problem for Thames Haven was that there was now a pronounced move (in part confirmed by legislative decrees) to slaughtering at the port of entry. This worked particularly in favour of the recently established Foreign Cattle Market at Deptford which had full slaughtering facilities. The LT&SR sought in 1877 to provide slaughtering facilities at Thames Haven (which had, as mentioned earlier, been proposed in 1865 but not provided) but this never came to pass as the London butchers were hostile to the notion of their having to travel to such a remote location to buy their meat. This proved a more important factor than the advantages of Thames Haven in avoiding the slow passage up the river, where the ventilation on the ships did not function properly bringing an appalling temperature and stink in the cattle decks by the time Deptford was reached.

The results are seen in the figures for 1875 - 1879 (6) : -

	Thames Haven		Foreign Cattle Market		Other London wharfs	
	Cattle	Sheep	Cattle	Sheep	Cattle	Sheep
1875	93,884	223,498	29,255	86,495	21,322	406,398
1876	105,204	182,627	21,860	38,714	20,472	559,493
1877	25,312	24,091	67,817	697,714	723	13,720
1878	33,938	38,364	60,675	699,911	2,217	317
1879	25,021	47,085	81,445	662,197	5,507	5,517

Thames Haven in fact retained a larger share of its traffic than the other London locations. These figures also show the actual numbers of animals being handled at Thames Haven both in the good years pre-1877 and in the poor years subsequently.

Thames Haven began with a continental traffic, primarily Holland, Denmark, and Germany, but from 1877 there are more frequent references to American cattle being landed here. (This too was subject to disease problems from time to time, ceasing entirely for some months in 1879 under government ban). From 1884 the total Thames Haven traffic improved again (although not back to 1867-76 levels) and most of this was now from Canada, the USA, Denmark, Sweden, and Norway. The transatlantic ships were larger than those used on the short sea continental routes, and had difficulties using the small piers at Thames Haven, leading the LT&SR to obtain parliamentary powers in 1880 and 1886 for a considerable expansion of the wharfage (see Chapter 6), but nothing was done immediately owing to the uncertainty of the times.

In 1888 traffic fell off somewhat owing to the Canadian boats having been enticed away to Liverpool and Hull, but hearts rose in March 1889 when the Privy Council announced the lifting of the longstanding restrictions on Dutch cattle as from 1st June. Since 1877 Dutch cattle had been banned unless slaughtered on entry, and the Dutch trade (which was larger than that from any other country) had therefore all gone to Deptford, with none at all at Thames Haven. Unrestricted importing was now to resume. The LT&SR reacted with extraordinary speed, the Chairman going to Thames Haven with the General Manager Arthur Stride on 21st March to agree on necessary improvements. Work was already under way, and by the time restrictions were lifted (after a postponement) on 1st September 1889, the LT&SR was fully prepared. These 1889 works (described in Chapter 6) were made under the 1886 Act powers and at £27,000 were much more extensive than the 1866 and 1876 improvements, such was the faith placed in the resumption of the Dutch traffic. It was hoped to attract some 150,000 cattle and a million sheep per annum. Alas it was to prove a false dawn. For the first ten weeks in September - November 1889 there was a large traffic which produced the greatest throughput ever seen at Thames Haven, but disease then reappeared in Holland and the ban had to be reimposed, with such business as remained reverting to Deptford. There was a brief lifting of the Dutch ban again in 1891/2, during which Thames Haven handled a good Dutch traffic again for a few weeks, but that was the end of it as far as Dutch dreams were concerned. A beneficial side-effect, though, was that the much-extended wharves of 1889 made it easier to handle the transatlantic ships, and Canadian ships returned again from 1891.

Unfortunately there was then a ban on Canadian cattle (unless slaughtered on entry) also, in 1893, and livestock traffic at Thames Haven almost ceased in that year. There was a resurgence in 1894-5, based primarily on Canadian and US *sheep* (which were not affected by the 1893 ban), but in November 1895 the government announced that as from 1 January 1896 *all* sheep as well as cattle would have to be slaughtered on entry. This was made permanent by the Diseases of Animals Act (Foreign Animals Order) 1896 and meant that livestock traffic at Thames Haven (and other ports without slaughtering facilities) came to a total and permanent end in the last days of December 1895. The large sum of money spent so dynamically in 1889 was to prove sadly wasted.

THE MAIDEN LANE CATTLE TRAINS

As mentioned earlier, the vast majority (if not all) of the livestock landed at Thames Haven were taken by special trains to Maiden Lane (NLR) from which it was only half a mile 'on the hoof' to the New Metropolitan Cattle Market.

The animals were accompanied on the ships by drovers from the country of origin, but they returned with the ship, and did not handle the animals in the UK. Both cattle and sheep were walked on and off the ships, the piers at Thames Haven being designed with different decks linked by ramps to enable this to be done at all states of the tide. The arrival of a ship at Thames Haven would be marked by the gathering of a little group of drovers and agents for the London salesmen at the pier; the ships were unloaded immediately on arrival and the animals put into covered lairs where they were fed and watered. There was a compulsory customs quarantine of 12 hours, and inspection by the Privy Council's vet.

The main market at the cattle market was held on Monday mornings and Messrs Phillips Graves & Phillips scheduled their ships to arrive at Thames Haven on Saturdays in order to minimise the time in England, the trains in this case running to Maiden Lane

on Sundays. But ships could of course arrive at Thames Haven on any day. The drovers would travel on the train if they had gone to Thames Haven, but some drovers would merely meet the train at Maiden Lane. Assistant drovers, notorious for their cruelty, would have to be casually employed for the drive from Maiden Lane to the Market (7).

Until 1880 the trains (like other 'LT&S' trains) were formed of GER locomotives and stock, although some NLR cattle wagons were hired to supplement the GER fleet when necessary. From the LT&SR's taking over direct working of its line in 1880, they were hauled by LT&SR 4-4-2T locos and formed mainly of the new LT&SR cattle wagons, the first 100 of which arrived in 1880 (with a further 50 following in 1891; 45 more were delivered in 1896 but this was after the Thames Haven traffic had ended).

Originally the trains ran via Stratford, with an NLR loco taking over for the Stratford - Maiden Lane section. But from the spring of 1876 they were run via Plaistow, with a change of loco there.

A picture of the trains can be gained from a December 1871 Accident Report when (thanks to the lack of Block Working) one of them was run into by a GER passenger train whilst standing at Victoria Park. The cattle train had left Stratford with an NLR loco at 9.45am and comprised 26 loaded cattle wagons and two brakes. In the brake with the NLR Guard were three LT&SR men who had come through from Thames Haven, 'two in charge of the cattle and one in charge of the train', and a drover. The rear van and rearmost wagon were 'knocked to pieces' by the impact of the GER train but it was reported that 'the cattle do not appear to have been much damaged, except that a calf was thrown over the bridge into the road below'.

There were never any timetabled services, the traffic being dependent on the unpredictable arrival of the ships. 1876 notes for three randomly-sampled days show :-

Sunday 6th February 1876 - two trains from Thames Haven, both worked by Johnson 0-6-0 No. 492, one of '31-35' wagons (stated to be average) and one of '36+' wagons. The same loco also worked the empties back.

Monday 7th February 1876 - two trains, loco 482.

Friday 5th May 1876 - no trains.

There must have been many days with no trains (and days on end with no trains, in the 'bad' years). The available figures suggest that something like 2,000 cattle and 4,000 sheep on average had to be moved per week in the busiest years. The 1884 WTT states that a maximum of 40 loaded or 50 empty wagons is applicable on the LT&S section.

DEAD MEAT AND PERISHABLES

The importing of 'dead meat' into the UK did not begin in a big way until the 1870s when developments in refrigeration began to make this traffic easier. By the late 1880s it was a major portion of the total meat importing business and by 1914 it had supplanted the import of live stock entirely. Thames Haven had a small share in the dead meat trade, particularly in the late '80s and early '90s, but was never really geared up for it.

Cheese also became a significant business at Thames Haven in these later years (and, to a lesser extent, other 'perishables' such as butter, eggs, bacon, and fruit). This cheese was brought over mainly in the Canadian cattle ships, or on other ships bound for upriver docks with general cargoes which found it beneficial to make a quick call at Thames Haven en route to offload perishables (if the ship was delayed in docking, the call at Thames Haven might mean the goods arriving a day earlier in the market). The cheese went to the LT&SR Commercial Road goods depot, which the merchants considered a very convenient place for them to go to inspect it. On one occasion in June 1894 there is reference to a 'special cheese train from Thames Haven' (which, somewhat ironically, ran into and killed some cows at Low Street), but one imagines that it was more often conveyed by the normal daily branch goods train.

ATTEMPTS TO ESTABLISH A GENERAL GOODS TRAFFIC

The LT&SR had never given up their 1860s hopes of establishing a general goods trade at Thames Haven. As noted earlier, Phillips Graves & Phillips had not established such a service in the event. In 1877 it was reported that there had been 'negotiations with more than one company', but silence then falls again for some years.

There was a small success in 1890/1 when the Perlbach Line began calling at Thames Haven three times a week on their regular

Hamburg - Tilbury service, but only to offload 'foodstuffs' (8).

A flurry of approaches followed in 1894/5. A Mr Breslauer came to the LT&SR in March 1894 regarding a proposed Thames Haven - Ostend service which seems to have been what eventually emerged in 1896 as the John Cockerill Line *Tilbury - Ostend* service. In November 1894 a Mr Tallermann put a grand scheme for the import of meat 'from the colonies' at Thames Haven, but the LT&SR seem to have been suspicious of him. Them in June 1895 Henry Crosse proposed a £200,000 plan for 'a new continental express route via Thames Haven', which also came to nothing.

THE LAST YEARS OF TRAFFIC AT THE PIER

After the 1896 ban on cattle and sheep, a small traffic in the importing of horses continued. There had always been a horse traffic (on the cattle boats) although the facilities were not ideal; the crane was not suitable for horses, and the Vange and Corringham village smiths had to be sent for when horses arrived to fix nails into the horses' shoes to enable them to walk down gangways.

The cheese traffic lasted until 1898 when it was reported that it had been lost to Tilbury where the London & St. Katharine Dock Co had offered very low rates.

Only odd references in the LT&SR minutes assure us of the continued existence of some shipping traffic after this :-
3.11.1898 Accidents .... James Maney, engaged in unloading a
  steamer at Thames Haven Wharf.......
5.4.1900 Henry James, Craneman in the company's service, injured
  whilst working the crane at Thames Haven wharf.

31.5.1900 Accidents.... A Thames labourer, assisting to unload a
  truck at Thames Haven pier.......
After 1900 calls by ships seem to have become very scarce and in 1905 the LT&SR minutes refer to the fact that 'practically no use is at present being made of the pier' as a reason for not repairing it. The LT&SR regarded the pier as still available for traffic until 1912, but if any ships actually called in these last years 1905 - 1912, there is no record of it.

Why had Thames Haven failed to attract any greater use by the shipping companies? There is no known contemporary analysis but one might note that
* This was a period (particularly pre-1888) of cut-throat competition between the London dock companies, with very low rates prevailing (so that the, presumably low, charges at Thames Haven were not especially attractive). After Tilbury docks opened in 1886 they were so little used that shippers had to be bribed to go there at 'loss-leader' prices, and some Thames Haven traffic was lost to Tilbury.
* The facilities for general goods at Thames Haven were not all that good, and it was possibly seen as being too far downriver to be used conveniently by lighters which were a fundamental part of the London system.
* There were (so far as one can gather) no servicing facilities for ships at Thames Haven so any longer-distance ships at least would have to go to an upriver dock as well for bunkering etc., thereby always reducing Thames Haven to quick calls for particular traffics where speed was of the essence.

LT&SR LIVESTOCK TRAFFIC

1869	£ 7,176	1877	£ 3,141	1885	£ 6,298	1893	£ 350
1870	£ 7,393	1878	£ 4,409	1886	£ 7,152	1894	£ 5,225
1871	£ 10,123	1879	£ 3,570	1887	£ 6,167	1895	£ 10,049
1872	£ 7,364	1880	£ 3,385	1888	£ 4,078	1896	£ 1,799
1873	£ 8,948	1881	£ 2,292	1889	£ 10,401	1897	£ 1,805
1874	£ 8,938	1882	£ 1,819	1890	£ 5,641	1898	£ 1,031
1875	nk	1883	£ 3,267	1891	£ 5,422	1899	£ 736
1876	£ 11,439	1884	£ 6,350	1892	£ 3,267	1900	£ 1,013

This table shows the LT&SR's total annual livestock traffic revenue for the 1869-1900 period (figures are not available pre-1869). There are no separate figures available for the Thames Haven traffic but the probability is that the 'other' traffic was under £1,000 in most years (it is not clear why the 1896 and 1897 figures are as high as they are; by the mid-1900s the figure is down to £300-£500). The table thus gives a good picture of the Thames Haven activity levels, which will be seen to accord entirely with what is known from contemporary sources of the factors affecting the cattle import trade. The figures come from the LT&SR half-yearly reports and have been added to give 12-month figures; in most years the July-December half had the heavier traffic, the greatest contrasts being in 1889 (£8,498 of the £10,401 total coming in the 2nd half) and 1895 (£7,253 of £10,049 in the 2nd half).

(1) Compare the words of the February 1865 LT&SR half-yearly report, that the branch had 'hitherto been used almost exclusively for the Margate and Ramsgate traffic during the summer'; also the comment of the Chairman, Eley, in December 1865 'up to a comparatively recent period the Thames Haven branch had only been opened during the summer and autumn months'. Both these suggest that there cannot have been any other significant traffic pre-1864/5. Per contra the November 1864 request wording suggests that Phillips Graves and Phillips were already using Thames Haven (which of course they could do without a lease); and there is a table in the report of the 1866 Parliamentary Select Committee on Trade in Animals of imports at each port in every week in 1865 which shows that Thames Haven was already importing regularly by the start of 1865. The already-existing P.G. & P. traffic is confirmed by Eley's comments in December 1865 'Messrs Phillips Graves & Phillips having brought their ships to Thames Haven a new traffic has been created, and it has now become absolutely necessary to have further facilities'. All this points to 1864 as the starting date. There is no evidence of any actual (as distinct from proposed) P.G. & P. general goods or passenger traffic; passengers would not normally travel on cattle boats which were very malodorous.
(2) GER Traffic Committee 7.12.1864, 4.1.1865. The word 'reduce' further suggests an existing traffic already in 1864.
(3) There were actually two agreements, one of 22.3.1866 between the LT&SR, Peto Brassey & Betts, and Phillips Graves & Phillips; and the other of 23.3.1866 between

Peto Brassey & Betts and Phillips Graves & Phillips. As ever with the pre-1875 LT&SR, the money details must have been complex, but no copies of either agreement are known. *Herapath's* 30.12.1865 reported that the LT&SR were to spend £2,500 on cattle lairs and sidings, Peto Brassey & Betts paying 5% on this until the end of their lease in 1875, and Phillips Graves & Phillips 5% thereafter. P.G. & P. were 'to expend not less than £5,000 on the construction of a new pier' within nine months.
(4) PRO BT31/1246/2965.
(5) It is not immediately evident why the LT&SR had to pay the Thames Haven Co such a large sum to end the lease, but it was presumably related to the sums spent by the Thames Haven Co in 1866 (£5,000 +) and 1876/7 (sum not known). The lease still had 20 years to run in 1883, per subsequent statements, so it would seem that it had only been extended to 1903 in the event, not 1908.
(6) Return under Section 5a of the Contagious Diseases (Animals) Act 1878, 29.7.1880 (Parliamentary Papers).
(7) Evidence on the livestock trade at Thames Haven given by John Irwin of the Thames Haven Company to the Transit of Animals Committee, 19.10.1869 (Parliamentary Papers).
(8) Stride, March 1891, Commons Committee evidence on LT&SR 1891 Bill. Stride does not actually name the Hamburg shipping line involved but there can be little doubt that it was Perlbach, who had been using Tilbury since c1888. There are no further references after 1891 so the Thames Haven calls may have been shortlived.

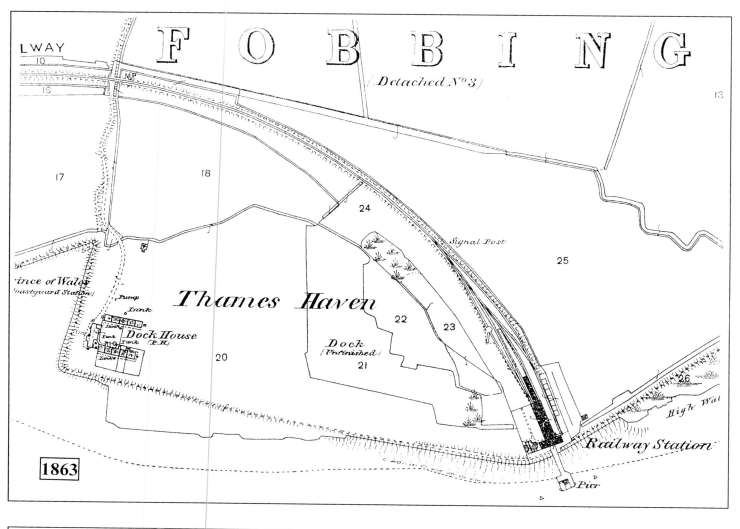

FOBBING *(Detached Nº 3)*

1863

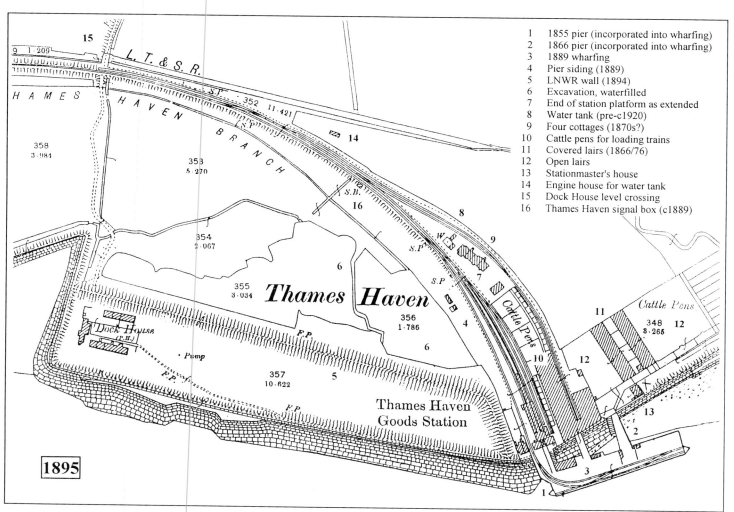

1895

1	1855 pier (incorporated into wharfing)
2	1866 pier (incorporated into wharfing)
3	1889 wharfing
4	Pier siding (1889)
5	LNWR wall (1894)
6	Excavation, waterfilled
7	End of station platform as extended
8	Water tank (pre-c1920)
9	Four cottages (1870s?)
10	Cattle pens for loading trains
11	Covered lairs (1866/76)
12	Open lairs
13	Stationmaster's house
14	Engine house for water tank
15	Dock House level crossing
16	Thames Haven signal box (c1889)

CHAPTER SIX

THAMES HAVEN STATION AND PIERS

Thames Haven station and pier were originally the only traffic location on the branch (until the Petroleum Storage Co's siding opened in 1878) and remained the most important centre of activity until the 1890s. The piers then fell into a 'limbo' in the 1900s with the end of the shipping traffic, and were in due course removed altogether in 1913/22. The old station buildings remained as staff accommodation until 1953.

THE 1855 STATION AND PIER

The station was wholly timber-built and comprised
- a 'head' building with the offices etc, about 75ft by 25ft, single storey, with a hipped roof.
- a 'trainshed' roof, 37ft wide and 125ft long, over a small 'concourse' area and a large part of the platform length.
- a timber 'island' platform with a line either side, originally 350ft long but extended, either in 1866 or 1876, to 550ft. Beyond the trainshed the platform had a canopy for a further 75ft, the rest being uncovered.

The west side platform had a loco run-round siding leading off it and a turntable was situated on this (1).

The only goods facility was one siding on the east side which had, from the start, cattle pens alongside it and a small open air cattle pound behind the pens.

Beside the main station building were a pair of houses also built in 1855, originally inhabited by the Stationmaster and Customs Officer.

The 1855 pier was 150 ft long, only 15ft wide for most of its length but with a 49ft pierhead. There was no pontoon and only one ship could call there at a time. This may have caused problems after the cattle traffic begun (i.e. in 1864-6, prior to the second pier being built, if a cattle boat was present when a passenger steamer had to call). By 1880 at least a crane was available.

Thames Haven was a public passenger station until the Margate trains ceased in 1880, and a public goods station although there was no public road access (2). In addition to the shipping traffic there was probably a small goods traffic from local farmers; there is a reference in 1904 to a wagon being loaded with hay here. Later there was a 'smalls' traffic for the industrial users as well as their private siding traffic.

THE CATTLE PIER AND LAIRS (1866/76)

There are no reliable plans for the c1870 period and it is not possible to disaggregate the improvements of 1866 (said to have cost £2,500) from those of 1876 (when £7,400 was spent on 'Thames Haven station', per the half-yearly reports, in 1876-8). The second pier, to serve purely as a cattle boat pier, does seem to have been built in 1866 (3); it was situated 80 yards east of the 1855 pier and was 172ft long, with a pierhead 49ft wide (as the 1855 pier's) equipped with a crane and small engine-house to provide power for it. At least some of the covered cattle lairage dated from 1866 also (4). At any rate there were after 1876 42,000 sq. ft. of covered lairage in three lengthy sheds, plus 14,200 sq. ft. of open lairage and pens adjacent. The lairage now provided accommodation for up to 1,800 cattle and 8,500 sheep, all paved and fitted with water and feeding troughs. In addition there were 16 acres of marsh available adjacent for grazing. The rail sidings were much expanded, including an additional cattle loading siding running directly alongside the eastern side of the block of covered lairs, to supplement the existing loading siding on its west side. The small pens alongside these sidings held 8 or 9 cattle each and it was claimed that a 35-wagon train could be loaded in $^1/_4$ hour. All these facilities can be seen on the 1895 OS map here.

THE ENLARGED WHARF FRONTAGE (1889)

Back in the 1850s Berkley had foreseen a 1200ft wharf frontage stretching away to the east of the station. That much never came to pass but, as noted in Chapter 5, it became clear that the small pierheads were far from suitable for large ships. The LT&SR's 1880 Act obtained powers for a modest 350ft wharf (much as actually built in 1889), but these lapsed in 1884, and when an improvement in the trade prompted a reapplication to Parliament in 1886 the powers gained were for the full 1200ft of Berkley's vision.

The existence of these 1886 powers proved a blessing when, in the summer of 1889, it became necessary to make improvements quickly to cope with the resumption of the Dutch traffic. The work was done by Mowlem's and cost over £27,000 even though only a 415ft wharf frontage was built. As the 1895 map shows, the new wharfage 'incorporated' the existing piers, and was directly served by rail sidings, the new 1889 siding to the wharves having to be squeezed between the station building and the staff houses. It is doubtful if these sidings on the wharf ever really justified their existence as only the deadmeat, cheese and other perishables could have used them. They were probably horse-shunted but no reference is known. The new wharf had 42 ft of water at high tide and 25ft at spring tide low tides; there were three 'decks' so that livestock could be walked off ships at any state of the tide. Three ships of the usual size could now be handled together. Two steam cranes were adver-

---

THAMES HAVEN, ESSEX.

615

Ships, cattle, sheep and all seem to have passed through Thames Haven unphotographed for over 30 years. This view of the station complex is probably c1920, but with little having changed since 1895 it still captures the feel of the 'cattle port' Thames Haven.

The photographer is standing near the old Dock House pub site.

The waterfilled excavated area at left partly represents the 1838/47 THD&R Co dock excavations but was much altered c1894. The 1894 LNWR additional river wall is at right foreground. In the station area beyond we see, left to right, the 1870s (?) staff cottages, the long roofs of the three main blocks of covered cattle lairs, the (cut-back) passenger station trainshed - a puny thing compared to the lairs! - the station houses, and the crane on the (soon to be removed) remnant of the piers. The scene in general should be compared with the 1895 OS map.
(Padgett Collection, Southend Museums Service.)

32

tised as available (presumably those from the existing piers) although in 1892 Stride was to note that the crane power here was inadequate and a 4-ton crane from Mowlem's should be acquired.

This 1889 work was the final expansion of the facilities. The LT&SR's 1891 Act revived the powers for the full 1200ft until 1896, and in October 1895 Stride was asked to prepare plans and estimates for this, but the ban on live cattle importing here was announced by the government in November.

DISMANTLING OF THE WHARF (1913/1922)

In January 1905 Robertson, the LT&SR Engineer, reported that the wharf, now hardly used, needed extensive repairs. This was 'fudged' until the autumn of 1906 when the Thames Conservancy (who, it will be recalled, had powers, under the THD&R Co's 1836 Act, to demand the removal of any pier etc, if considered dangerous) pressed for action. In December 1906 the LT&SR Board agreed repair work estimated at £9,500, and Samuel Williams & Sons of Dagenham Dock put in a tender for this. Nothing seems to have been done. In November 1907 it was reported that subsidence was affecting the pier but only in January 1909 was an order to Messrs Williams, for concrete piles, approved. Again however nothing is recorded as having been done.

On 24th September 1909 the pier was hit and 'seriously damaged' by the Tyser Line steamer *Nerehana*. They offered £500 compensation but the LT&SR, forgetting for the moment that it had no real interest in the pier, threatened court action, and got £1,100.

Silence then descends again until 25th January 1912 when Robertson again reported to the LT&SR Board on the condition of the pier. The Board decided that the pier 'should be closed to traffic as soon as possible'. As there was effectively no traffic it is difficult to see that anything would have prevented immediate implementation of this 'closure'.

In October 1913 the Midland Engineer reported that the 'removal of the wrecked portion of Thames Haven pier' was about to begin. However some of the wharf remained after this 1913 dismantling (including the 1885 pier) and can be seen on the 1919-survey map at the end of this chapter (5). The war had given people more important things to fret about, but in 1921/2 the Port of London Authority began making noises again and in April 1922 the Midland Engineer was told by his Board to remove the residue of the pier(s) also, which seems to have been done in that year. This was the final end of Amsinck's dreams.

STAFF

The station originally had a resident stationmaster but this ceased in 1878 when the LT&SR's Goods Superintendent C. A. Noble took direct control of this station, no doubt on account of the low traffic. By the 1890s there was a Stationmaster again, Charles Cottee, who resigned in 1901 owing to ill health, receiving 15s a week pension. The real man-in-charge for over four decades was Foreman Thomas Robert Cooling who was said, on his retirement in 1910, to have been at Thames Haven since its opening.

The Stationmaster got a new larger house (in 1889?) but as it was salubriously located overlooking the cattle lairs, this may not have been welcomed! Four single-storey cottages were also built (date not known) opposite the far end of the platform, and the Customs took one of these. This left the original two station houses free for other members of the station staff.

Although traffic at the station itself was next-to-nothing by the mid-1900s, this did not mean the staff were left in idleness, as the stationmaster and clerks had to handle the paperwork for the increasing private siding traffic on the branch. The stationmaster's office in the 1855 passenger station building also remained the hub of branch operating, although with the opening of the CLR in 1901, and the Shell (Anglo-Saxon) and LATHOL 'Reedham' Sidings in 1916-18, shunting activities gravitated more towards the Dock House LC vicinity, the sidings at the passenger station becoming seen increasingly as mere dead-end storage sidings.

In 1915 there were eight staff

E.B. Griggs	Station Agent	Age 37
A. E. Reeves	Clerk	28
H. Rayment	Clerk	24
S. Moss	Checker	26
S. Baldwin	Temporary Porter	50
J. Spooner	Temporary Porter	35
J. Cole	Relief Clerk	35
F. Taylor	Relief Clerk	24

and with the wartime increase in traffic (Chapter 7) they were becoming heavily pressed. 'The place is a difficult one to staff owing to the absence of houses in the district, and appears to be considerably understaffed', noted the 1915 Midland report; 'Griggs is frequently on duty for 24 hours or more at a stretch'. One can well imagine the unpopularity of Thames Haven as a posting, but nothing has come down to us to elucidate the strange isolated life that those sent there must have endured in Victorian times, with no shop in reach and only the Dock House pub as a refuge. From 1899 Kynochtown, and then the Shell housing, brought other human beings within an easier walk.

1921 figures give the station's 'coaching' debit as a mere £26 (all for parcels), but the goods debit, at £368,432, was much the biggest on the LT&S section - almost all private siding traffic.

The opening of 'Thames Haven Halt' in 1923 (Chapter 9) brought a further new place of action away from the old station. In the interwar years most of the cattle lairs were removed (6), the station roof and platform decayed, and Margate and Rotterdam became even remoter in the inherited memory; but still the clerks beavered away in the old station offices, time warped in 1855 whilst the tanks of Shell and LATHOL closed in ever closer on both sides.

THE LNWR CONNECTION

One of the most 'unlikely' pieces of the history of Thames Haven is the fact that for many years the London & North Western Railway owned far more property here than the LT&SR ever did. The LNWR purchased this land in 1870, from Thomas Brassey, who had no doubt had notions of some future development but was now giving up active involvements owing to his age (7). (See map p.37.)

Clearly the LNWR, which did not have good direct access to Thames shipping, had intentions of some kind of dock development, but the Continental war put ideas on the backburner at the time the land was brought, and the scheme never seems to have recovered from this initial discouragement. A decade later, Arthur Stride the LT&SR General Manager reported in January 1881 that he had just visited Thames Haven with a party of LNWR and NLR directors and 'discussed the possibility of establishing a through service from Willesden to the LT&SR'. In 1882 Counsel told a Commons Committee that the LNWR would 'have docks there'; but after this silence falls again.

This did not, however, mean that Euston could *forget* its Thames Haven property. Like the THD&R Co before them they were all too often troubled with the bother and expense of having to repair the river walls under the demands of the Commissioners of Sewers of the Fobbing Levels. In 1894 they were obliged to spend no less than £3,717 building a new wall inland of the old for a considerable distance (see the 1895 25 inch map here), but having done the work they went to court claiming that the Commissioners were not entitled to make such an order. They lost the case and then seem to have decided, as the Thames Haven Dock Co had in the end of

Thames Haven station staff under the LMS. Stationmaster Draper takes the conventional centre position, and at left is Foreman Jack Burr who would have been responsible for the 'Pilot Guard' function in working the branch. The group is posed by the corner of the 1855 station building.

1859, that owning property in these parts was more bother than it was worth. The 58 acres were offered to the LT&SR first in 1901, but with their maritime traffic being moribund by then they saw no use for it, and the land was sold by the LNWR in 1902 to the London & Thames Haven Oil Wharves Ltd, for £16,600. So ended another might-have-been.

THE THAMES HAVEN POWER STATION SCHEME

By s.8 of the LT&SR Act of 1911, powers were obtained to build a power station, to supply electricity for the electrification of the LT&SR line, on LT&SR land (1895 OS map parcels 348 & 349) at Thames Haven station. The Bill had been opposed by London & Thames Haven Oil Wharves who were concerned at the idea of the branch, to which their storage tanks were so close, being electrified. However Stride placated them by assuring them that the electrification on the branch would be 'insulated' (whatever that meant - the type of electrification had still not been decided). They also got a pipe subway under the line.

The power station was never built (and indeed the branch has never been electrified).

THE LMS DUNKIRK SERVICE PIER PROPOSALS

From 1927 to 1932 the LMS and their French partners the Nord ran a Tilbury - Dunkirk shipping service. Details were given in an article in *Midland Record* No. 5 and it only remains to note the relevance of this to Thames Haven.

The Nord were against Tilbury, considering it could be handicapped by river fogs, and had initially (c1925) pressed for Thames Haven to be used instead, but the LMS, having just *removed* the wharf here, were understandably opposed to this, and succeeded in getting Tilbury accepted so that the service could begin without any expensive works. Unfortunately the fears about fog were proved correct too often and in 1929-31 various schemes were drawn up (8), both by Euston and by the French, for possible new wharfage at Thames Haven, all very much along the lines of the 1889 arrangements. However it was decided to abandon the service instead.

THE END OF THE OLD STATION AND EXPANSION OF 'THAMES HAVEN YARD' (1953-6)

The old station building was getting in a bad way by the 1940s and plans were drawn up for its replacement. The first plans, dated 1947, were for a new building of 'concrete hut units' immediately adjacent to the old buildings, and a new concrete 'loading platform' in lieu of the existing station platform, but this was not proceeded with. Instead it was decided in 1951 to provide a new building at the Dock House Level crossing, closer to the new centre of activities. This 60ft long single storey brick structure, on the site of the 1922 Halt hut, was built in 1953 (9) and can be seen in the photograph at p.54. It became known as the 'Yard Inspector's Office' (later 'Supervisor's Office'), the branch having been put under the control of the Stanford-le-Hope stationmaster some time in this period. The clerical functions were also transferred elsewhere.

The old station buildings were evacuated when the new block came into use, and were demolished in 1954, probably just failing to reach their centenary (10). The 1855 staff houses adjacent also went. The station platform and the cattle pens loading bank followed in 1955 (11), and with the remaining cattle lairs shed, and the stationmaster's house, also going around this time, the 'old', after 60 years of little change, was effectively all swept away in this one fell swoop in the course of a couple of years.

At the same time plans were being drawn up for the expansion of siding capacity to cope with the booming oil tanker traffic (Chapter 10). These additional sidings were installed in 1955/6 (12) and the location became known as 'Thames Haven Yard' henceforth. The sidings were now numbered 1-14 from the south side and comprised (as shown on the track layout plans at the end of Chapter 10):-

1-4   New sidings 1955/6 (3 and 4 partly on the site of the 1889 pier siding)

5-8   The existing former platform lines and sidings of 1855 and 1866.

9   A new 'Cripple Siding' (with a 'Wagon Repair Shop' adjacent) laid on the site of the recently removed cattle pens.

10   Existing siding.

11-14 New sidings 1955/6 (11 and 12 partly on the site of old sidings).

This gave siding capacity for around 300 more (4-wheel) tankers.

However this soon proved insufficient itself, and only a few years later (13) another three sidings were installed on the north side, Nos. 15-17. The sidings now filled almost the whole area of additional ground taken by the LT&S in 1855 and mostly vacant until as late as 1955. It was therefore fortunate that no further expansion was to be needed after this.

For footnotes see p.36

DOCK HOUSE HOTEL, SHELL HAVEN, ESSEX. 689.

The terminus buildings, in LMS days, after the platform canopy and trainshed had been dismantled except for the last 30ft or so of the trainshed over the 'concourse', as seen here. (This was done at an unknown date between 1895 and 1919). The lean-to 'shack' extension behind the van body was of 1860s-80s vintage and housed a coal store and Mess Room. The eastern end of the main building housed the lavatories, hence the small window. River wall at left, 1855 staff houses behind the trainshed. The clerestory coach at right was presumably part of the then Workmen's set.

right The terminus in (probably) the 1930s, still in reasonable shape. Some years after the canopy went, the platform itself had been cut back in the 1920s to the original 1855 length. At far left is the 1855 goods siding with the derelict remains of the original set of cattle pens. At far right, looking a little rough, is the additional 1889 siding put in for access to the wharf, but cut short by the station houses when the wharf was removed in 1922. The branch Workmen's set is stabled in the platform in this morning view.

left When the old Dock House pub had to be abandoned it was replaced by a new and more substantial 'Dock House' built c1900 adjacent to the level crossing. This view looking south over the crossing was taken c1922 and shows in the background some of the wartime army huts built for troops manning the 'Block houses' erected in the vicinity. The prefabricated sections of these huts had arrived by train in 1915. The military left at the end of the war leaving their huts behind them.

The pub's landlord at 1914 was R. J. (Dick) Eastabrook the former LATHOL piermaster. Although definitely a step up on the old pub, it was still, inevitably, troubled by drunken violence from the ship's crews who formed one of its primary clienteles. Like its predecessor it was more often known as the 'Pig & Whistle' (or the 'Pig') by its customers.

At bottom left corner is the 'branch' running line, then, curving away to the south, the additional connection just put in at this date to the LATHOL sidings.

This pub was in turn replaced by the new, more upmarket, 'Haven Hotel' further up the road in 1924, and became a LATHOL Staff Hostel.

(Padgett Collection, Southend Museums Service)

Another view of the Dock House level crossing area, from the east, with Thames Haven Halt the main feature in the foreground. Undated but probably c1950; the Halt area and the lamps are still well-maintained. At centre distance is the Dock House public house, and at right the Shell offices. The points in the immediate foreground are the connection for the 1922 carriage siding for the Workmen's set.

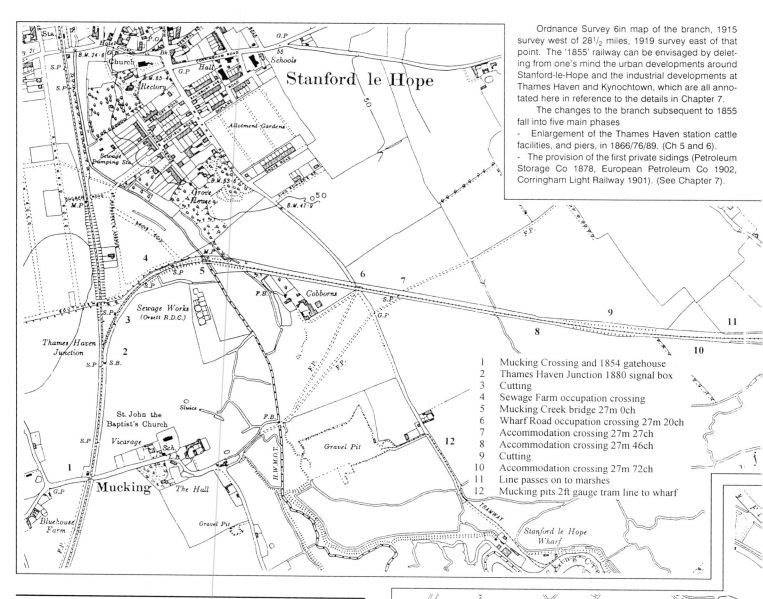

Ordnance Survey 6in map of the branch, 1915 survey west of 28½ miles, 1919 survey east of that point. The '1855' railway can be envisaged by deleting from one's mind the urban developments around Stanford-le-Hope and the industrial developments at Thames Haven and Kynochtown, which are all annotated here in reference to the details in Chapter 7.

The changes to the branch subsequent to 1855 fall into five main phases
- Enlargement of the Thames Haven station cattle facilities, and piers, in 1866/76/89. (Ch 5 and 6).
- The provision of the first private sidings (Petroleum Storage Co 1878, European Petroleum Co 1902, Corringham Light Railway 1901). (See Chapter 7).

1   Mucking Crossing and 1854 gatehouse
2   Thames Haven Junction 1880 signal box
3   Cutting
4   Sewage Farm occupation crossing
5   Mucking Creek bridge 27m 0ch
6   Wharf Road occupation crossing 27m 20ch
7   Accommodation crossing 27m 27ch
8   Accommodation crossing 27m 46ch
9   Cutting
10 Accommodation crossing 27m 72ch
11 Line passes on to marshes
12 Mucking pits 2ft gauge tram line to wharf

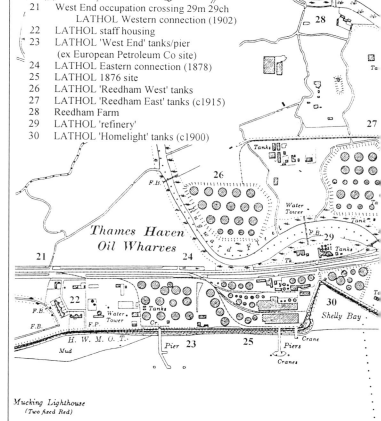

21 West End occupation crossing 29m 29ch
    LATHOL Western connection (1902)
22 LATHOL staff housing
23 LATHOL 'West End' tanks/pier
    (ex European Petroleum Co site)
24 LATHOL Eastern connection (1878)
25 LATHOL 1876 site
26 LATHOL 'Reedham West' tanks
27 LATHOL 'Reedham East' tanks (c1915)
28 Reedham Farm
29 LATHOL 'refinery'
30 LATHOL 'Homelight' tanks (c1900)

(1) The turntable is shown in the 1860s OS plan but not on the November 1855 TH&DR Co deposited plans. However the latter are a little imprecise in the trackwork details. Had the turntable not been there when the line was inspected in 1855, this would almost certainly have been commented on adversely: the Board of Trade regularly insisted on turntables at branch termini at this period, and the Thames Haven line was to be worked by tender engines. It is nowhere specifically mentioned in the records and only its size, position, and necessity point to its being a locomotive turntable.
(2) Still listed as 'G' in the 1956 edition of the RCH Handbook. The date of formal closure to public goods traffic (if there ever was one) is not known.
(3) Herapath's 3.11.1866 reports that 'strenuous Exertions will be made to induce Shipowners to the New Pier.'
(4) In 1869 it was stated that the cattle 'go under sheds' (ref. Chapter 5 note 7).
(5) In disagreement with the 1919 OS map, the Midland 1920 2 chain survey plan shows a significant proportion of the 1889 wharfage still in situ also. Borley wrongly states that the pier was removed, i.e. in toto, in '1912'.
(6) Local historian F. Z. Claro stated in a newspaper article that these lasted until the 1953 flood, but all but one block are gone by the 1939 OS. Probably this one block did last until after the 1953 floods; it is still shown on a 1951 plan.
(7) The land was purchased under s.11 of the LNWR Additional Powers Act 1870. Part of the land was ex-Oil Mill Farm land, sold by the THD&R Co to Samuel Sharpe in 1861 and resold by him to Brassey in 1869.
(8) Plans in Railtrack Archive, Waterloo, several versions, mostly undated but one for 'Scheme A' is dated January 1930 and another has December 1929 stamp date; those for Schemes 'B' and 'C' must be later. There are also French plans for a wholly new pier on Canvey Island with a railway from Benfleet, dated December 1930. One of the Thames Haven plans has a note 'soundings were taken in December 1926'.
(9) Scheme Plans 51 LSF 253 and 52 LA 7172/7173. No work commenced at time of Frank Church's March 1952 photographs. 1954 plans show the new building as an existing structure and this is confirmed by the photographs of the old station derelict in April 1954. A second storey was added later in (?) 1964.
(10) Still there derelict in April 1954, shown as already gone in February 1955 plan.
(11) February 1955 plan 55LSF121 is for removal of the platform and cattle pens bank. Gone by 1957 OS and 1957 photographs.
(12) In a January 1955 ER report it is stated that 'an extensive increase in the siding accommodation has now been authorised, the contract let and work should start in the near future'. All the new sidings are there by the 1957 OS.
(13) Exact date not known. These sidings are shown on a 1960 ER branch plan, but not on the 1965 OS 25in.

- A rush of extra facilities for increased traffic in c1915-18 (Miners Safety siding 1916, LATHOL Reedham sidings 1918, Shell siding 1916). (See Chapter 7).
- The provision of the 'Halts' for the Workmen's service in 1922. (See Chapter 9).
- Additional private sidings for Shell (Curry Marsh) in 1949 and Fisons in 1959, on the up-to-then undeveloped western half of the branch, plus the enlargement of 'Thames Haven Yard' in the 1950s.

This was all largely 'accretion', and the branch in the 1960s & 1970s still bore its infrastructural history behind the veneer of the new 'oil railway'. More recently, however, change and decline have been more destructive of the past.

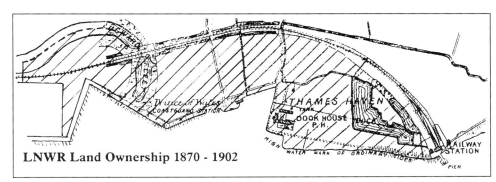

LNWR Land Ownership 1870 - 1902

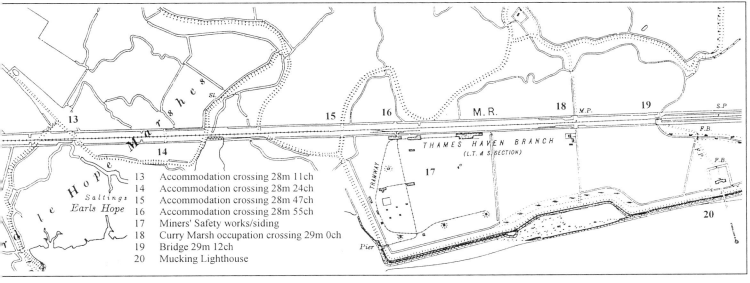

13 Accommodation crossing 28m 11ch
14 Accommodation crossing 28m 24ch
15 Accommodation crossing 28m 47ch
16 Accommodation crossing 28m 55ch
17 Miners' Safety works/siding
18 Curry Marsh occupation crossing 29m 0ch
19 Bridge 29m 12ch
20 Mucking Lighthouse

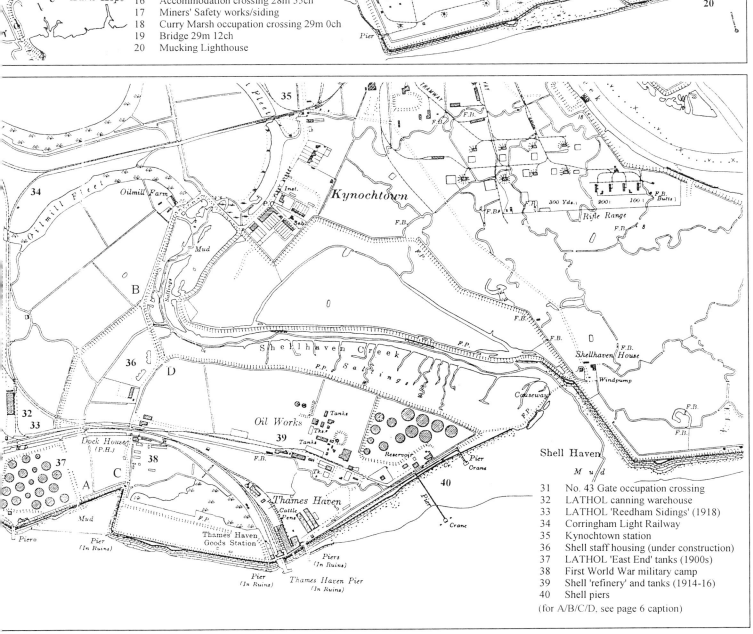

31 No. 43 Gate occupation crossing
32 LATHOL canning warehouse
33 LATHOL 'Reedham Sidings' (1918)
34 Corringham Light Railway
35 Kynochtown station
36 Shell staff housing (under construction)
37 LATHOL 'East End' tanks (1900s)
38 First World War military camp
39 Shell 'refinery' and tanks (1914-16)
40 Shell piers
(for A/B/C/D, see page 6 caption)

left The abandoned terminus building was fully derelict by 3rd April 1954 (when it was descended upon by an SLS Railtour). The stops put in on the westernmost siding when the wharves were demolished are seen at left, and behind the building's roof are the gun emplacements from which the photograph below was taken. (Edwin Course)

middle Another April 1954 view, showing the appalling state of the timber passenger platform in later years. (Edwin Course)

below The track layout at the terminus itself did not change (apart from the removal of the sidings on the wharves when the latter were demolished) after 1890 until the big changes of the mid-1950s. This view was taken on 19th July 1952 from the 1939-45 war gun emplacement towers on the river wall and shows all five sidings at the terminus well-filled with Shell-BP, BP, 'National', and 'Regent' tank wagons, plus a few other wagons. A late piece of Saturday shunting is in progress before the week comes to an end. The 1855 cattle pen bank is seen again at bottom. The passenger platform is largely hidden by the tankers but can be glimpsed at left. At left upper is part of the remaining portion of the 1838/47 excavations which had been filled in to some extent in the interwar years and was shortly to be filled in altogether to extend the LATHOL tank site. Beyond the water tank at right upper many more tank wagons can be seen in the Shell private sidings. (Frank Church)

CHAPTER SEVEN

PETROLEUM AND EXPLOSIVES: THE PRIVATE SIDINGS, 1878-1939

The branch's 'third life', as the home to new industrial activity producing private siding traffic, was something that had never been anticipated at all by the THD&R Co - indeed it could not have been, for the oil industry had not then existed. The 'Prize Fight Special' in 1862 had already seen the line gaining traffic in one very minor way because of its remoteness from civilisation, but from the 1870s on this factor became the key to the growth of traffic which in due course made it a very successful railway, as both the oil industry and the explosives companies were looking for out-of-the-way sites with cheap, flat, land and good transport links. Thames Haven was 'right' on all fronts.

UK oil importing began in the 1860s and the industry came to Thames Haven in 1876. But in the earlier decades the only major market for oil was as paraffin for domestic lighting, and the industry remained relatively small until the growth of road transport brought much increased petroleum demand from the 1900s on.

The explosives industry came to Thames Haven in 1890 but was to prove shortlived here, as both the works involved closed in the post-1918 slump, leaving the vicinity to the oilmen alone, as has remained the case still up to the present day.

These traffics therefore 'overlapped' with the cattle traffic in the years from 1876 up to 1895.

THE PETROLEUM STORAGE CO AND LONDON AND THAMES HAVEN OIL WHARVES

Up to the 1940s the dominant influence in the oil industry at Thames Haven was the London & Thames Haven Oil Wharves Ltd. This company was established in 1898, but the activity at this site derived from two separate predecessor companies.

The most important of these was The Petroleum Storage Co Thames Haven Ltd set up in 1876. Petroleum in these first years was being imported in barrels from Russia and the USA, in sailing ships, and was a dangerous cargo. The Petroleum Act 1871 was passed to tackle the dangers, and under this Act the Thames Conservancy made byelaws prohibiting ships carrying petroleum from proceeding upriver beyond Mucking Lighthouse. This meant that Thames Haven was effectively the only place on the north bank where the ships could call. Initially they moored at special buoys in the river and offloaded into lighters, but inevitably somebody was going to have the bright idea of establishing a pier and storage site at Thames Haven instead. (No attempt seems to have been made to use the existing Thames Haven station pier for petroleum ships). The man in question was the sober and respectable Edward Hunter of Blackheath who nevertheless claimed that he had a 'heavenly

vision' telling him to go down the Thames in a boat and look out for a certain group of trees, and buy the land in question. This purchase was done in March 1876, nine acres at Rugward Marshes, between the railway and the river wall, half a mile west of Thames Haven station (see 1895 OS map below). His co-promoter Timothy Gittins, a Liverpool businessman, was already having talks with Arthur Stride, the newly appointed LT&SR General Manager, in June 1875. The agreement of the Thames Conservators was gained for a pier, and in June 1876 the company was registered, with a nominal capital of £100,000, and took over the land. In August an agreement was made with the well-known contractor William Eckersley to build a 300ft pier, workmen's and custom officers' dwellings (not built), and warehouses. As the company had not yet raised enough money for the whole, Eckersley was to do only £12,000 of work initially and take ⅓ of his payment in shares. In April 1877 a further £10,500 was authorised. A private siding connection with the LT&SR was seen as essential for transporting the petroleum to London; this was arranged for quickly enough, but when the company asked Stride in May 1877 to have the junction put in, the LT&SR started worrying that the company had ideas of 'carrying on a cattle and general goods trade' also, in competition with the Thames Haven Co. They were told that the siding must be for petroleum traffic only, which was accepted. Eckersley completed his work early in 1878 and the private siding was brought into use in April (1).

This was the first private siding on the branch. It was also the first place in the UK where ships could discharge petroleum without the use of lighters. Initially all the storage was underground, for oil in barrels, but the first storage tanks (of the modern type) were built in the 1880s, when the first bulk shipping in tankers began. The first rail tank wagons also appeared at this time.

The company also took a lease in 1877 of some LT&SR - owned land at Abbey Mills, where they had a private siding from 1880 (see photograph Vol. 1 p.28) for direct rail transport from their Thames Haven siding. This depot functioned until 1937, having been largely devoted to 'motor spirit' from the 1900s on.

The company attracted trade at Thames Haven successfully and the mooring buoys in the river had gone out of use by 1880 as ships were using the pier in lieu. Nevertheless there were 'problems' and in 1881 the company went into liquidation at Hunter's petitioning. The LT&SR was told that a replacement company was to be set up, and talks were held with those involved. In May 1882 another company, the London & Thames Haven Wharfage Co Ltd, was indeed registered. However this company was never 'activated',

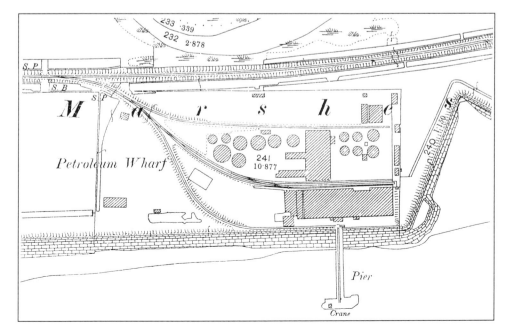

1895 25in plan (reproduced at 100 yards to the inch - 69% of original scale) showing the London & Thames Haven site, still confined at this time to land bought in 1876. The pier was built 260ft long; the contract had been let for a 300ft pier but there were last minute economies. The railway siding on the pier is accessed via a wagon turntable. The pier crane was primarily for lifting barrels. There are 14 oil storage tanks here which tallies well with the recorded 1898 figure of 15. Note the 1878 LT&SR signal box at top left, and signals. The land to the east (upper right) was still LNWR-owned at this date.

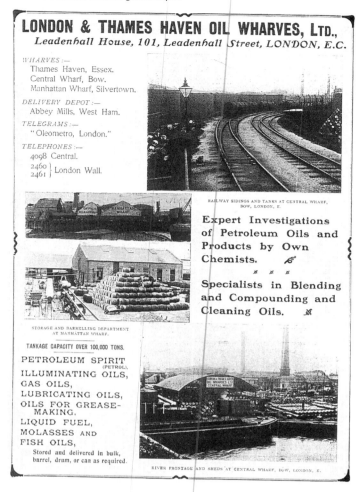

and it seems that Hunter actually carried on the business himself in 1881-94.

A further new company, The London & Thames Haven Petroleum Wharf Ltd, was formed in 1894 and took over the site, the Abbey Mills lease, and the business, from Hunter. Hunter and other members of his family remained principal shareholders. Finally in 1898 this company was wound up and **The London & Thames Haven Oil Wharves Ltd** formed to take over (2). Edward Hunter himself had died shortly before this and there were now new men in charge. Alfred C. Adams was Managing Director until the 1920s when the Russian-born Nicholas Anfilogoff, who became a well known public figure in South Essex, succeeded him.

In 1902 the site was enlarged by purchasing from the LNWR all the land south of the railway between the original site and Thames Haven station. This enabled more tanks to be built and the storage capacity was increased dramatically:-

8,000 Tons	1898	(15 tanks)
13,000 Tons	1899	
100,000 Tons	1907	
800,000 Tons	1926	(190 large tanks, plus small tanks)

There was no significant further increase after this until postwar.

Further London depots were established at Central Wharf, Bow, and Manhattan Wharf, Silvertown. These were served primarily by barge.

In 1907 plans were drawn up for extensive 'deepwater wharves' on the ex-LNWR land just west of the station, and LT&SR support was sought for this. In 1910 work started but was abandoned after a few weeks, owing to a general lack of enthusiasm amongst other parties. However additional small piers for oil tankers were built here.

In 1911 the European Petroleum Co's Thames Haven site was taken over (see below), as a result of which LATHOL now had a river frontage one mile long, and a second private siding connection.

LATHOL were essentially Wharfingers providing storage for oil companies and distributors - they did not engage in the oil trade themselves. However they did build a small refinery for their customers' use around 1914, the first refinery functional at Thames

Haven. It should perhaps be explained at this point that all primary refining of crude oil up to the 1920s, and most up to the 1950s, was done in the countries of origin; only in the postwar period has it become the normal practice to bring oil to the UK as crude oil for refining here. The refineries existing at Thames Haven pre-1950, and most of those elsewhere in the UK at this period (3), were generally for the purpose of producing specific products from 'topped' oil (oil which had already undergone primary refining in the producing area).

'Motor spirit' (petrol) became the most important aspect of importing at Thames Haven; almost all of the petrol sold in the London area was coming through here. It was imported as a finished product. The rail traffic at the LATHOL sidings amounted to £21,820 in 1913/14 (increasing to £36,208 in 1914/15 as the demands of war took hold). There were by then twelve oil companies using the LATHOL facilities, of which the British Petroleum Co, and the Anglo-American Oil Co (a subsidiary of the Standard Oil Co of New Jersey, the biggest US company; later renamed ESSO), were much the most important. LATHOL's 'own' rail traffic was a minor thing by comparison; only coal, ships' stores, and ironwork for new tanks (all inwards). This was not for the most part handled in the private sidings, but at unloading 'platforms' which had been erected on the branch running line itself (see Chapter 8).

LATHOL also brought up much land north of the railway, for future expansion. Most remained unused until sold to Shell in 1947 for the 'West Site', but part was used for a new tank farm site (the Reedham Site) in 1915. An additional private siding connection (LATHOL's third) was put in for this in 1914 (4), at a cost to the Midland of £2,400, LATHOL paying 8% interest on half this sum. This became known as 'Reedham Sidings'.

A fourth LATHOL siding connection followed in 1920 (5), at Dock House level crossing. This was originally meant to be a temporary facility whilst six storage tanks were built nearby, but it was in the event retained for permanent use and later extended westwards to join up with the original 1870s sidings. It was no doubt found useful because it enabled transfer movements between the LATHOL sidings and the sidings at the terminus without occupying the 'branch' line.

After 1920 there were no major changes to the LATHOL site, or its rail sidings, for many years. However the number of tanks continued to increase in the 1920s, and the refinery capacity was enhanced. The use of barrels (or cans, latterly) gradually declined, but much oil was still going out in cans, in open wagons, in the interwar years. From the 1920s road tankers were much used for deliveries to London and East Anglia, but rail traffic still increased, because of the ever-increasing total demand for fuel. Nevertheless the general picture of the oil trade at Thames Haven in the interwar years was one of steady, rather than spectacular, growth, followed indeed by some decline in the 1930s when LATHOL lost some of its best customers.

The sidings appear to have been horse-shunted initially but soon after 1918 three fireless locos were acquired by LATHOL ex-Gretna and Morecambe munitions factories. The full locomotive stock will be found listed in an Appendix at the end of this book.

THE EUROPEAN PETROLEUM CO

The second company to be established at Thames Haven, originally as a rival to LATHOL but then taken over by them, was the European Petroleum Co Ltd. This was an offshoot of the Western Trading Co, which in 1896 sold to the new company (for £895,000) its oil wells in Baku, Russia, Rumania, and Galicia; fourteen steamships; fifty rail tank wagons (acquired in 1896 under hire purchase agreements with the Bristol Wagon Co, and the North Central Wagon Co); the goodwill of the business; and land at Thames Haven on which a refinery of 52,000 tons p.a. capacity was under erection. The land in question was immediately west of the LATHOL site, and it had been acquired in 1895/6 (6). The new company took over the site in June 1897 at which time £14,000 had been spent there, but the refinery was not complete, and it appears that it never was completed. A pier was however built.

It is not clear that any active trading was done at the Thames Haven site prior to 1901. In 1900 the 1896 company was wound up and a new company with the same name registered, controlled by quite different interests; Herbert Pease of the famous Darlington iron and railway family was Chairman. Agreement was now quickly made with the LT&SR for a private siding and this was put in in the winter of 1901/2 (7).

After a few years the company decided to pull out of Thames

THE JETTY, SHELL HAVEN, ESSEX. 691.

Haven. The 1900 company was dissolved in 1911 and the assets elsewhere transferred to a new company, The European Oilfields Corporation Ltd. LATHOL bought the company's Thames Haven site in 1911, and it quickly became just another part of the LATHOL site, primarily just a tank farm area. The 1902 siding became known as the 'LATHOL Western Connection' and the 1878 siding as the 'LATHOL Eastern Connection'.

SHELL

The Shell conglomerate was founded in the 1890s by Marcus Samuel, who got into oil via a general import/export business but found it starting to overwhelm his other activities, so that a separate company, The Shell Transport and Trading Co Ltd, had to be set up in 1897. (The 'Shell' name derived from the fact that Samuel's father had run a curio shop in London specialising in oriental sea shells which were then in vogue; there was no connection with the name 'Shellhaven'). In 1903 a working agreement was come to with the rival Dutch company, The Royal Dutch Petroleum Co, and all the Shell companies have been jointly UK/Dutch owned since that time. A joint marketing company, The Asiatic Petroleum Co was formed in 1903, and in 1907 two new 'operating companies' were set up (one in each country, but both jointly owned). The UK operating company was The Anglo-Saxon Petroleum Co Ltd and this took over all the UK storage and transport facilities. It was, therefore, Asiatic and Anglo-Saxon who became involved at Thames Haven, the latter owning the site but the former dealing with the railway as the sales arm.

In 1911 Anglo-Saxon bought the portion of Oil Mill Farm between Thames Haven station and Shellhaven creek. A pier was built, and in 1914-16 a refinery and tank farm, although Shell also made use of the LATHOL facilities. When commissioned in 1916 the refinery produced fuel oil for the Admiralty, but with demand

SHELL HAVEN, ESSEX. 692.

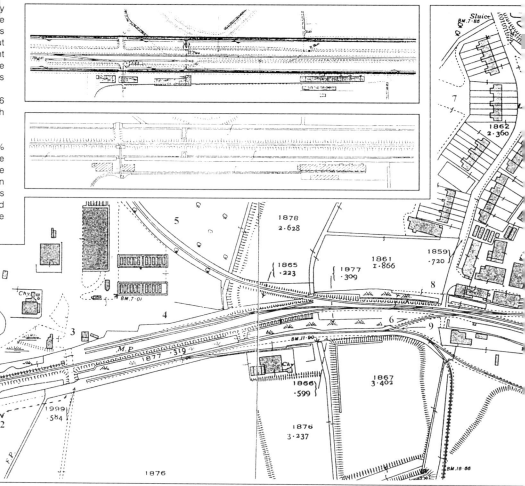

right upper 1917 Midland Railway 2chain survey (reduced to 100 yards to the inch) showing the railway arrangements at the Miners Safety Works after the installing of the private siding in 1916 (but before the 'Halt' was provided). For the arrangement of the works generally see the 1919 OS map. The narrow gauge tramways served the various 'Magazines' scattered around the site, and pier.

right lower The 1895 OS showing the pre-1916 arrangement with loading platform on the branch running line itself.

below OS 25in map, 1939 revision, reduced to 69% original scale (100 yards to the inch). Changes since the 1895 and 1919 maps are annotated, but the growth of the 'Shell' site is particularly to be noted. In common with a number of printings of maps of this area in the 1930s-50s period, all oil tanks are omitted for 'security' reasons. The internal rail sidings in the LATHOL 'Reedham' site are also omitted.

for this dropping after the war, it was modified in 1919 to produce bitumen which was the main product here in the '20s. Further improvements in the interwar years enabled the production of printing ink for newsprint, luboils, asphalts, 'Mexphalte', and other products.

Initially rail transport was facilitated by a 'tramway' laid up to a loading place on the LT&SR station sidings, but in 1916 a private siding connection was put in, joining the branch at the Dock House level crossing. This was known variously as the 'Asiatic Petroleum' or 'Shell Mex' private siding (8). Initially there were only two sidings, holding 20 and 23 wagons, within the Shell gates, but a substantial internal system built up in due course (see 1939 OS map).

The operations were successful but it was really only after 1950 that they became a very big business.

Owing to the frequent reorganisations and renamings of the many companies within the Shell group, the responsibility for the Shell Haven site and the transport arrangements here passed between several different 'companies' over the decades; this however was of legal rather than practical significance, and it will suffice to refer simply to 'Shell' henceforth in this account.

THE MINERS' SAFETY EXPLOSIVES WORKS

The Explosives Act 1875 had made it obligatory to build new explosives works on remote sites. The Miners' Safety Explosive Co Ltd was formed in 1888 (9) by Sir George Eliot MP, who had started as a pit boy at North Biddick Colliery (which he now owned) and had a great interest in the development of safer explosives. He had made an agreement with the Belgian company Les Explosifs Favier for the right to market their improved types of explosives in the UK and the British Empire. Sir George and Les Explosifs Favier owned between them the vast majority of the new company's capital. The factory was built in 1890 (in fact it comprised only a few small detached blocks) on the Stanford-le-Hope marshes, between the branch line and the river. It was a small works for specialist products and only 20 - 30 people were employed. A loading platform was provided on the branch (10) where the rail traffic, coal inwards and explosives (ammonite) outwards, had to be unloaded/loaded from trains en route. A narrow gauge tram system conveyed materials from the 'platform' around the site. The traffic was never great - 200

tons of ammonite out per month in 1915 - but the use of the 'platform' was no doubt less than ideal and a private siding agreement was sought. The siding was installed in 1916 (11) and a replacement 'platform' erected alongside the siding.

However the factory was closed in 1927 (12). The company was taken over by I.C.I. and the work transferred to the Cooke's Explosives Ltd factory in Penrhyndeudraeth. The private siding was left in situ until taken out of use on 14th June 1939. The site remained vacant for many years until incorporated into the Shell complex in the 1960s.

KYNOCH'S EXPLOSIVES WORKS AND THE CORRINGHAM LIGHT RAILWAY

It is intended to give a full account of the Corringham Light Railway in a future work; what follows here is, therefore, only a brief outline.

G. Kynoch & Co Ltd were major ammunitions manufacturers with their main works at Witton, Birmingham. Seeing a need for a new plant in the south east, they purchased Borley Farm, by Shellhaven Creek, in 1895, and built a factory complex there in 1897. The LT&SR was hostile initially, for reasons unknown, but in February 1897 Arthur Stride the LT&SR Managing Director met A. T. Cocking, the Managing Director of the new works, and was

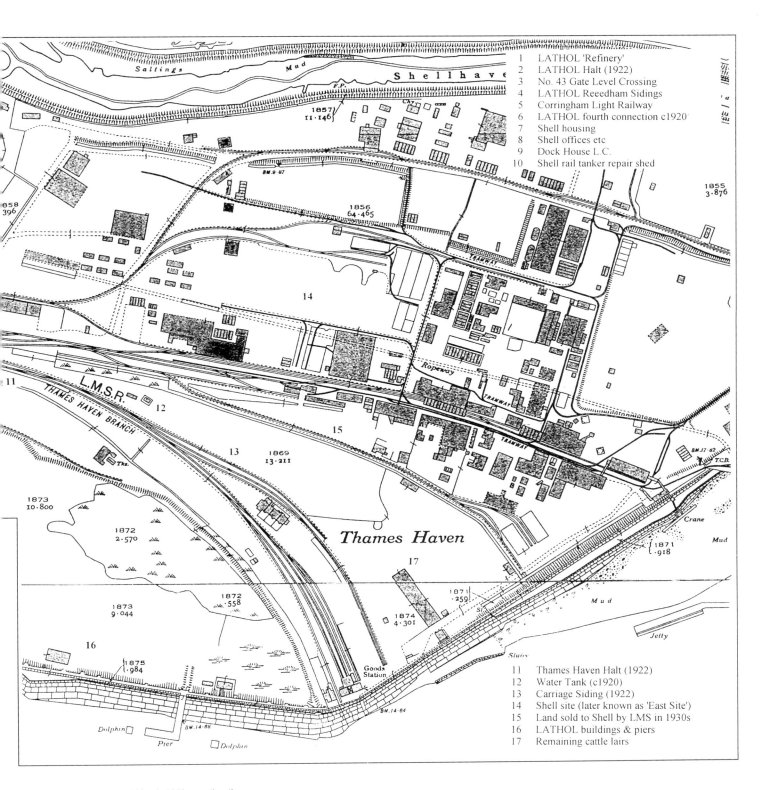

1 LATHOL 'Refinery'
2 LATHOL Halt (1922)
3 No. 43 Gate Level Crossing
4 LATHOL Reeedham Sidings
5 Corringham Light Railway
6 LATHOL fourth connection c1920
7 Shell housing
8 Shell offices etc
9 Dock House L.C.
10 Shell rail tanker repair shed

11 Thames Haven Halt (1922)
12 Water Tank (c1920)
13 Carriage Siding (1922)
14 Shell site (later known as 'East Site')
15 Land sold to Shell by LMS in 1930s
16 LATHOL buildings & piers
17 Remaining cattle lairs

Shell No. 19 again, on 2nd March 1959, sporting the new 'Shell Refinery Company' name and a replacement exhaust since the 1952 photograph at page 3. The loco is shunting the internal sidings with the points set for the short headshunt road, which enabled such shunting to be done without affecting the 'BR' operations. For a full listing of the Shell locomotive fleet see Appendix. (Frank Church)

left An early wooden-framed Shell/BP tank wagon, No. 19, at Thames Haven in July 1952. No. 3781 at left exemplifies the later steel-framed design. Shell and British Petroleum entered into a joint marketing arrangement in the UK in 1931 (lasting until 1976), hence the joint wagon fleet. In the 1930s they had 55% of the total UK market between them. This wagon is probably at the head of a just-arrived train, with the shunter uncoupling the 'barrier wagon'. (Frank Church)

43

persuaded that the traffic would be beneficial. The 600 employees settled mostly in new housing in Corringham and in the company village 'Kynochtown' built by the works gates in 1897-9.

Kynochs decided in 1898 that a rail link with the Thames Haven branch was necessary, and also wanted a line from Corringham to the works to run workers' passenger trains. A Light Railway Order application was made in November 1898, under the name of the 'Corringham Light Railway', and the order was made in July 1899. The CLR was a separate entity from Kynochs in law but in reality it was promoted by and wholly owned by Kynochs.

With no significant engineering works involved, the line was quickly and cheaply built during 1900. The section between the works and the LT&SR at Thames Haven station was opened for goods traffic in January 1901 (it never had a passenger service, although proposals were to be made, as described in Chapter 9). The passenger service between Corringham and Kynochtown was formally inaugurated in June 1901 and operated as an isolated service, not impacting on the LT&SR at all. Legally it was a public service and some LATHOL and Shell men did use it as well as the Kynochs workers. A small amount of public coal and other goods traffic was also dealt with, via Thames Haven and the LT&SR.

Now that the Thames Haven branch was a goods-only line, there was no problem at all with the 'junction' at Thames Haven station, which was effected with simple hand points and no signalling. Because the CLR was a statutory railway company there was no 'Private Siding Agreement', but in operational reality the CLR was only a glorified private siding, from the LT&SR's viewpoint.

A vague impression had been given in 1899 that the CLR would be worked by the LT&SR, and provision had been made in the Order for this. It was then revealed in the local papers in January 1901 that the LT&SR might be taking over the CLR altogether, and indeed the LT&SR's 1901 Act provided for this. However it seems there was no intention of any immediate takeover. In May 1902 Stride gave a report to the LT&SR Board on the subject; the Directors resolved that they wished to inspect the CLR before deciding, but afterwards the matter was never heard of again. It is really quite surprising that the idea of the LT&SR working the line had been floated at all; the lightly-laid track was unsuitable for LT&SR locos, and Kynochs would have had to acquire a locomotive anyway to shunt the internal works sidings (laid in, at the same time, in 1900/1). In the event the CLR bought two locos in 1901 and these were used for both the CLR and the Kynoch's works shunting.

The CLR did not actually bring the LT&SR much traffic in the first years. The coal for Kynoch's works was all brought in by

sea, and the majority of the manufactured ammunition went up river by barge to Woolwich Arsenal (13). In 1913/14 the year's rail traffic was only £95 inwards (cordite paste) and £648 outwards (cordite and gunpowder). The war changed this, partly because coal had to be brought in by rail and partly because of the vastly increased ammunition production. The 1914/15 figures were £1,487 inwards and £4,445 outwards. Even so this was only one twentieth of the total Thames Haven branch goods traffic.

At the end of the war there was a huge slump in the demand for ammunition, and the industry had to undergo rapid rationalisation. Kynoch's merged with Eley, Noble, and the works were closed completely in 1919. The CLR remained in existence as a separate company in law.

CORY BROTHERS

In 1921 the Kynochtown works site (including Kynochtown village) was sold to Cory Brothers Ltd, hitherto coal shippers and merchants but now branching out into the oil fuel trade. The CLR remained a separate entity legally, but the whole shareholding was taken over by Cory representatives. Kynochtown was renamed 'Coryton'.

In 1923 Cory's built oil storage tanks and a small refinery on part of the site (south of the explosives works site). As a result oil tankers became the main CLR goods traffic exchanged with the LMS at Thames Haven. Cory's trade remained relatively small-scale and it was only after the Mobil takeover in 1950 (Chapter 10) that traffic grew.

The CLR Corringham - Coryton passenger service continued until 1952, although little-used after bus services began. The Corringham line was lifted in 1952 and the CLR reduced to the Coryton - Thames Haven section.

THAMES HAVEN JUNCTION BALLAST SIDING

The last private siding for consideration in this chapter was somewhat different in origin, insofar as when first opened in 1885 it had been an LT&SR ballast siding. Like many such sidings it was closed after a few years (14).

In the years after this, commercial sand and gravel pits were opened in the Mucking area (as in many places near the river), and in 1931 the siding was restored, now as a private siding for the Stuart Sand & Shingle Co. From the end of the siding a narrow-gauge tramway ran to the pits and on to Stanford Wharf.

The siding closed around 1956 (15).

(1) According to an interview with W. Levett, the former Miners' Safety Works Manager (who knew Hunter), in the *Grays & Tilbury Gazette* 17.6.1933, the first ship to land oil at Thames Haven was the sailing vessel *Chegnito* in September 1876. If this is correct it is not clear which pier the ship used or how the oil was transported away. The private siding connection seems to have been put in in autumn 1877, as Easterbrook Hannaford & Co. were paid £300 for the signalling in November (they would not have been paid prior to completion), but it was only on 10th April 1878 that Stride informed the Board of Trade that the siding was 'complete and fit for use'. Hutchinson inspected the week after (PRO MT6 205/12). The PSA is dated 26.2.1878. For more information on the company see PRO BT31/2242/10665.
(2) For the 1894 company see PRO BT31/5768/40416. The files of the 1898 company cannot be traced at the PRO or at Companies' House.
(3) Crude oil refineries were commissioned at Grangemouth, Llandarcy, Fawley, and Ellesmere Port in the 1920s/30s, but as at 1938 four-fifths of UK oil was still refined, before shipping, in the producing areas. Shell had no UK crude oil refinery prewar.
(4) Exact date not known. Approved by MR Traffic Committee 18.5.1916 and Way & Works Committee 22.6.1916. An MR plan for the 'proposed sidings' is dated 12.1.1918, and the Private Siding Agreement is dated 23.4.1918, both of which point to a 1918 installation date. The sidings appear on the 1919 OS and the 1920 MR 2 chain survey. They were overlooked by the compilers of the MR Distance Diagrams until the 1922/3 amendments.
(5) Exact date not known. Approved by MR Traffic Committee 14.10.1920 and Way & Works Committee 18.11.1920 (as a temporary siding). Not shown in 1919 OS or the April 1920 MR 2 chain survey. Private Siding Agreement dated 26.11.1920.
(6) Cf the fact that this site is still empty marsh on the 1895 OS map. For the companies see PRO BT31/6813/47927 (1896) and BT31/16400/65935 (1900).
(7) Private Siding Agreement dated 16.12.1901. The Engineer's records give expenditure on this siding beginning January 1902. It was not put up for BOT inspection as the branch was no longer a passenger line. On 12.6.1923 a new PSA was made between the LMS and LATHOL for both this connection and the 1878 connection (the original 1878 agreement for the latter having become lost by both parties in Midland days).
(8) Exact date not known. Approved by MR Traffic Committee 24.6.1915 and Way & Works Committee 22.7.1915 (both refer to 'Anglo-Saxon Petroleum Co'). The siding appears as an existing feature on a January 1918 MR plan, the 1919 OS and the 1920 MR 2 chain survey. It was overlooked by the compilers of the MR Distance Diagrams

annual amendments until the 1922/3 edition. The Private Siding Agreement is dated 29.11.1915.
(9) For the 1888 company see PRO BT31/4128/26594. After the death of Sir George Eliot the original company was wound up and a new company of the same name registered in 1898; see BT31/ 31618/57426.
(10) Date of platform not known; there is no reference as such to its provision, but as the works' location would have been pointless without rail facilities, it is to be imagined that the platform was an original 1890 facility. It is shown on the 1895 OS. According to the recollections of W. G. Styles in *Panorama* No. 29, the LT&SR initially refused to carry ammonite.
(11) Exact date not known. Approved by MR Traffic Committee 18.5.1916 and Way & Works Committee 22.6.1916. The siding is included in the 1916 amendments to the MR Distance Diagrams, and shown on the 1917 MR 2 chain survey. The Private Siding Agreement is dated 15.6.1916.
(12) Exact date not known. The LMS Traffic Committee noted in July 1927 that the works had closed.
(13) The LT&SR had built 25 gunpowder vans in 1904. They were marked 'When Empty Return to Thames Haven', so they must have been intended for Kynoch's and the Miners' Safety Traffic.
(14) Opened around January 1885 (the LT&SR asked for 'provisional sanction' on 17.1.1885 but the work was already completed and inspected by February, Hutchinson's report being dated 9.2.1885). No information on date of closure but the siding had gone by the 1895 OS.
(15) Opened around May 1931 (MoT minute to inspect is dated 14.5.1931). The application had come from W. Cory & Son in 1930 (LMS plans date stamped 18.7.1930, Railtrack Waterloo) but the Private Siding Agreement of 6.6.1931 was with the Stuart Sand & Shingle Co. Inspected (after the usual delay for the period) on 31.3.1934. The siding and the narrow gauge system are shown on the 1939 OS (not reproduced here). In the 1956 RCH Handbook the siding is listed as Stuart (Thames Mouth) Sand and Shingle Co. Ltd; with W. Cory & Son, the East Sussex Reclamation Co, the Lower Hope Development Co, Mucking Hall Dairy, Mucking Hall Farm, and F.W. Surridge as additional users. By the 1957 OS the siding is shown as 'Disused' and the narrow gauge system has gone.

CHAPTER EIGHT

GOODS TRAIN WORKING 1855-1947

LT&SR DAYS

Information on the LT&S goods services generally (for which see Volume 2, Appendix B) is scanty owing to the small number of surviving WTTs, but the picture so far as the Thames Haven branch is concerned is reasonably clear.

In the first years of the LT&S the whole goods traffic was very poor and could be accommodated in only one, or two, trip workings from London to Southend and back. These ran initially from Brick Lane (1854-8), then from Mint Street (1858-61), then from Goodman's Yard (1861-86). It has to be assumed that these trains diverted via Thames Haven when necessary, but (as noted earlier) there was precious little goods traffic at Thames Haven in the first years, if any. When the large scale cattle business began in 1864/5 it was (as noted in Chapter 5) handled in special trains to Maiden Lane, run at short notice depending on shipping arrivals, so although the branch now had a worthwhile goods traffic (until cattle importing ended in 1895), it was not something that impacted on the regular goods trains. Probably it was only with the opening of the Petroleum Storage Co's Siding in 1878 that any other goods traffic of substance materialised.

By 1884 (the first surviving WTT) there were four daily (Mon-Sat) goods trips on the LT&S system, one of which ran from Plaistow (now becoming the centre of goods operations) to Thames Haven :-

Plaistow	6.30am		2.0pm
Abbey Mills Jn	6.33/6.45		-
Bromley	6.48/7.0		1.50/1.55 (E&B)
Abbey Mills Jn	7.3/7.15		1.23/1.48
Plaistow	7.18/7.20		1.15/1.20
Barking	7.30/7.40		12.37/1.7pm
Rainham	7.55/8.15		12.2/12.22
Purfleet	8.25/8.35		11.28/11.50
Grays	8.50/9.20		11.9/11.15
Low Street	9.35/9.45		10.50/10.55
Thames Haven Jn	(9.52)		(10.43)
Thames Haven	10.5am		10.30am

The Abbey Mills call would have been for the petroleum depot opened there c1880 for traffic from the Petroleum Storage Co's siding at Thames Haven (no other goods train is shown as calling at Abbey Mills). The siding at Thames Haven was presumably shunted by the train on its up working. Of course the Thames Haven branch traffic was only a minor portion of this trip's total purpose.

By 1890 there were significant quantities of cheese, other dairy products, and dead meat being carried from Thames Haven to Commercial Road, much of which must be assumed to have been conveyed on the ordinary goods trip. This quickly died off after 1895 but the goods trip now gained additional traffic from the Miners' Safety works (opened 1890, and served by a 'loading platform' - see Chapter 7 and below), Kynoch's (brought to Thames Haven station by Corringham Light Railway locos from 1901), and the European Petroleum Co's Siding (1902) which must (like the Petroleum Storage Co's Siding) have been shunted by up trains.

None of this was big business at first, though, and with the end of all specials the branch was very quiet in the early 1900s with only the one daily train seen. The 1908 WTT still shows only one train on the branch (although the LT&SR goods workings at large were much expanded by this date). This now ran from Plaistow at 4.41am, reaching Thames Haven at 12.35pm and leaving at 1.15pm (corresponding to the 1914 6.56am infra).

As well as calling at the two oil sidings, the 1.15pm up working also 'called' at the Miners' Safety (this is specifically stated in the 1908 and 1913 WTTs). One is forced to assume that goods were loaded/offloaded at the 'platform' by the Miners' Safety employees, whilst the train waited for them, as with a 'station truck' in a normal goods train.

Trains were worked by GER locos up to 1880, then by LT&SR 4-4-2Ts in the 1880s and 1890s, then more often by LT&SR 0-6-2Ts from the 1900s. Plaistow shed took the leading role from the 1880s in branch goods operations.

WARTIME EXPEDIENTS (1914-16)

With oil importing growing the private siding traffic soon started to grow faster and the branch began to take on fully its 20th-century role as an oil line, the 'old' being cast off finally at the same time with the dismantling of the pier. In June 1914 a second daily train was added by diverting to Thames Haven the 1.52pm from Plaistow which had previously terminated at Stanford-le-Hope.

The full timings of the two trains, as given in the June 1914 WTT, were (Sunday excepted) :-

Plaistow	6.56am	1.52pm
Little Ilford	7.4/9.4	2.1/2.45
Tilbury Docks N Jn	9.38/10.15	3.30/4.25
Tilbury Docks	10.18/10.35	4.29/4.40
Low Street	10.48/11.3	4.52/5.10
Thames Haven Jn	(11.9)	(5.17)
Thames Haven	11.20am/1.0pm	5.30/6.0pm
Thames Haven Jn	(2.25)	(6.38)
Low Street	2.31/2.41	6.47/6.52
Tilbury Docks	2.50/3.0	-
Grays	-	7.9/9.5
Little Ilford	3.45/4.42	9.44/10.18
Plaistow	4.49pm	10.27pm

Taking advantage of the existence of two trains per day, the Midland decided to adopt a new method of working for the works traffic on the branch from 2nd June 1914, owing to the growing traffic. The main problem arose not from the two private sidings en route (ex Petroleum Storage Co and European Petroleum Co, both now belonging to LATHOL) but from three 'loading platforms' which LATHOL had been allowed, not long before this, to erect on the branch itself (following the precedent of the similar Miners' Safety Works' 'platform') (1). Quite how these were served originally is not clear; with the branch being quiet in the 1900s, ad hoc arrangements were no doubt made which it was not deemed necessary to commit to print.

From June 1914 the method was for the 1.0pm up to drop off en route, at the three LATHOL 'platforms' and the Miners' Safety 'platform', any wagons or empties for them. The companies' men then had about 4 hours to load or unload them, after which they were 'collected' by the afternoon down train which of course had to push them in front of the loco back to Thames Haven. This involved the line being obstructed for the four hours, which did not matter in terms of the train service, but had to be provided for from a 'signalling' viewpoint, otherwise the signalman at Thames Haven Junction might absent-mindedly give the staff to another (unexpected) train or engine, which could set off down the branch in full confidence and collide with the standing wagons. Therefore, a 'Branch Pilotman' was appointed who travelled on all trains and held the Staff in his possession. The Pilotman was required to 'make himself thoroughly acquainted with the position of the trucks left on the line by the 1.0pm goods train and arrange to protect each lot with detonators' (in case he forgot them after all!). The proceedings were not to be allowed in fog or snow, and 'the line must be cleared before dark' (which was quite impossible in the winter months, given the timings of the afternoon train). If anything went wrong the first wagon that the 1.52pm down collided with would be one full of loaded explosives at the Miners' Safety platform!

This decidedly non-standard way of running a railway was replaced, by late 1915, by another just as non-standard. In the '1915' working arrangements the train on arrival at Thames Haven immediately shunted any wagons for the 'platforms' and pushed them back to the furthest point, the Miners' Safety platform, dropping off the front wagons there and then proceeding back to Thames Haven again dropping off the rest at the LATHOL platforms in batches. (Although not specified, this must surely have been done by the morning train, which had 1hr 40mins at Thames Haven, and the benefit of daylight). The companies' men had only an hour or so to load/unload, yet we are told that there were now 2-4 wagons per day at the Miners' Safety, and 11-23 at the LATHOL platforms. The main traffic was inwards coal, so there must have been some frantic shovelling. It might also be borne in mind that the Miners' Safety men were loading explosives. Then, before its return to Plaistow, 'the engine runs up the branch from Thames Haven, pushing all the wagons it comes across to the furthest point [i.e. Miners' Safety], where they are coupled up and brought [back] to the Thames Haven depot [sic] to be sorted and marshalled for dispatch'. The 'Branch Pilotman' was no longer needed as the staff was in the driver's possession throughout the time the wagons were blocking the line. We are not told specifically how traffic for the two oil sidings was handled in the '1914' and '1915' systems, but it would not have been a problem as any of the up movements could still have shunted these sidings en-route - note that both up trains are allowed considerable excess time between Thames Haven and the junction.

The '1915' system also had obvious defects and in December 1915 the Midland Railway officers carried out a full investigation of the branch (2). Because of the war (which meant more coal coming in by rail rather than by sea, in particular) the branch traffic had grown from 36,835 tons in/42,521 tons out in 1913/14, to 66,363 tons in/65,676 tons out in 1914/15. It was decided that the 'platforms' must be done away with, and this was acted upon. The Miners' Safety had a private siding installed in 1916 and LATHOL were made to take all wagons into their sidings henceforth (it is not really clear why they had preferred to use the 'platforms' anyway). Another change in 1916 was the introduction of 'Pilot Guard' working whereby the eastern end of the line (including the LATHOL private sidings) was now effectively within Thames Haven 'station limits', under the Foreman's control, so that these sidings could now be shunted as convenient. This working is described further in Chapter 11.

The June 1916 WTT still shows only the two booked trains per day, but by January 1917 a third train had been introduced, a through trip from Brent (Midland) at 4.51am returning from Thames Haven at 8.45am. It is also known that much of the oil traffic during the war was sent in additional specials.

By 1914 trains were having to be divided on arrival at Thames Haven for the loco to 'run round', owing to the short distance between the two crossovers then existing. However in 1916 an additional crossover was provided at the Dock House crossing to eliminate this problem.

Some time around 1920 (3) a shunting loco was introduced at Thames Haven for a day shift (1921 timings - Tilbury 8.55am, Thames Haven arrive 9.15am depart 4.35pm, Tilbury 4.55pm). From 1923 this duty was performed by the loco of the branch workmen's service (see Chapter 9).

THE INTERWAR YEARS

The three trains a day continued after the war, although the Brent trip was changed to mid-afternoon. The winter 1925/6 timetable tabulated here will serve as an example.

Brent Loaded Sdgs	-	-	2.55pm
Plaistow	9.18am	3.4pm	-
Barking	-	-	(4.11/4.26)
Low Street	10.27/10.42	-	(5.41/5.46)
Thames Haven Jn	(10.56)	(4.14)	(5.54)
Thames Haven	11.10am/12.0	4.27pm/6.20pm	6.7pm/7.0pm
Miners Safety Sdg	12.7/12.17pm	6.26/6.36	-
Thames Haven Jn	(12.23)	(6.46)	(7.13)
Low Street	-	6.56/7.0	-
Little Ilford North	1.27/1.39	-	8.26/8.45
Plaistow	1.50pm	8.18pm	-
Brent Empty Sdgs	-	-	10.5/10.15
Brent South Sdgs	-	-	10.20pm

NOTES. On Saturdays the first up train leaves Thames Haven at 1.0pm and does not call at Little Ilford. 9.18am down calls Low Street to take up parcels. 3.4pm down on Weds and alternate Thurs calls Low Street to pick up cash box. Light Engine movements omitted (but none of them were related to these three goods train workings).

For several years around 1930 a fourth train was run (11.57am Plaistow, return 2.50pm Thames Haven to Little Ilford), but this did not become a fixture (4). It will be noted that all the trains were now dedicated purely to Thames Haven branch traffic (whereas up to late LT&SR days Thames Haven had merely been one call on an multi-station trip working). This was to remain the case subsequently.

None of the trains were now allowed extra time to shunt the LATHOL sidings on the branch en route (nor is there any mention of these sidings in the WTT) (5). However the shunting loco now present at Thames Haven in the daytime, or the train locos during their time at Thames Haven, were available to deal with traffic to and from the LATHOL sidings as an untimetabled shunt move.

The ballast siding opened on the branch at Thames Haven Junction in 1931 had its own additional service, e.g. in 1934 3.0pm empties Grays to Junction siding arrive 3.31pm, returning 3.58pm loaded to Grays. (After the war, however, it was served by calls on an up working from Thames Haven).

In the days when the western half of the branch still bore a largely agricultural air, ex-LT&SR 0-6-2T 2233 heads west near Curry Marsh with a train of 22 loaded oil tankers and a barrier wagon, c1937.

(Frank Church collection)

LMS tender locos were often used in addition to the LT&SR 0-6-2Ts, and were turned on the Tilbury triangle, as the turntable at Thames Haven was long since removed. The 2.55pm Brent, which was worked by Cricklewood locos and men, was booked to 'turn loco' on its down journey; but the 6.30pm up did so in the up direction instead. Whichever direction was favoured, it meant that the Tilbury - Thames Haven leg had to be tender-first in one direction.

THE 1939-45 WAR: BACKGROUND

The 1914-18 war had brought a big increase of traffic to the branch, but the 1939-45 war was to have more drastic (and variable) effects. These can only be understood by reference to Government oil policy at large in the war years (6).

Prior to the outbreak of war it had been assumed that most shipping, including oil tankers, would be diverted from East Coast to West Coast ports in war conditions. It was also considered that oil storage in the south-east was too vulnerable to air attack. LATHOL (who had excess capacity in the late 1930s owing to loss of customers, and were in a bad way financially as a result) had offered in 1939 to make capacity available for government use at Thames Haven, but this had been rejected. The idea of building new, protected, underground oil storage facilities on a general basis was investigated but found impractical; hence storage also was to be concentrated on the West Coast.

In the event things continued very much on a 'business as normal' basis in the 'phoney war' period. The West Coast oil ports (Avonmouth, Swansea, and Stanlow [Ellesmere Port]) had not been properly equipped to handle extra tonnage, and were also somewhat thrown out by the convoy system which meant that ships arrived together in inconvenient bursts of activity instead of at regular intervals. It was also pointed out that all these three ports were dependant on entry by a single lock gate which could be destroyed by enemy action (to insure against which emergency ocean tanker ports were built at Port Talbot and Bromborough in 1940/1, and jetties outside the docks at Avonmouth).

The dangers of war were brought home in late 1939 when the S.S. *Arinia*, bound for Thames Haven, struck a mine in the Thames and exploded with the loss of all crew. In June 1940 a bomb landed only 20ft from the Thames Haven branch, and whilst it did no significant damage it was put down in the records as the first bomb of the war to affect LMS property. There were four serious raids on Thames Haven in September 1940, the worst on the 5th and 6th when 21 LATHOL tanks were hit. But despite a spectacular blaze which took six days to put out, and smoke columns that could be seen from the French Coast by approaching enemy pilots, the damage done was much less than had been feared. Few HE bombs actually hit tanks - the ancillary pipework between tanks was worse affected - and incendiary bombs mostly failed to ignite the oil even when they hit a tank. In accordance with general policy, many tanks had been 'sterilised' (filled with water instead of oil) both as a means of preventing fires spreading and as a supply of water for firemen.

The normal pumping facilities of the site enabled oil to be transferred quickly from tanks close to the burning areas, and indeed half the oil from tanks which were actually on fire themselves was recovered by pumping. The one thing not done that ought to have been done prior to this was the provision of ARP brick walling around the tanks to prevent penetration of the sides by shrapnel; this ARP walling was now done belatedly in late 1940.

From 7th September the raiders turned their main attentions to Central London (although there were to be two further raids on Thames Haven in April 1941). By the time air raids generally ceased in June 1941 it was calculated that only 3% of the UK's national oil stocks, and 5% of tank capacity (some tanks being destroyed whilst empty), had been lost. LATHOL themselves had lost only 18,000 tons of oil by bombing in six raids (plus some losses at Shell and Cory's). A further 8,000 tons were lost in April 1941 when the S.S. *Lunula* struck a mine when berthing at LATHOL No. 4 jetty, the most tragic incident to occur here, as the whole crew of the *Lunula* and an assisting tug, and the LATHOL Berthing Master Captain Pearson, were killed. No. 4 jetty was destroyed and all the other jetties badly damaged.

From September 1940 there was a big reduction in the amount of oil handled in the Thames estuary. This was primarily for shipping reasons; the theory that the west coast would be safer for oil *storage* had been scuppered by the fall of France which enabled the enemy to bomb western areas with ease, and indeed Llandarcy had been bombed as well in September 1940. At the height of the 'diversion' policy in 1942 and early 1943, 94% of oil was imported via west coast ports. This brought severe problems to the railway system, despite the adoption of large-scale 'block-train' working for oil traffic for the first time and a consequent big increase in the productivity of rail tank cars (now 'pooled' under central control). The government therefore built a number of long-distance pipelines for the movement of fuel oils, the first of which opened in November 1941 from Avonmouth to Walton-on-Thames, and became the main fuel supply route for London. (The Walton-on-Thames site was chosen because it enabled barge distribution to the many waterside industries which had previously been supplied by barge from the Thames estuary sites).

From late 1940 to mid 1943, therefore, activity at Thames Haven was at a low ebb. Jack Whittington, a fireman at Tilbury shed in 1941-3, regularly worked to Thames Haven with the morning workmen's train, and recalls a scene of faded glory, with bombed storage tanks being cut up for scrap and little rail tank traffic. Nevertheless LATHOL, Shell, and Cory's all continued in active business, and ships continued to come here as necessary. The Shell Bitumen and Luboil plants were kept in full production (after a government analysis of the overall national production capacity for these products).

Everything changed quite the other way in 1943-5. With air raids over - there were actually one or two (lesser) raids on Thameshaven in 1943/4, but this did not affect the overall judgment

A further September 1940 view (see also back cover). Here we look north-west over the LATHOL Western connection/West End level crossing area. One of the tanks on the LATHOL 'Rugward West' tank farm (built in the interwar years and therefore not shown on the 1919 OS) is burning, and firemen and their vehicles are seen on the track leading down to the level crossing. The piece of 'Semi-detached London' in the foreground is the LATHOL senior officers' housing area.

(Thurrock Museum Collection courtesy R.E. Reynolds)

TIMETABLED GOODS SERVICES 22.5.1944 ufn

Weekday service shown. The same trains run from Reading/Neasden on Sundays, but some of the timings differ.

arr   Thames Haven   dep

		arr	dep		
6.32pm	Reading	1.10am	2.45am	Empties Reading	*The WTT also shows Light Engine moves from Tilbury to Thames Haven at 11.27am SO, 3.5pm SX, 4.10pm SO (all coupled to down trains), and from Thames Haven to Tilbury at 10.10am and 9.45pm.*
8.5pm	Reading (D/H)	2.15am	4.0am	Empties Neasden	
12.50am	Neasden	4.45am	5.55am	Empties Acton C.W.	
12.5am	Reading (D/H)	6.37am	8.30am	Empties Reading	
2.5am	Reading (D/H)	8.10am	10.40am	Empties West End	
2.35am	Reading (D/H)	10.0am	2.45pm	Ripple Lane	
10.0am	Plaistow (& Ripple Lane)	11.55am	5.30pm	Empties Reading	
9.33am	Reading	3.35pm	7.5pm	Plaistow	*D/H - Double Headed.*
2.32pm	Plaistow (& Ripple Lane)	4.35pm	7.45pm	Empties Reading	
10.33am	SO Reading	6.51pm	9.25pm	Empties Neasden	
12.33pm	SX Reading	6.51pm	11.40pm	Empties Reading	
2.3pm	Reading	8.30pm			
6.15pm	Neasden	10.10pm			

All down Reading/Neasden trains call at Woodgrange Park for water, and most call at Tilbury for loco/crew change up and down.

of the situation - the government decided in 1942/3 to take over the now underused oil storage capacity in the Thames estuary and the Solent for military purposes. In October 1943 it was agreed that the Thames Haven tankage would be used by the Air Ministry for aviation fuel to supply the many airfields in East Anglia, and a pipeline was built from Thames Haven to RAF main depots at Saffron Walden, Thetford, and Hethersett, with further direct branches to those airfields nearest to it (the other airfields remaining served by road from the main depots). This pipeline was brought into use in spring 1944; its design capacity of 95,000 tons per month was to be well used, as around one million tons of aviation fuel was pumped from Thames Haven between the pipe's commissioning and June 1945. The fuel was initially brought in to Thames Haven partly by rail from Avonmouth and partly by ship. However in late 1944, after the invasion of Europe, it was possible to reopen the Channel for shipping at large, and the last months of the war the aviation fuel was all brought direct by ships to Thames Haven and the special trains from Avonmouth were no longer required. Further details of the rail operations are given below.

A lesser (but not insignificant) LATHOL government contract in the war years was for the filling and stockpiling of Jerry Cans. These were stored on vacant land at Curry Marsh (where the Shell West Site was built after the war) and a narrow gauge railway was provided in connection with this. Thames Haven was not used for the bulk storage of fuel for 'Overlord', which was concentrated at the Isle of Grain sites.

1939-47: TRAIN SERVICES

The established 3-train service was continued in the September 1939 timetable, but the morning trip from Plaistow (and return) ceased in February 1940, and the existing Plaistow and Brent trips in 1941. From May 1941, with oil operations much reduced, only one train a day ran, at 11.57am from Plaistow, returning 4.15pm from Thames Haven.

Ripple Lane up and down yards opened in 1940 and from then on most Thames Haven branch services called there en route from Plaistow or, in some cases, ran to/from Ripple Lane only. Some

continued to call at Little Ilford.

For a few months in 1942 there were additionally two through trains a day from Avonmouth (plus an 'as required' service from Ellesmere Port) (7). This was at the time when shipping at the east coast ports and the Thames was most severely restricted and was the start of the process of bringing oil *in* to Thames Haven by rail, which was soon to be much expanded.

After several months back to one train a day, May 1943 saw an increase to three Plaistow trips a day (8), probably in connection with the first phase of government storage build-up at the Thamesside installations. This was followed in October 1943 - on the decision to use Thames Haven for aviation fuel stockpiling - by the most dramatic development ever to occur in the branch's train services. Eight trains a day from Reading, via Cricklewood and the T&FG line, plus a corresponding seven trains a day of empties westbound (a couple of them timetabled to West End sidings or Acton Canal Wharf only), were put on to bring fuel from Avonmouth (9). This required the branch to be opened 24 hours a day 7 days a week; previously the branch had always shut at night, and there had been no Sunday traffic for many years. Several of the trains were double-headed; there are no known references to the motive power but one imagines that Cricklewood locos were used for the LT&S leg. Water stops were made at Woodgrange Park, and crews changed at Tilbury in each direction. The timings are shown in detail in the tabulation here. From January 1944 a further two trains (ex Ellesmere Port?) were added from 'Neasden LNER Sidings' via the T&FG, with a corresponding two trains of empties westbound. The branch was now being used primarily for the new, unwonted, role of bringing *in* oil.

From the start of the Reading trains, the Plaistow trips were reduced from three to two a day, at new timings. These Plaistow trips remained concerned primarily with the established job of carrying oil products away from Thames Haven.

The Reading and Neasden trains all ceased in or about October 1944 (10) when full scale direct shipping to Thames Haven resumed. After the busiest year in its life to date the branch sank back to the two Plaistow trips only in the 1944-7 period.

(1) The LATHOL 'platforms' in question were at 29m 66ch (North side), 29m 77ch (North side, just west of No. 43 gate LC), and 29m 78ch (South side, east of LC). The first two were relatively lengthy and well-used, primarily for coal. The last was very short and used for ships stores. There was a fourth LATHOL loading 'platform' at Thames Haven station itself (30m22ch, South side) but being within station limits this was more easily dealt with from an operating viewpoint. It was used for barrels.
(2) PRO RAIL 491/788/1.
(3) Not in July 1916 WTT, in July 1921 WTT.
(4) The summer 1934, winter 1934/5, and summer 1935 WTTs show the three 'established' trains still at the same or nearly the same departure times as in 1925 and only minor differences in intermediate timings. The 1157am down/2.50pm up does not appear in any of these timetables, nor in late 1930s timetables.
(5) The Miners' Safety siding did appear in the WTT from its opening in 1916 to its closure in 1927, no doubt because it was outside the Thames Haven Pilot Guard's shunting area. The two Plaistow trains are shown as calling there in the up direction. Similarly the Shell Curry Marsh sidings, and the Fison's siding, opened in BR days, have specific entries in the WTTs, they too being outside the Pilot Guard's area. The

LATHOL sidings, within the Pilot Guard's area, never appear in the WTTs after the 'Pilot Guard' system was introduced in 1916.
(6) The information here is derived primarily from D. J. Payton-Smith, *History of the Second World War: Oil*, HMSO 1971.
(7) These three trains appear in the 4.5.1942 WTT and are then shown as 'suspended' in the 5.10.1942 WTT. The exact product(s) carried, and the length of time these trains actually ran, are not known.
(8) The regular WTT reissue of 3.5.1943 still contains only the 11.57am from Plaistow, but the 31.5.1943 amendments delete this train, replaced by three trips leaving Plaistow at 6.0am, 10.7am and 2.32pm.
(9) The Reading trains first appear in the LMS WTT reissue of 4.10.1943. There is no surviving GWR Freight WTT for this period in the PRO set. No reference has been found to these trains outside of the WTTs themselves.
(10) The trains are included in the 2.10.1944 WTT reissue but the January 1945 amendments note them as 'suspended' as from 2.10.1944. The 7.5.1945 WTT includes all the paths as (Q). The 1.10.1945 WTT does not include the trains at all.

CHAPTER NINE

THE WORKMEN'S TRAIN SERVICE (1923-1958)

Apart from the Corringham Light Railway opened in 1901, which was really only of use to those living in Fobbing and Corringham, no provision had been made for any means of transport for the officials and staff of the various works that had grown up in the area since 1876. There were no proper roads, either. What happened in consequence was described by the former Miners' Safety Manager W. Levett in an interview with the *Grays & Tilbury Gazette* in 1923 :-

'the branch line was treated very much like a highway, and the track was in constant use by pedestrians and cyclists, whilst the officials of the works at Thames Haven and other places were conveyed to and fro on trolleys. This was quite safe as, after the cattle trade came to an end, there was only one train a day. It was quite exciting to see a trolley, propelled by a white sail, moving along the metals. The keepers of the old lighthouse [Mucking] or the customs officials were responsible for this innovation, which however proved too much for the long-suffering railway company, and the practice was stopped. As business increased, the number of people using the railway footpath grew.....'

In September 1905 the *Railway Magazine* had carried a short piece on the sail trolleys, with an illustration (showing the trolley to be of the usual P. Way type):-

'When the wind is favourable a mast and sail are put on the trolley. With a good breeze a speed of from 20 to 25 mph can be obtained with perfect safety'.

One wonders if it was this publicity that made the LT&SR clamp down! The practice was not especially dangerous; the trolley users had to look out for the semi-predictable appearance of the few trains that were then running, and pull the trolley off the line smartly if necessary.

The pedestrians and cyclists, however, were not controllable and the 1915 MR report on the branch notes:-

'Alongside the track is a well defined footway, and I am told the public have used the path for very many years for walking and cycling, as the principle means of access from Stanford-le-Hope to Thames Haven'.

The normal access point was at Stanford Wharf Road (Mayes Crossing). This included the trolley users, who shied off attempting to join the main line at the junction!

THE PROPOSED 1902 SERVICE

Stanford-le-Hope was the key place, both because many of the workers lived there, and because it was the nearest station on the LT&SR, where those that lived further afield could join any Thames Haven transport service.

In October 1902 Stride submitted to the LT&SR Board 'proposals for a train service between Stanford, Thames Haven, and over the Corringham Light Railway, involving the construction of a temporary platform at May's Crossing (sic) on the Thames Haven branch, and the expenditure of a small sum upon the platforms at Thames Haven station to adapt them for the traffic'.

This is a little vague but suggests that it was proposed to run a purely local service from Mayes Crossing, rather than from Stanford-le-Hope station (which would have involved an inconvenient reversal at the junction), and that it (or a separate train in connection) was to continue on to Kynochtown after reversing at the old Thames Haven station. It is not clear why the platform at Mayes Crossing should be 'temporary'.

The Engineer's monthly expenditure statements actually show the expenditure of significant sums on 'May's Crossing station, Thames Haven branch' from October 1902 on. Possibly a timber platform was built (and later removed)? However nothing further is heard of the idea in the minutes, and clearly the proposal was abandoned after a few weeks.

The Corringham Light Railway records confirm this. Their line between Kynochtown and Thames Haven had not been inspected by the Board of Trade so far, as there had been no passenger traffic over it. But in October 1902 they gave notice of their intention to open it to passengers on 18th November. This was then postponed in favour of 13th February 1903, but the inspection

was called off again, on the excuse that the LT&SR had not finished their works for the service and the inspection of both company's works might best be done at the same time. Nothing is heard after February 1903.

THE FIRST WORLD WAR

In the war years, when the activity at Kynoch's works was vastly expanded, the workforce grew to several thousands. Many were accommodated in hut camps at Kynochtown village itself, and Herd's Farm near Corringham CLR station. Others however had to come in from afar daily. They were conveyed by horse brakes between Stanford-le-Hope station and Corringham CLR station, whence they completed their trip on the CLR - neither fast nor convenient!

It has been claimed in print, more than once, that special trains were run from London to Thames Haven (or even Kynochtown via the CLR) in the war years, for Kynoch's workers. However no real evidence has ever been provided for this (1). The only reference found to additional trains on the LT&S line is the running of an extra 8.10am Stanford-le-Hope to Southend on Sunday mornings for 'Kynoch's workpeople', presumably those on night shift, as from January 1917.

Around the end of the war, Shell started running lorries for their workmen to and from Stanford-le-Hope station via the Manorway, which was only an earth track at the time. The workmen simply stood in the back of an open lorry.

INTRODUCTION OF THE WORKMEN'S SERVICE (1923)

It was evident that regular employment in the oil industry in particular would continue to grow, and in 1921 the idea of a workmen's train service on the branch was raised again. Although there is no specific comment, it is likely that the oil companies took the initiative on the matter. In March 1921 the Midland Railway Traffic Committee agreed that in order to provide a service for workers at the Miners' Safety works, LATHOL, and Shell-Mex, four halts should be provided, plus signalling alterations (the introduction of Tablet working - see Chapter 11 for details) and a carriage siding at Thames Haven station for stabling the trainset during the daytime. The estimate was £4,140 of which the three employers were to pay £2,680 and the Midland £1,460. The three companies also agreed to 'guarantee the Midland company the expense of engine power and staff in connection with the running of the service' (i.e. pay a subsidy if revenue was less than working costs), and 'relieve the Midland company of all liability in respect of accidents arising from the non-provision of proper platforms at the Halts' (which shows that it was intended from the start to have ground-level halts only). An agreement was signed on this basis, formally dated 4th November 1922.

The four halts were all simply surfaced areas with small hipped-roof timber shelters, and lamp posts for oil lighting (electric at the LATHOL Halt). 600ft long halts were originally intended when scheme plans were drawn up in 1921, but this was economised in the event.

MAYES CROSSING HALT (the same site as the 1902 proposed halt) was situated at 27m 16ch, west of the Wharf Road level crossing, on the north side of the line. It was provided for the benefit of people living in Stanford-le-Hope and working at Thames Haven, and was therefore an 'originating' point, whereas the other three halts were essentially 'destination' points. The surfaced area was 450ft long and 12ft wide. The MoT inspection report states that it was 'provided with a booking office and shelter for the staff'. The hut was identical to those at the other halts but it does seem from this, and the existence of properly dated tickets, that this halt was staffed (presumably for a brief period only, before the morning down train's arrival) in the interwar years, as would really be necessary in the circumstances. It was not staffed in the BR period, however.

This halt is also referred to 'Halt No. 1' in some railway documents (2). The halts do not seem to have had nameboards and passengers and staff were thereby the more prone to refer to them by

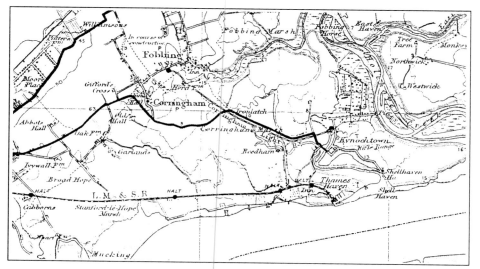

above The Halts are all shown on this 1930 reprint 1in map. This map is actually based on the 1914/19 revision of Essex, hence the Kynoch's works are shown, and 'Kynochtown' not 'Coryton'. The Halts however have been added in the course of 'minor corrections 1924-1929': Mayes Crossing at left, Curry Marsh (which had actually closed three years before this map was printed), LATHOL, and finally Thames Haven Halt (by the 'Inn'). London & Thames Haven Oil Wharves Halt is shown about 1/10in west of its actual site; this error was corrected in a 1930s revision. The various oil installations are very poorly shown and not named. The improved 1920s Manor Way motor road from Corringham to Coryton shows up well. If the Corringham Light Railway is included, there are six 'stations' in the Thames Haven vicinity on this map! However the Thames Haven branch Halts were not shown on the 1in maps from 1940 on.

right upper   LMS on-train issue ticket (in reality probably 'on-platform', as there was no way in which the guard could go round the train, which was always non-corridor compartment stock). It was *impossible* to get from Thames Haven to Mayes Crossing and back in the same day! - hence the deletion of 'and back' for use of the ticket as a single, one assumes to a passenger who had arrived at Thames Haven by other means. There was apparently little or no ticket checking on the branch in later years, but most passengers would have got tickets at fully-staffed stations elsewhere on the LT&S.

(Courtesy Godfrey Croughton)

right lower   Return ticket Tilbury to Thames Haven, dated 22nd August 1936. Latterly the ticket would have been 'Early Morning Return', rather than 'Workman'.   (Courtesy Godfrey Croughton)

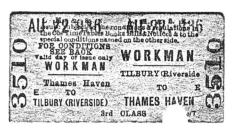

This is the only known pre-1939 view of the Thames Haven Workmen's train, and also the only one of the morning down train (which of course was at an inconvenient hour for photographers!). 2222 (ex 71 *Wakering*) is standing at Thames Haven Halt just after arrival at 7.38am. The leading coach is a Midland 6-wheeler, the rest LT&SR 4-wheelers. It is impossible to tell how many further 4-wheelers there are out of sight, but if there were many more the rear of the train would be over the level crossing. There was an incentive for drivers to stop short so that they could use the crossover here. The heads in the 6-wheeler were no doubt enthusiast friends of the photographer. The date is not recorded, but Plaistow became 13A in 1935 and 2222 was renumbered again in 1939, so let us say 'c1937'. The 0-6-2Ts were the normal locos for this service ; they were mostly Plaistow locos on paper although it was a Tilbury shed job.

(Frank Church collection)

Mayes Crossing Halt, looking west, in November 1950. By this date the 1922 Waiting Shed/B.O. and the fencing were in decay, and the ten lamp posts had ceased to illuminate. The condition of the 'road' in the foreground shows well enough why it was deemed unsuitable for heavy Fisons lorry traffic.

(Frank Church)

Thames Haven Halt looking west on 4th November 1950; the opposite view to that seen previously at p35 bottom, with Dock House level crossing and (ex) public house in the foreground here. At left is the 1916 Shell siding connection, still in its original form at this time, with one of the Shell fireless locos visible. The Shell 'East Site' belches smoke in the background.   (Bob Cogger)

other names colloquially.   Mayes, it might be noted, was the landowner in the 1830s.

CURRY MARSH HALT at 28m 57ch was located between the Miners' Safety siding and the main line, on the south side of the main line. It was only 200ft long and 10ft wide, owing to the site constraints, and could not accommodate the full length of the long trains used initially, passengers being instructed to join the rear three coaches on down trains and the front three on up trains. Two white boards were fixed east of the halt to show drivers of down trains where to stop. The MoT inspection report says that this halt was 'provided with a shelter for the staff' but one wonders if this was a confusion as there is no evident reason for needing staff here. The name 'Curry Marsh' came from Curry Marsh House, just east of here, which had an occupation crossing at 29m 0ch. It is surprising that the name 'Miners' Safety' was not used given that the halt was entirely for the use of workers there. Also known as 'Halt No. 2'.

LONDON AND THAMES HAVEN OIL WHARVES HALT at 29m 74ch, was on the north side of the line, west of the level crossing later known as No. 43 gate crossing, which was the main road access to the LATHOL site. It was 450ft by 12ft (as Mayes Crossing) and had a 'shelter for the staff' (same comment as above applies). Also referred to as 'Halt No. 3' (3).

THAMES HAVEN HALT at 30m 21ch was on the south side of the line, east of Dock House (Manor Way) level crossing. Again at was 450ft by 12ft and had a 'shelter for the staff' (4). Also referred to as 'Halt No. 4', and colloquially as 'Shellhaven' or 'Pig Halt'.

The train service began on 1st January 1923 (5). The intro-

duction of this service was deemed to make a MoT inspection necessary and this was eventually carried out in April 1925.

The trainset used initially comprised 17 old four-wheelers (giving a capacity of 600) which had been fitted with double footboards in consequence of the ground level halts.

The service comprised only one down train in the morning and one up train in the late afternoon (at midday on Saturdays). It ran from Tilbury by which means people living anywhere on the LT&S system were able to connect into and use it. The timings were

	MON - SAT	SAT	MON - FRI
Tilbury	7.7am	12.38	5.38
Low Street	7.15	12.33	5.33
Mayes Crossing Halt	7.23/7.25	12.22/12.24	5.22/5.24
Curry Marsh Halt	7.29/7.31	12.18	5.18
LATHOL Halt	7.33/7.35	12.14	5.14
Thames Haven Halt	7.38	12.10pm	5.10pm

As there was already a loco going down Light Engine from Tilbury to Thames Haven for a shunting shift, the Midland was probably exaggerating the 'engine power and staff' costs! The Workmen's train loco now took over the full shunting turn as well (6), except that on Saturdays, when the up Workmen's ran at midday, it was necessary to send another loco LE from Tilbury at 11.30am to provide shunting power at Thames Haven in the afternoon, returning at 4.35pm.

The Workmen's train had to carry a Guard, and as he had

nothing to do at Thames Haven, it was the practice in most years (except when some other train or loco left at the appropriate time) for the loco of the Workmen's to return light at 7.45am to Thames Haven Junction, leaving the Guard there to find his own way back to Tilbury, the loco then returning immediately at 8.0am to Thames Haven to commence shunting. The 1920s WTTs show the 3.4pm Plaistow - Thames Haven goods stopping at Tilbury Docks station 'to pick up Guard', which we may take to be the Guard for the up Workmen's, who thereby had 43 minutes 'recovery time' at Thames Haven in case of the goods running late. On Saturday the Guard probably came down on the 11.30am Light Engine although this is not specified.

THE WORKMEN'S SERVICE 1923-1958

Apart from the Saturday return service being retimed to 12.20pm around 1950, the timings of the trains never varied by more than a minute or two in the whole of the 35 years for which the service operated.

In 1926 there was a 'crisis' which nearly caused a premature end to the service. The causes are not known but the three firms gave notice to the LMS that they wished to terminate the agreement. However after negotiation matters were resolved. Mr Looker MP asked a parliamentary question in April and stated that the service was being used by 'over 400' workers from London, Gravesend and other places - the only known reference to usage at this period.

When the Miners' Safety works closed in 1927, Curry Marsh Halt (which had no other use) was closed also (7). This also required the making of a new agreement between the LMS and the remaining two companies, Shell-Mex and LATHOL.

The trains called also at East Tilbury from its opening.

Whilst the passenger timings remained the same in the war years, the locomotive arrangements were changed several times. In 1940-3 with freight traffic falling off and less shunting work required, the loco began running back to Tilbury Light Engine at 11.0am SX, and a different loco and crew left Tilbury at 1.30pm SX to shunt for three hours in the afternoon before returning with the up Workmen's. But when freight traffic increased again in 1944 the previous arrangement was reverted to (and indeed an additional Light engine was run from Tilbury at 3.5pm SX to shunt at Thames Haven in the evenings after the up Workmen's had left, the first time that shunting cover had been needed here after 5pm).

At the very time that the service began, the 'Manor Way' from Corringham to Thames Haven was transformed into a modern motor road. This was an inevitable and necessary step but it did mean that those living in Stanford-le-Hope and Corringham could now cycle to Thames Haven much more conveniently, to the detriment of the new rail service and the CLR. (It also put an end to the cycling along the railway!). As noted above workers from further afield did patronise the new rail service in good numbers for some years, but in due course regular bus services began along the Manor Way, from Grays and Southend, and usage of the train was well in decline by BR days, the two old bogie coaches now used being more than enough.

The service was withdrawn as from the new timetable of 9th June 1958 (8). The Halts, being what they were, soon ceased to have any visible presence as such.

left Most photographs are of the 12.20pm up train on Saturdays. Frank Church photographed this train on three occasions in the 1950s. This is the first occasion, 15th March 1952; 41984 (ex 73 *Cranham*) is just pulling away from Thames Haven Halt, a minute or two after the front cover upper photograph was taken. The first coach appears to be E14040M as in the 1954 views, the second is an LT&SR vehicle but not a brake, hence the need for an (unidentifiable) brake as a third vehicle. In the foreground is the extra LATHOL connection of c1920. (Frank Church)

below Unusually, 4-4-2T 41946 was on the workmen's train on 4th November 1950, and is seen here between the old station and the Halt. The water tank seems to have been built around 1920, replacing that seen at far left of the photo at p.32. It was looked after by the Tilbury pumpman who went by bike to Low Street every morning to check the pump there (which supplied Tilbury shed) and then proceeded to Thames Haven by the Workmen's service. A. W. Starvis the pumpman in the 1940s was notorious for his dislike of any crew who made his life harder by *using* the Thames Haven tank! 1952. (Bob Cogger)

this page Frank Church's next visit was on an unrecorded date in the spring of 1954. In the first view 0-6-2T 41991, its shunting work completed for the day, is taking water prior to returning to Tilbury with the 12.20. Next we see the coaches in the platform at the old station before the loco couples up. Despite the provision of the special siding in 1922 it is evident from photographs that, by 1950 at least, the coaches were often left in one of the old station platform roads during the day (although this was not always possible as oil tankers might be occupying these roads). The two coaches here are (nearer) E23245M, 52ft 9¹/₂in LT&SR Brake Third No. 60 of 1912 (one of the coaches made up from two of the LT&SR/District joint stock coaches of 1901), and (further) E14040M, 46ft LT&SR Third No. 288 of 1910 (withdrawn in 1955). The telegraph pole on the platform is still carrying wires to the offices in the old station building.

In the lower view the train is seen at Mayes Crossing Halt. Since the 1950 photograph, the lamp standards have been removed altogether, and nature has generally taken a little more control.

A further 1954 view appears on the front cover (lower photo).   (all - Frank Church)

Frank Church's final visit was on Saturday 12th October 1957. A different train set was now in use, comprising two ex-Midland Thirds and an ex-NSR Brake Third. In the first view 41992 is waiting with the train in what had been the south side platform road, but the platform had been demolished the previous year (possibly the timbers at right are remains of it). The additional sidings of 1956 are seen in the foreground. The nearest coach is identifiable as E14258M.

The second view shows the Brake Third, E24129M.

The lower photo is taken from the level crossing at Thames Haven Halt, from exactly the same spot as the front cover upper photograph, with the train awaiting departure. Here also there has been change since 1952, with new lighting and (at night) the new Inspector's Office of c1953 (built on the site of the 1922 waiting shed) to which the staff had moved from the old station building. There is also a helpful new notice board which tells the workmen that their stationmaster is Mr J.E. Cobb at Stanford-le-Hope.

The branch's last remaining 'mystery' of any significance is this ticket, which can be dated by the 'LNER' title and other details to the 1948-50 period. It is not itself an issued ticket but the 0670 number proves that at least 750 were printed. 'Issued at Stanford-le-Hope' may be interpreted as 'accounted for at Stanford-le-Hope' whose stationmaster was responsible for the branch in the 1950s. No station called 'Shell Haven Halt' ever existed and no other reference to this name is known in railway sources. However the 1948-50 date suggests that it might have been intended for the additional proposed halt at the Shell West Site as referred to in the text at the end of this chapter. Shell were by this time referring to their whole site as 'Shell Haven' so the name would have been appropriate enough. (Godfrey Croughton)

On Saturday 10th January 1953 the winter sunshine had drawn Henry and Richard Casserley to visit the branch and travel on the 12.20. On this occasion the train was hauled by 'Jinty' 47458 (a type introduced to the LT&S section in penny numbers from 1920, and more numerously in BR days). The coaches are the same two as in Frank Church's 1954 visit, in reverse order. This photograph gives a good view of the timber platform of the old station. The Casserleys boarded the train here without any objection being raised; no doubt a few others did from time to time, although the ordinary 'workmen' were not likely to prefer it to the Halt. The old station was therefore still seeing a little passenger use!

(H.C. Casserley)

41963 making ready for departure with an SLS Railtour on 3rd April 1954, between the Halt and the old station. The ground at right was to be used for some of the 1956 additional sidings. Several other railtours have visited Thames Haven since, the only passenger trains in the years since 1958.

(Ken Nunn, Courtesy LCGB)

PROPOSED NEW HALT FOR SHELL WEST SITE

When plans were drawn up in 1947 for the new 'Curry Marsh Sidings' for the Shell West Site Refinery (see Chapter 10), they included the provision of an additional Halt, with a raised platform, at that point (29MP). The purpose of this is not elucidated upon but one imagines that it was intended initially for bringing in some of the large number of contractors' men involved in building the plant, who were billeted all over South Essex. However the Halt is scrubbed out from a revised 1949 plan and it seems clear that no raised platform, at least, was built (9). Local recollections are that the contractors' men were brought in daily by road coaches, and the surviving WTTs for the 1948-51 construction period do not mention any additional stop by the Workmen's train.

(1) There is no reference to any such passenger trains in the July 1916, October 1917, or October 1919 WTTs, or in the Midland weekly notices for 1918 (where they would be mentioned if they had been newly introduced since the last WTT, or if they were only running occasionally). The Midland December 1915 report on the Thames Haven branch also states that there is no passenger service on the branch, which is irrefutable evidence that there was no service of any kind, at that time at least.
(2) The name 'Broad Hope Halt' has been seen in print but seems to be a delusion arising from the fact that the Bartholomew's map has the word 'Halt' immediately below the name 'Broad Hope' which is actually the name of a farm nearly a mile further east (see the 1in map extract here). It is unlikely that anyone ever used this name for the Halt. The names 'Wharf Road Halt' or 'Stanford Road Halt' (or similar) were probably used by some locals, as 'Mayes Crossing' was a piece of railway rather than local terminology. A myth has also grown up that there was an 'LT&SR station' at this point, called 'Mucking'. This seems to be due to the erroneous inclusion of such a station on the map of the LT&SR system in H. D. Welch's Oakwood history of the LT&SR.
(3) The MR weekly notices in December 1922 state (somewhat vaguely) 'A workmen's platform will be provided on the down side on the Thames Haven side of the level crossing at the LATHOL works'. However the 1922/3 amendments to the MR Distance Diagrams state that the Halt is at 28m 74ch which (on the usual basis of a mid-point mileage) indubitably means *west* of the (No. 43 Gate) level crossing. The 1925 MoT inspection report only gives distances to the nearest 1/4 mile and says '30 miles' here, which is unhelpful. The OS 1in maps in the interwar years show the Halt west of the level crossing (see excerpt here for further detail). The WTTs never give mileages for the Halts, which only appear as footnotes. Overall therefore there is good evidence for

the Halt being (immediately) west of the level crossing. The 1939 OS 25in map (Chapter 7) appears to show the Halt here. It is also shown on a (non-scale) '1955' track plan in MT114/534 (as '43 Crossing Halt'). See also back cover photograph.
However the April 1921 scheme plan for the halts shows that it was originally intended to provide this halt on a quite different site (28m 55ch) nearly 1/4 mile to the west, on the down side, with a foot exit at its west end close to the LATHOL 'eastern connection'. It is also shown in this position in an (undated but 1920s) LMS 'Rating Plan', and in a 1960 signalling plan of the branch. One suspects that the authors of these plans were copying from the 1921 plan without realising the halt had not in the event been built there.
(4) Noted as 'B.O.' on the 1923 plan (for the new LATHOL siding connection here) in the LTS Section Private Sidings book (Railtrack archives). It is just possible that staff were present to issue tickets here in the first years (in case there were passengers for the evening up train who had not arrived with return tickets?). Possibly the hut was used by the train guard for this??
(5) The MR weekly notices December 1922 state that the service will begin on 1st January. It is not in the October 1922 WTT, but it is in the June 1923 WTT.
(6) It appears from the June 1923 WTT that initially the loco and crew off the down Workmen's returned Light Engine to Tilbury at 12.30pm SX, with another loco leaving Tilbury at 12.30pm SX to shunt in the afternoon and return with the up Workmen's. But this was soon changed (by 1925) to having the loco remain at Thames Haven.
(7) Exact date not known. Curry Marsh Halt still appears in the September 1926 WTT but is not in the July 1927 WTT.
(8) Specific evidence is a little thin, but the trains are shown in the September 1957 WTT, and not in the June 1958 WTT. The report of a 28.1.1958 site meeting, in an ER correspondence file on the branch, notes that 'the present workmen's service will be discontinued with the commencement of the summer timetable 1958 and the branch can therefore be considered as a goods line'. A note (made 1960?) on ER S&T diagram SE 60 L140 states 'Workmen's passenger trains ceased June 1958'. Frank Church was told that the 12.10.1957 train was the 'last Saturday train'; this may well be correct but there is no other evidence available.
(9) The original plan LMS 2737-47 (of 1947), and the slightly later plan 2848-47 which is of December 1947, are entitled 'Proposed Siding Accommodation and Halt' and show a 660ft long proposed halt with raised platform at 29m 01ch (centrepoint) (blocking Curry Marsh occupation crossing). The revised plan 11-49 (of January 1949) has the words 'and Halt' deleted from the title and the platform is scrubbed out on the plan. It is not evident why a raised platform had been considered necessary, unless the Halt was intended to be served by trains other than the regular branch workmen's set. S&T plan SE 60/140 shows a 330ft Halt, marked 'New Halt', at much the same point (actually immediately east of Curry Marsh LC, 29m 04ch midpoint), but there are 'problems' generally with this plan and its sources! No other post-1949 plan shows anything. The absence of any halt here in the 1955 branch plan in MT 114/534 is near-proof that no 'halt' existed, but there remains the possibility that trains sometimes stopped here on an ad hoc basis.

CHAPTER TEN

THE OIL BOOM YEARS (1948-1993)

Within a few years of the end of the war both Shell and Mobil built large new refineries at Thames Haven and oil traffic began to increase rapidly to figures well above prewar levels.

THE SHELL 'WEST SITE' REFINERY (1950) AND CURRY MARSH SIDINGS

In 1948 the Shell Petroleum Co Ltd (the Asiatic Petroleum Co, renamed in 1946) decided to build a crude oil refinery, for processing Kuwait crude, on previously unused marshland on the north side of the branch to the west of the LATHOL installations. This reflected a general tendency for European companies at this time to switch refining from the countries of origin to new home refineries. The new refinery became known as the 'West Site' (with the original Shell installations by Thames Haven station becoming the 'East Site'). 704 acres were purchased from LATHOL, who owned a large amount of unused land here, in 1947. As part of the land purchase agreement Shell undertook not to carry on 'the business of an oil storage installation or of a wharfinger' on this site, and entered into a 100-year tankage hire and service agreement with LATHOL for the additional storage capacity needed.

The primary Crude Distillation Unit on the West Site, with a capacity of 2 million tons per annum, was brought into use in 1950, the rest of the new refinery facilities following in 1950/1. To serve this new site, 'Curry Marsh Sidings' were installed in 1949 (1), comprising two reception sidings on the north side between $28^1/_2$m and 29m, leading to the new Shell internal system within the West Site. These sidings were at the same mileage as the former Miners' Safety works, but there had never been anything on the down side here before.

In 1959 a second West Site CDU was commissioned, together with a West Site Fertilizer complex incorporating an Ammonia Plant and Nitric Acid Plant. The Ammonia Plant was in connection with the new Fisons works (and was closed when that was closed; the whole Fertilizer Complex was closed by 1977).

In 1969 the Shell Refining Co purchased the LATHOL tankage and jetty facilities at Thames Haven for £21m, bringing to an end the life of the company which had 'made' Thames Haven more than any other, and making Shell the main player here. The LATHOL site became known as the 'Central Site'. Many of the facilities did not meet current Shell standards and an improvement programme was initiated.

Total Shell refining capacity here was in due course increased to 4-5 million tons per annum.

THE MOBIL REFINERY (1953)

1950 also brought a new force in the form of The Vacuum Oil Co (renamed The Mobil Oil Co Ltd in 1956). Founded in the USA in 1866, Vacuum had begun UK operations in 1885 and set up a UK company in 1901, but had not owned any refinery in the UK prior to this. In 1950 Vacuum bought the Coryton site from Cory's and commenced work on a large refinery here to process Middle East crude, which was brought into operation on 31st January 1953 (the afternoon before the East Coast floods, which submerged the site within hours!). Vacuum had only sold vehicle luboils in the UK previously, but began petrol sales in 1952 in preparation for the new refinery's output. The refinery was planned for $^3/_4$ million tons per annum but was soon exceeding this (and was up to 8 million tons per annum by the 1970s).

On 1st September 1950 the Corringham Light Railway passed into the effective ownership of Vacuum (but remained legally a separate company until 1969, when the line was transferred to the direct ownership of Mobil under a Light Railway Transfer Order). The section of the CLR between Thames Haven station and Coryton was reballasted and resleepered in 1951 in order to take the much heavier tanker traffic that would now be using it. The rail sidings within the Coryton works had to be much extended to serve the new refinery.

Coryton village remained through the 1950s and 1960s (and escaped further renamings!). However further expansion of the refinery was then planned which required the removal of the village, which was depopulated in 1970, all the houses removed and a new 'Fluid Catalytic Cracker' built on the site.

THE FISONS PLANT AND SIDINGS (1959)

A wholly new business came to the branch in 1959 with the opening by Fisons of an ammonium nitrate plant, situated on the south side of the line between Mayes Crossing and the Shell West Site. This plant had been planned from 1955 in combination with the expanded (1959) Shell facilities, and used waste gases supplied from the Shell plant. The ammonium nitrate had to be transported to other Fisons plants at Avonmouth and Immingham for use in the manufacture of fertilisers, and this had to be done quickly to ensure that it was still in a liquid state on arrival. Fisons acquired 45 rail tankers for this purpose and a private siding was laid in on the branch at $28^1/_4$m. For details of the train services operated see the photograph caption opposite and the 1962 WTT.

However the plant proved shortlived and these trains (which ran latterly to Avonmouth and Tavistock Junction) ceased running around 1970. The siding was retained for the use of the new owners of the site (British Dredging).

TRAIN SERVICES 1948-1968

By 1949 it had become necessary to increase the service (from the 2 trips of 1947) to three down and four up workings. These continued to be worked on the 'traditional' Plaistow/Ripple Lane basis, with remarshalling and transfer to onward services there, the traffic to each destination not yet being enough to justify 'block train' working (as practised briefly during the war). The additional up train was needed because of the up trains being loaded tankers and the down train only empties. The September 1949 WTT shows the following trains:-

DOWN

8.5am Ripple Lane - Thames Haven 9.50am (calling Curry Marsh)

11.20am Ripple Lane - Thames Haven 12.50pm (calling Thames Haven Junction siding if required)

1.53pm Plaistow/2.35pm Ripple Lane - Thames Haven 3.45pm (one hour later on Saturdays)

Engine & Brake Tilbury 2.50pm - Thames Haven 3.12pm (on Saturdays, from Grays 1.32pm)

UP

10.50am Thames Haven - Ripple Lane 12.5pm/Plaistow (SX) 1.8pm

2.0pm Thames Haven - Ripple Lane 3.28pm (Saturdays departs 2.45pm and extended to Plaistow)

4.0pm SX Thames Haven - Ripple Lane 5.25pm/Plaistow 6.22pm

6.50pm Thames Haven - Ripple Lane 8.14pm and Plaistow 9.8pm

Apart from a few trains being timetabled to call at Curry Marsh sidings, the established post-1916 practice of running all trains complete to/from Thames Haven Yard, and distributing to/from the various Shell sidings by untimetabled local shunt movements, continued in BR days (until the 1983 changes described later).

The 1955/6 timetables show no change of major significance. The real 'boom' came in the years after 1958 when car ownership in the UK increased fastest and petrol supplies had to be expanded accordingly. The railway's 'Modernisation Plan' urge for more use of 'block trains' coincided happily with this increased petrol demand, which now enabled the running of economic-length complete trains of tankers to a single destination - the destinations in question being, mostly, the oil companies' major inland tankage/distribution depots, from which customers were supplied by road. Thames Haven's primary supply areas were the West Midlands and the WR London Division, particularly the Shell/BP depots at Thame, Northampton, and Rowley Regis/Langley Green, and the Mobil depots at Tile Hill/Hawkesbury Lane. There was also traffic for the Southern (particularly Salfords, which served Gatwick Airport) and East Anglia (particularly Royston and Cambridge) although most fuel for East Anglia went by road. Other destinations proved more shortlived. In addition to those destinations served by rail on a regular basis it was also sometimes necessary, in bad weather in the winter, to run trains at short notice to depots normally served by coastal shipping, such as King's Lynn.

The first 'block train' (in 1958) was actually an ESSO working to Neasden for the Underground power station; it was the June 1959 timetable (tabulated here) that saw the start of the block trains to inland distribution depots. Total weekday departures from Thames

The opening of the Fisons factory (south of the railway) caused Mayes Crossing Halt to be wiped off the face of the earth in 1959 when the Wharf Road (occupation) level crossing was replaced by a (public) road underpass, in anticipation of a much-increased lorry and car traffic here. These views were taken on 24th May 1959 when work was not much advanced (the underpass was not ready when the factory opened). The first is from much the same spot as the 1954 view at page 53 (the nearest telegraph pole here is the same one as appears above the loco cab there). The line was slewed to the north for the duration of the work, the old track (right) being left in situ, disconnected, as it was to be restored to use on completion. Note the signal wire run for Thames Haven Junction up distant.

The lower photo is looking north over the crossing towards Stanford-le-Hope. The slewed line crossed north of the old, hence the distance to the far gatepost.			(Frank Church)

The diverted line at Wharf Road features again in this 28th May 1959 photograph of 9F 92194 on the then-newly-introduced Fisons service. The eastern end of the diversion is seen here, with Thames Haven Junction distant at right. The Fisons tankers were formed into two sets one of which left on Monday Wednesday and Friday evenings for Avonmouth, and the other on Tuesday Thursday and Saturday evenings for Immingham, returning empty the next evening in each case. With departures around 8pm (and arrivals back here in the small hours) they were not the most readily-photographable of trains, and Frank Church was not to be favoured with good light on this particular evening. The Avonmouth trains were 8F-worked, the Tilbury men taking over at Acton; the Immingham trains were worked by a 9F from Immingham shed with crew changes at March and Stratford. The locos ran light to and from Tilbury shed for servicing, temporary facilities having to be provided for them latterly after Tilbury closed as a shed.

(Frank Church)

above J1 65552 at Tilbury East Junction with the 10.50am Thames Haven to Ripple Lane on Saturday 29th August 1953, with the regulation two 'barrier wagons' at the head of the tankers. Several locos of this class were active on the LT&S in the 1950s, after the ER takeover.

(Ken Nunn, courtesy LCGB)

right 41985 shunting tanks at Thames Haven Yard on Saturday 3rd April 1954.

(Ken Nunn, courtesy LCGB)

Haven increased from 6 in 1958 to 8 in 1959, 12 in 1961 (when 220 wagons were leaving Thames Haven per average day) and 14 in the 1962/3 timetable set out in detail here (plus a couple of trains running odd days only). By 1962 half the trains were 'block trains', the remainder still running to Ripple Lane (where the new Hump Yard had opened in 1958) or Brent for transfer to forward services for destinations which could not justify a complete train.

The sidings at Thames Haven Yard were much expanded in the 1955-60 period (as described in Chapter 6). Another major development was the start of 24 hour opening of the branch in September 1959, something which had previously only been known briefly in 1943/4, but which was now (weekends excepted) to become a permanent feature of the line. The main inspiration for this was the way in which departures of the additional services were largely concentrated in the late afternoon and evening, in order to arrive at the destination in the early morning to enable unloading during the daytime working days of the depots. With Thames Haven Junction box and the Thames Haven Yard Inspector and staff working two shifts only, and due off duty at 10pm or so, time started to run out on the busier evenings by 1959. After 24-hour working was introduced departures continued into the night, and it also became the practice for many of the down empties to be timed to arrive back at Thames Haven at night time.

The traffic boom also coincided with the dieselisation of the LT&S system. Based at the new (1959) Ripple Lane depot, the Brush Type 2 diesels gradually took over the Thames Haven services from Plaistow and Tilbury depots' steam power. Some of the earlier 'block trains' were steam-worked, but by 1962 the only steam on the branch was on the Royston 'block' service and the Fisons trains. Devons Road depot Type 1 diesels also had a small role in the workings in the early 1960s. The imbalance in the number of down and up trains became more noticeable as traffic grew; despite dieselisation there were limits on up loaded tanker trains because of the gradients on the Barking flyover and the Tottenham & Forest Gate line, and the 1962/3 timetable reproduced here shows 14 daily up workings but only 7 daily trains needed for the down empties. This meant a lot of Light Engine mileage, which was exacerbated by the new service pattern; there were no arrivals of empties in the afternoon/evening, so all the departures in that period needed Light Engine movements from Ripple Lane. (In contrast, with the service run up to the late 1950s, based on simple 'trips' from Plaistow to Thames Haven and back, very little Light Engine mileage had been necessary). However this undesirable aspect was outweighed by the generally more economic working with diesels and by the fact that Ripple Lane men now worked through to such distant parts as Didcot, Rugby, and Cambridge on the 'block' trains.

THAMES HAVEN TIMETABLED SERVICES 15.6.1959-13.9.1959 (Mon-Fri service)

		arr	dep	
5.15am	Ripple Lane	6.36am	7.17am	LE Ripple Lane
12.15pm	Ripple Lane	1.50pm	2.10pm	Brent
			3.40pm	Ripple Lane
2.56pm	LE Tilbury Tn N. Jn	3.25pm	4.25pm	Ripple Lane
1.35pm	(Q) Neasden	4.20pm	6.45pm	(Q) Neasden
4.15pm	Ripple Lane	5.10pm	6.15pm	Northampton
7.30pm	Ripple Lane	8.30pm	9.0pm	Acton
8.2pm	LE Purfleet	8.50pm	9.45pm	Acton
9.5pm	LE MWFO Tilbury	9.30pm	10.5pm	Hawkesbury Lane

(Fisons trains omitted here).

Saturday service has some differences.

No services on Sundays.

(Q) – runs when required.

THAMES HAVEN TIMETABLED SERVICES 10.9.1962-16.6.1963 (Mon-Fri service)

		arr	dep	
12.15am	MX Ripple Lane	1.10am	1.25am	LE Ripple Lane
9.15pm	MX Royston	1.55am	3.5am	Ripple Lane
2.20am	MX Acton [MO from R.L.]	4.24am		
12.15am	MX Rugby	4.40am	5.15am	LE Ripple Lane
3.15am	WThO Brent	4.55am	5.35am	WThO LE Ripple Lane
			5.50am	Seabrooks Sidings
5.15am	MX Ripple Lane [MO is LE]	6.9am		
7.54am ‡	Ripple Lane	9.22am		
			9.40am	Rowley Regis
9.29am*	(Q) Ripple Lane	10.17am	11.15am*	(Q) Ripple Lane
			12.10pm	Ripple Lane
11.54am	Ripple Lane	12.49pm	1.40pm	Brent
1.45pm	LE Ripple Lane	2.30pm	3.10pm	Ripple Lane (and Brent MThO)
3.18pm	LE Tilbury Tn N. Jn	3.52pm	4.40pm	Ripple Lane
3.29pm	LE Ripple Lane	4.18pm	5.20pm	Ripple Lane
4.24pm	LEs Ripple Lane	5.16pm	⌈6.15pm	Rugby [for Tile Hill]
			⌊7.10pm	Acton
6.10pm	TThO LE Ripple Lane	7.8pm	7.40pm	TThO Nechells
7.4pm	LE Ripple Lane	8.10pm	8.40pm	Royston
8.45pm	E&BV Tilbury Engrs Sdgs	9.10pm	9.40pm	Acton [for Thame]
9.10pm	LE Ripple Lane	10.8pm	10.40pm	Rowley Regis
9.33pm	LEs Devons Road	11.8pm	11.35pm	Northampton
10.24pm	Ripple Lane	11.25pm	11.50pm	E&BV Stanford-le-Hope

Saturday service differs (13 arrivals, 7 departures, plus LEs).

No services on Sundays.

(Q) – runs when required.

* - to/from Curry Marsh only.

‡ - calls en route at Curry Marsh 8.48am/9.13am.

FISONS SERVICES (10.9.1962-16.6.1963 WTT)

7.5pm TThSO Avonmouth – Fisons Siding 2.42am WFO/1.55am Sun.
    LE Fisons 2.55am WFO/2.5am Sun. to Tilbury
8.5pm MWFO Immingham – Fisons Siding 3.50am TThSO
    LE Fisons 4.0am TThSO to Tilbury
    LE Tilbury 7.15pm Mon-Fri/6.10pm SO to Fisons
8.12pm MWFO Fisons Siding to Avonmouth
8.12pm TThO/7.15pm SO Fisons Siding to Immingham

In both the 1959 and 1962 WTTs, Light Engines are specified in the WTT as being for/from the services shown opposite here; in cases not involving LE movements, it is only <u>assumed</u> that the up train is the return locomotive working of the down train shown opposite it.

On a better evening than he was to be favoured with when trying to photograph the Fisons train two days later, Frank Church was on Stanford-le-Hope marshes to catch D 5509 on this (unidentified) up working on 26th May 1959. At this point the line was built outside the old river wall for some distance and the THD&R Co had to build a new stretch of wall along the south side of the line (right). The river defences at this vulnerable spot were improved c1980. In the background are the chimneys of the expanded Shell 'West Site'.

(Frank Church)

Diesel shunters were infiltrating by the mid-50s (although the shunting at Thames Haven was still primarily the job of the loco off the Workmen's train, until that ended in 1958). 12108 is seen here beside the 1953 Inspector's Office on a gloomy Monday 9th January 1956, with three barrier wagons.

(Frank Church)

TRAIN SERVICES 1968-1983

Traffic was still increasing into the 1970s; the 1971/2 WTT tabulated here shows 23 departures from Thames Haven daily. With the run-down of Ripple Lane Hump Yard (from 1968), the timetabling of trains to/from Ripple Lane for remarshalling ceased (or all but ceased) for several years. The great majority of the traffic was, by this date, handled by 'block train' workings; these were still the province of Ripple Lane depot and indeed most of them still called there briefly for loco or crew change. For the rest of the traffic, two or three workings a day to/from Temple Mills were introduced, that yard having taken over Ripple Lane's remarshalling functions.

Around 1974 (2), however, there was a major change in the method of working Thames Haven 'block' traffic. All these trains were now timetabled to/from Ripple Lane only, where thay 'lay over' in the new (1971) East and West sidings before/after the extra-LT&S leg of their journey. This simplified crew arrangements and all but eliminated the large amount of Light Engine working that had existed in the years prior to this, albiet largely because the loading of the down empties workings was now well below the locos' limits. A driver would now work two or three Ripple Lane - Thames Haven - Ripple Lane 'trips' in the course of a shift, with roughly an hour's turnround time at Thames Haven. The Temple Mills services were unaffected by all this; they were incorporated into the new 'Speedlink' system in the 1980s. The 1987/8 timetable opposite shows the principle of the post-1974 service pattern.

THE SHELL 'SHELLHAVEN' TERMINAL (1983): THAMES HAVEN YARD REDUCED IN IMPORTANCE

In 1978 Shell commenced on a 'Streamlining Plan' for the Shell Haven site, where the mixed Shell/LATHOL ancestry had left a legacy of duplicate facilities scattered about different parts of the refinery. This was certainly true of the rail facilities which involved *four* rail tanker loading areas - East Site (the original Shell sidings of 1916), Central Site (the original LATHOL sidings), Reedham (ex LATHOL), and West Site (Curry Marsh). Shell was still committed to rail transport at this time (though Shell distribution of bitumen by rail ceased in 1980) and it was decided to replace all the existing loading facilities by a wholly new rail terminal on the south side of the branch on the original LATHOL site, which was cleared of all existing buildings and tanks, also seeing most of the previous rail sidings (some of which dated back to 1878) being removed for the new layout. The new Shell Haven Oil Terminal ('Shellhaven Sidings' in railway parlance) was commissioned in March 1983, and involved a major resignalling of the branch (Chapter 11). The existing Shell sidings elsewhere were left in situ, but in due course rusted into unusableness.

In a further rationalisation exercise, the whole of the Shell 'East Site' was subsequently demolished and the sidings removed, so that by 1990 the refinery bore a decidedly newer face, with operations concentrated on the post-1949 'West Site', and nothing left from earlier years save for some of the 'Reedham' tank areas.

The razing of the 'East Site', and all of the ex-LATHOL tanks south of the railway, led to Thames Haven (station) Yard, hitherto increasingly 'crowded in' by the busy oil installations on both sides, suddenly becoming left in a sea of desolation, with little human activity left in the immediate area. With Shell traffic now running direct into and out of the new terminal, instead of using Thames Haven Yard, the railway's own activity at Thames Haven Yard was itself much reduced after 1983. Instead of being the heart of the branch operations, it was now restricted to Mobil traffic. The sidings used for traffic purposes (Nos 1-4, 11-14, and 15-17) were remodelled at the stops end to run into loco-run-round headshunts (instead of the previous dead-end sidings which had to be shunted from the Dock House LC end). (See trackplans pp62/63). Mobil locos now ran direct from the refinery into Thames Haven Yard sidings (instead of being restricted to CLR metals) and performed any shunting work still necessary at Thames Haven Yard, enabling the BR shunting loco to be withdrawn.

THE BOOM ENDS: TRAFFIC AND TRAIN SERVICES SINCE 1983

The prudent historian does not attempt to dwell at too much length on the events of the last decade. However a summary must be given of the rather dramatic changes in the branch's fortunes in recent years.

In the 1960s and early 1970s it might well have been thought that the railway oil traffic boom was likely to continue forever, but both in the UK at large, and for Shell Haven in particular, this did not prove to be the case in the event. Pipelines began to be installed for the most important flows, and the growth of the motorway system made road transport more viable for medium distance flows. By the time the new Shell terminal opened in 1983, a marked decline in rail traffic was already evident. The 1985 WTT shows 17 branch departures per day and by the 1987/8 WTT tabulated here this was down to 13 per day, with the branch closed for 48 hours weekly (0600 Saturday - 0600 Monday). This 1987/8 timetable shows the 1970s 'Ripple Lane shuttle' service still in operation; from 1983 trains had been timetabled variously to/from either Shellhaven Sidings or Thames Haven Yard (or either, as needed by the demands of the day's traffic). In practice the trains actually ran on any particular day were becoming more and more subject to *ad hoc* changes according to the refineries' customer demands; the oil companies' own inland rail distribution depots, which had provided such a large regular baseload rail traffic in the 1960s and '70s, were fading in importance, and some were now closed altogether (e.g. Royston in 1982) as the double transhipping involved was no longer viable.

Around 1991 there was another volte-face in the train working, with a reversion to the pre-1974 system of having all trains timetabled as through workings to the destination. (This enabled Ripple Lane East sidings to be taken out of use, and West sidings run down). The majority of services were now timetabled to run on only 1-3 days a week (though to simplify rostering, in several cases the same path was followed daily on the LT&S leg, with the train continuing to different destinations on different days).

The gradual decline of traffic was turned into a massive collapse in 1993 when Shell, in the face of the increasingly negative BR attitude to freight, decided to cease rail distribution at Shell

THAMES HAVEN TIMETABLED SERVICES 4.10.1971-30.4.1972

DOWN

		from	Arr Thames Haven
2145 SX	(Class 7)	Temple Mills	0019
2255 SX	COY	Acton	0040
1620 MWFO	COY	North Walsham	0330*
2347 MX	COY	Coventry	0446
0308 MX	COY	Acton	0505
1950 TFO	COY	Barton-on-Humber	0523
0435	(Class 8)	Dagenham Dock	0542
0410	(Class 7)	Temple Mills	0618 SX/0633 SO
0350 MX	COY	Langley	0615SO/0734SX
0450 SX	COY	Cambridge	1156‡
0940	(Class 8)	Temple Mills	1220
0950 SX	COY	Royston	1320
1126 SX	(Class 8)	Temple Mills	1339
1015 SX	COY	Thatcham [or 1145 Southall]	1500
1030 SX	COY	Richborough	1620
1324 SX	COY	Thame	1654
1322 SX	COY	Salfords	1754
1812 SX		Ripple Lane	1905
2035 SX	COY	Royston	2359

UP

dep Thames Haven		to
0106 MX/0207 MO	COY	Richborough
0125 MX	COY	Salfords
0219 MSX	COY	Kings Lynn
0238 MX	COY	Thame
0353	COY	Royston
0412	COY	Thatcham (or Southall)
0737SX/0817SO	COY	Salfords
0836	COY	Thame
0924	COY	Didcot or Southall
1026 MSX	COY	(destination not stated)
1045 SX	COY	West Drayton Staines
1047 SO	(Class 8)	Temple Mills
1117 SX	COY	Hawkesbury Lane
1312 SO (Q)	COY	Salfords
1342 SX	(Class 8)	Temple Mills
1413 SX	COY	Royston
1623 SX	COY	Didcot
1719 SX	(Class 8)	Temple Mills
1825 TThO	COY	Kingsbury
1908 SX	COY	Cambridge
1950 SX	COY	Brent
2055 SX	COY	Southall
2150 SX	COY	Langley
2227 MWFO	COY	Curry Marsh to Wensum
2243 SX	COY	Southall
2306 TFO	COY	Barton-on-Humber
2325 SX	COY	Bromford Bridge

Light Engine movements are no longer shown in the WTT by this date, hence the presentation of this tabulation as a simple list of arrivals and departures, with no correlation of the two. 'Suspended' trains (of which there are 6) are omitted here. No services on Sundays (it will be seen that the branch now closes at the end of Saturday early turn). The days of the week noted for nighttime down trains are those of the arrivals at Thames Haven. Fisons Siding is still shown in the WTT but without trains.

COY – Company Block Train.   (Q) – Runs when required.
‡ Calls at Curry Marsh 11.14/11.45   * To/from Curry Marsh only.

THAMES HAVEN TIMETABLED SERVICES 5.10.1987-15.5.1988

			Thames Haven arr	Thames Haven dep			
2355 SX	COY	Ripple Lane	*0045	*0145 MX	COY	Ripple Lane	
2318 SX	(Class 9)	Leyton	0140	0240 MX	(Class 9)	Ripple Lane and Leyton	
0125 MX	COY	Ripple Lane	*0215	*0305 MX	COY	Ripple Lane	
0145 MX	COY	Ripple Lane	*0235	*0325 MX	COY	Ripple Lane	
0525 MO	Light Engine	Ripple Lane	0605	†0642 MO	COY	Ripple Lane	
0542 SX	COY	Ripple Lane	0636	0730 SX	COY	Ripple Lane	
0625	COY	Ripple Lane	*0715	*0825 SX	COY	Ripple Lane	
1042	COY	Ripple Lane	1132	1232 SX	COY	Ripple Lane	
1140 SX	COY	Ripple Lane	*1230	*1334 SX	COY	Ripple Lane	
1214 SX	(Class 7)	Speedlink Temple Mills	1330	‡1420 SX	(Class 7)	Speedlink, Ripple Lane and Temple Mills	
1425 SX	Light Engine	Ripple Lane	1507	1551 SX	(Class 7)	Speedlink, Ripple Lane and Willesden Brent	
1640 SX	COY	Ripple Lane	*1730	*1840 SX	COY	Ripple Lane	
1930 SX	COY	Ripple Lane	*2030	*2140 SX	COY	Ripple Lane	
2045 SX	COY	Ripple Lane	*2135	*2235 SX	COY	Ripple Lane	

All departures are the return locomotive working of the arrivals shown on the same line. No Light Engine movements. No services on Sundays. Down trains from Ripple Lane West, Up trains to Ripple Lane East.

COY – Company Block Train
* May start from/terminate at Shellhaven Sidings instead of Thames Haven Yard
† Starts from/terminates at Shellhaven Sidings not Thames Haven Yard
‡ Scheduled to start from/terminate at Shellhaven Sidings, but may start from/terminate at Thames Haven Yard

Haven. (Rail traffic at the other Shell refinery, Stanlow, continued until 1998). The expensively-built 1983 facilities were mothballed after a life of only ten years. The branch was therefore left with only the Mobil traffic at Thames Haven Yard, which has amounted to roughly 10-15 trains a week in the years since 1993 (about one-tenth of the traffic levels in the 1970s). With goods traffic elsewhere on the LT&S also in decline, the Shell pull-out signalled the end of Ripple Lane loco depot, which was closed in January 1994, since when the Thames Haven traffic has been worked by Stratford Depot.

The oil refining industry itself has fallen into rapid flux in the late 1990s, owing to massive overcapacity in Europe. After four decades of 'stability' at Thames Haven, 1996/7 saw the Mobil refinery sold to BP. This has not had any fundamental effect on the level of rail operations but has brought changes in the destinations served. As at late 1998 these were

Barnwell Junction (BP depot)	3 times a week
Brownhills (Charrington depot)	3 times a week
Langley (Total depot)	once a week
Littlemore (BP depot)	once a week
Whittington (Celtic Oil depot)	once a week
Ferrybridge Power Station	once a week
Lostock Works Northwich	once a week
Rugeley Power Station	once a week

Even more dramatically, in June 1998 it was announced by Shell that the whole Shell Haven refinery was to be closed by late 1999 owing to overcapacity. Shell operations are to be concentrated on the larger Stanlow refinery which has been processing 12 million tons per annum in recent years compared to Shell Haven's 5 million. With Shell rail traffic already ceased, this did not of course have any impact on the railway per se, but it did mean that the whole LATHOL/Shell oil saga begun in 1876 will come to an end in 1999, and the BP (as it is now) refinery will be left as the sole remaining industrial plant in the vicinity of the branch.

(1) No reference has been traced to the exact opening date of these sidings. They appear in the September 1949 WTT. There are no copies of the 1948, or summer 1949, WTTs in the PRO set. LMS CE New Works Section plan 2848-47 of December 1947 was drawn up for the scheme, and replaced by a revised plan 11-49 of January 1949, annotated subsequently 'as laid in'. (The siding layout is actually the same in both plans).
(2) The author has not had access to all WTTs of this period as those for 1971-5 are missing in the PRO set. After 1975 the freight timetables were changed to two volumes, one for 'Mandatory' trains and the other for 'Conditional', but the Ripple Lane-Thames Haven workings do not appear in either of these; they must have been listed in Local Trip Circulars, none of which are known to the author. (The Mandatory WTTs show no Thames Haven services at all, the Conditional WTTs show only the Temple Mills services, or some of them). Only from the mid-1980s do the main Thames Haven trains reappear in the WTT.

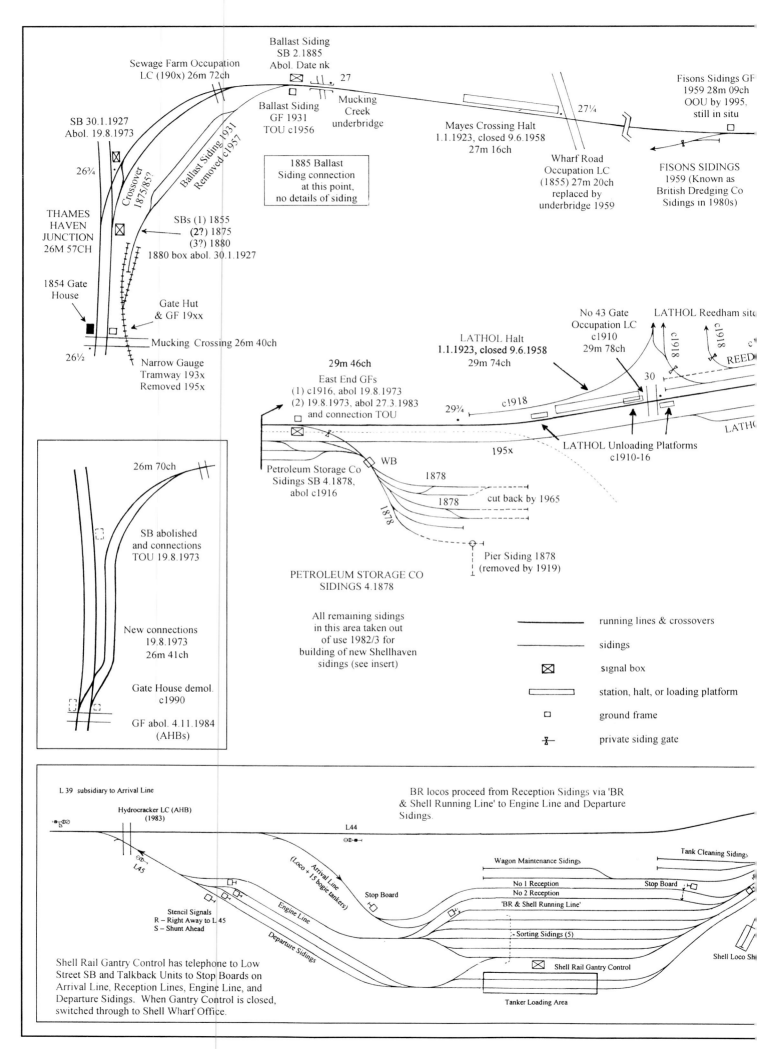

Sewage Farm Occupation
LC (190x) 26m 72ch

Ballast Siding
SB 2.1885
Abol. Date nk

27

SB 30.1.1927
Abol. 19.8.1973

Ballast Siding
GF 1931
TOU c1956

Mucking
Creek
underbridge

26¾

Crossover 1875/85?

Ballast Siding 1931
Removed c1957

1885 Ballast
Siding connection
at this point,
no details of siding

Mayes Crossing Halt
1.1.1923, closed 9.6.1958
27m 16ch

27¼

Fisons Sidings GF
1959 28m 09ch
OOU by 1995,
still in situ

THAMES
HAVEN
JUNCTION
26M 57CH

SBs (1) 1855
(2?) 1875
(3?) 1880
1880 box abol. 30.1.1927

Wharf Road
Occupation LC
(1855) 27m 20ch
replaced by
underbridge 1959

FISONS SIDINGS
1959 (Known as
British Dredging Co
Sidings in 1980s)

1854 Gate
House

Gate Hut
& GF 19xx

26½

Mucking Crossing 26m 40ch

Narrow Gauge
Tramway 193x
Removed 195x

No 43 Gate
Occupation LC
c1910
29m 78ch

LATHOL Reedham site

c1918

c1918

LATHOL Halt
1.1.1923, closed 9.6.1958
29m 74ch

c1918

29m 46ch

East End GFs
(1) c1916, abol 19.8.1973
(2) 19.8.1973, abol 27.3.1983
and connection TOU

29¾

c1918

30

REED

26m 70ch

SB abolished
and connections
TOU 19.8.1973

New connections
19.8.1973
26m 41ch

Gate House demol.
c1990

GF abol. 4.11.1984
(AHBs)

Petroleum Storage Co
Sidings SB 4.1878,
abol c1916

WB

1878

1878

cut back by 1965

195x

LATHOL Unloading Platforms
c1910-16

LATHO

1878

Pier Siding 1878
(removed by 1919)

PETROLEUM STORAGE CO
SIDINGS 4.1878

All remaining sidings
in this area taken out
of use 1982/3 for
building of new Shellhaven
sidings (see insert)

running lines & crossovers

sidings

signal box

station, halt, or loading platform

ground frame

private siding gate

L 39 subsidiary to Arrival Line

Hydrocracker LC (AHB)
(1983)

BR locos proceed from Reception Sidings via 'BR
& Shell Running Line' to Engine Line and Departure
Sidings.

L44

Tank Cleaning Sidings

L45

Arrival Line
(Loco + 15 bogie tankers)

Wagon Maintenance Sidings

No 1 Reception

Stop Board

Engine Line

Stop Board

No 2 Reception

'BR & Shell Running Line'

Stencil Signals
R – Right Away to L 45
S – Shunt Ahead

Departure Sidings

Sorting Sidings (5)

Shell Rail Gantry Control

Shell Loco Sh

Shell Rail Gantry Control has telephone to Low
Street SB and Talkback Units to Stop Boards on
Arrival Line, Reception Lines, Engine Line, and
Departure Sidings. When Gantry Control is closed,
switched through to Shell Wharf Office.

Tanker Loading Area

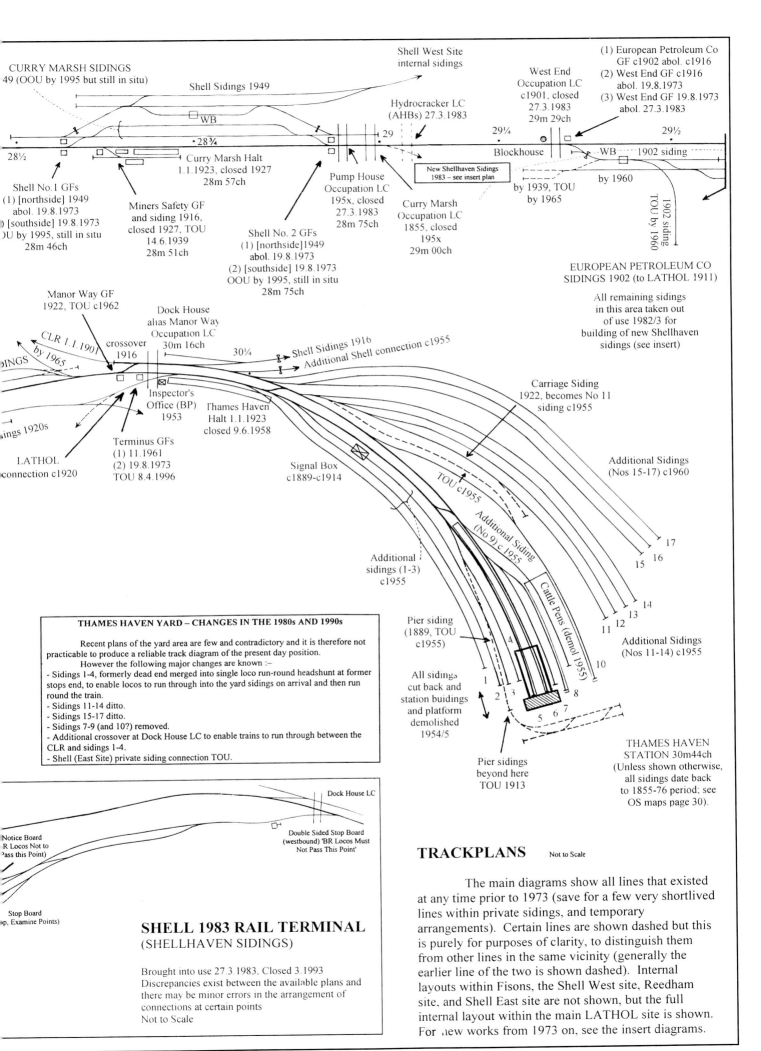

CURRY MARSH SIDINGS
.49 (OOU by 1995 but still in situ)

Shell Sidings 1949

Shell West Site
internal sidings

West End
Occupation LC
c1901, closed
27.3.1983
29m 29ch

(1) European Petroleum Co
GF c1902 abol. c1916
(2) West End GF c1916
abol. 19.8.1973
(3) West End GF 19.8.1973
abol. 27.3.1983

Hydrocracker LC
(AHBs) 27.3.1983

WB

·28¾

29

29¼

29½

Blockhouse

WB 1902 siding

28½

Curry Marsh Halt
1.1.1923, closed 1927
28m 57ch

New Shellhaven Sidings
1983 – see insert plan

by 1960

Shell No.1 GFs
(1) [northside] 1949
abol. 19.8.1973
) [southside] 19.8.1973
OU by 1995, still in situ
28m 46ch

Miners Safety GF
and siding 1916,
closed 1927, TOU
14.6.1939
28m 51ch

Pump House
Occupation LC
195x, closed
27.3.1983
28m 75ch

Curry Marsh
Occupation LC
1855, closed
195x
29m 00ch

by 1939, TOU
by 1965

1902 siding
TOU by 1960

Shell No. 2 GFs
(1) [northside]1949
abol. 19.8.1973
(2) [southside] 19.8.1973
OOU by 1995, still in situ
28m 75ch

EUROPEAN PETROLEUM CO
SIDINGS 1902 (to LATHOL 1911)

All remaining sidings
in this area taken out
of use 1982/3 for
building of new Shellhaven
sidings (see insert)

Manor Way GF
1922, TOU c1962

Dock House
alias Manor Way
Occupation LC
30m 16ch

Shell Sidings 1916
Additional Shell connection c1955

CLR 1.1.1901
by 1965

crossover
1916

30¼

DINGS

Inspector's
Office (BP)
1953

Thames Haven
Halt 1.1.1923
closed 9.6.1958

Carriage Siding
1922, becomes No 11
siding c1955

ings 1920s

LATHOL
connection c1920

Terminus GFs
(1) 11.1961
(2) 19.8.1973
TOU 8.4.1996

Signal Box
c1889-c1914

TOU c1955

Additional Sidings
(Nos 15-17) c1960

Additional Siding
(No 9) c 1955

Cattle Pens (demol 1955)

Additional
sidings (1-3)
c1955

17

15 16

14

13

11 12

Pier siding
(1889, TOU
c1955)

4

Additional Sidings
(Nos 11-14) c1955

All sidings
cut back and
station buidings
and platform
demolished
1954/5

10

1

2 3

5 6 7

8

Pier sidings
beyond here
TOU 1913

THAMES HAVEN
STATION 30m44ch
(Unless shown otherwise,
all sidings date back
to 1855-76 period; see
OS maps page 30).

THAMES HAVEN YARD – CHANGES IN THE 1980s AND 1990s

Recent plans of the yard area are few and contradictory and it is therefore not practicable to produce a reliable track diagram of the present day position.

However the following major changes are known :–
- Sidings 1-4, formerly dead end merged into single loco run-round headshunt at former stops end, to enable locos to run through into the yard sidings on arrival and then run round the train.
- Sidings 11-14 ditto.
- Sidings 15-17 ditto.
- Sidings 7-9 (and 10?) removed.
- Additional crossover at Dock House LC to enable trains to run through between the CLR and sidings 1-4.
- Shell (East Site) private siding connection TOU.

Dock House LC

Notice Board
R Locos Not to
Pass this Point)

Double Sided Stop Board
(westbound) 'BR Locos Must
Not Pass This Point'

Stop Board
p, Examine Points)

SHELL 1983 RAIL TERMINAL
(SHELLHAVEN SIDINGS)

Brought into use 27.3.1983. Closed 3.1993
Discrepancies exist between the available plans and
there may be minor errors in the arrangement of
connections at certain points
Not to Scale

TRACKPLANS   Not to Scale

The main diagrams show all lines that existed
at any time prior to 1973 (save for a few very shortlived
lines within private sidings, and temporary
arrangements). Certain lines are shown dashed but this
is purely for purposes of clarity, to distinguish them
from other lines in the same vicinity (generally the
earlier line of the two is shown dashed). Internal
layouts within Fisons, the Shell West site, Reedham
site, and Shell East site are not shown, but the full
internal layout within the main LATHOL site is shown.
For new works from 1973 on, see the insert diagrams.

CHAPTER ELEVEN

SIGNALLING AND OPERATING

The method of working the branch has been changed frequently, partly in response to the considerable fluctuations in traffic levels over the years, and partly because of the changes from passenger to non-passenger status and vice-versa. Although no public passenger trains ran after 1880 the line was effectively perceived as a passenger route until some time in the 1890s when it became realised that passenger trains would not run again (1). After some three decades as a goods line it then became a passenger line again (as far as Thames Haven Halt) in 1922, remaining so until 1958; but even then it remained a 'line equipped for passenger train working over which there is no scheduled passenger service', as the now-heavy goods traffic made it inappropriate to relax standards merely because the Workmen's train had ceased running.

The single line working will be discussed first, followed by details of the signal boxes and other signalling installations.

ELECTRIC TELEGRAPH WITHOUT STAFF (1855-1875)

The branch was equipped with the Electric Telegraph from the start, like the rest of the LT&S system, and it was also almost certainly intended from the start (under Bidder's influence) to signal the trains on the single line by telegraph. However when Major Wynne inspected the line for the Board of Trade on 27th April 1855 he was not satisfied with the proposed working, and reported that, whilst the line had been built well,

'I am however compelled to report that in my opinion the Thames Haven Railway cannot be opened without danger to the public owing to the uncompletion (?) of the working arrangements for it as a single line'.

In the manner of that time, the report does not clearly specify the problem in question; was the telegraph not complete, or was Wynne objecting to telegraph working in principle? However on 30th April Wightman the LT&S line manager gave an understanding that

'the trains will be so regulated that not more than one engine in steam will be allowed on the line at the same time, between the junction and the terminus'.

This was what the Board of Trade liked to hear and Wynne approved the opening that same day.

Although there are no detailed operating instructions for the 1855-75 period, it can be assumed that the working was not 'OEIS' in the sense we would use the term (i.e. where the first train has to get back to the junction before another train can leave), but rather 'block working without train staff', as commonly used on new single line routes in the 1850s. The ordinary 'speaking' telegraph instruments in the signal box at Thames Haven Junction and the station office at Thames Haven terminus, also used for all other types of messages, would have been used for train signalling as well; on such a quiet line this would have caused no difficulty.

ELECTRIC TELEGRAPH AND TRAIN STAFF AND TICKET (1875-1916)

By the 1870s the Board of Trade was firmly hostile to working single lines without a Train Staff, and as soon as Arthur Stride became manager in 1875 he introduced 'Train Staff & Ticket' working, on top of the telegraph block working (2). The instructions are given here. Whether the existing 'speaking' telegraph instruments continued to be used, or separate 'block' instruments were introduced for train signalling, is not clear; the former seems most likely, at least initially.

All points on the line were originally unlocked handpoints as per 1850s practice, but the additional Junction Ballast Siding (1885) and Petroleum Storage Co (LATHOL Eastern) (1878) connections were worked by interlocked 'signal boxes' in accordance with updated practice, and the Train Staff had an 'Annett's Key' added to release the latter (non-block post) box, and also the ground frame at the 1902 LATHOL Western connection. Trains on a 'Ticket' could not shunt these sidings, but this is unlikely to have caused difficulties very often at this time.

(Details are given later but it might be noted at this point that Thames Haven Station, which had still been uninterlocked at the time the regular passenger service ended in 1880, was fully interlocked, with a signal box, in c1889; so the branch, in practice goods-only but probably still perceived as a 'passenger' line as this date, did meet the requirement of the Regulation of Railways Act 1889 for full interlocking. However this period of full interlocking perversely coincided with the branch's quietest years! and by 1916 the signal boxes on the branch were gone and the line definitely regarded as a

---

Regulations for working the Single Line between Thames Haven and the Junction with the Main Line at Stanford-le-Hope.

In all cases a train staff, or train staff ticket is to be carried by each train or engine to and fro, and without this staff or ticket no train or engine is to be allowed to travel on this Line.

No train or engine must be permitted to leave either end of the Single Line unless the staff is then at the same end, and IS ACTUALLY SEEN BY THE ENGINEMAN BEFORE HE STARTS.

The station master, or officer in charge of the Thames Haven Station during the station master's absence, and the signalman at Stanford-le-Hope Junction, are the sole persons authorised to receive and deliver the staff or ticket.

Upon a train or engine being ready to start from either end, and no second train or Engine being intended to follow it, it is the duty of the person in charge of the staff to give it to the engineman, but it must not be given until the station master or signalman, as the case may be, at the other end has been advised by telegraph that the train is about to enter the Single Line, and the receipt of such advice by such station master or signalman has been duly acknowledged.

The all right or caution signal being shown at the fixed signals, or the order to start being given by the guard or other person, WILL NOT be an authority to the driver to start unless he has the train staff or ticket.

If other trains or engines are intended to follow in succession before the staff can be returned, a train ticket stating "Staff following" will be given by the officer in charge of the station or the signalman at the junction to the engineman of the leading train or engine, THE STAFF BEING SHOWN TO HIM; and so with every other except the last train or engine; the staff itself being given to the engineman of the last train or engine as stated above.

AFTER THE STAFF HAS BEEN SENT AWAY NO OTHER TRAIN OR ENGINE MAY ENTER ON THE SINGLE LINE UNDER ANY CIRCUMSTANCES WHATEVER UNTIL THE RETURN OF THE STAFF.

above These instructions come from the 1884 WTT but probably date from 1875; 'Stanford-le-Hope Junction' was a rather archaic nomenclature by the 1880s. They essentially reflect standard British practice but LT&SR men had not been involved in Staff & Ticket working before and were therefore presumably deemed to need everything spelt out in full. Note the expression 'advised by telegraph that the train is about to enter the single line'. The 1870s LT&SR Block Regulations (as with most companies at that time) were on the basis of 'open block'; a signalman did not 'ask for line clear' but sent 'warning' that a train was coming, and the signalman in advance had to refuse it if necessary. This was changed in the 1890s to the modern 'closed block' system of working.

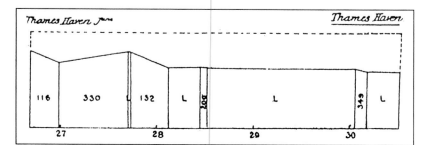

left Gradient Profile of the branch.

goods line where full interlocking was not needed).

The increase in traffic at the start of the 1914-18 war brought about the further complication of the 'Branch Pilotman' system from 2.6.1914. Details of this were given in Chapter 8. From a signalling viewpoint it was a somewhat peculiar system, but then it was only a response to the decidedly peculiar practice of leaving wagons for several hours at different points on the running line in the middle of a 'block section'! Strictly speaking it could be said that the branch was actually operated on the 'Pilotman' system in this period and not on the 'Train Staff and Ticket' system at all; if the Pilotman travelled on all trains as instructed there was no actual need for a Staff, and no Tickets could be issued. But the whole thing seems to have been regarded as a superimposed temporary 'fudge' rather than a change of principle in the signalling system, and appears to have ended in late 1915 when the goods train working was altered again, to a timetable that could be worked within the normal bounds of the TS&T system.

The war brought a further quasi-signalling imposition as the LATHOL premises were given military protection with a 'Blockhouse' erected at the west end (see trackplans). A notice of 4.9.1914 stated that

'All trains on the Thames Haven branch in either direction are to stop upon arrival at the boundary of the London and Thames Haven Oil Wharves Ltd, and only proceed upon receiving permission from the NCO in charge of the military picket on duty at each end of the oil wharves premises'.

The military had their camp next to the Dock House public house, the eastern boundary of the LATHOL property. How zealously they actually carried their train-halting function does not seem to have been recorded! The military presence presumably ended in autumn 1918.

TRAIN STAFF AND TICKET PLUS 'PILOT GUARD' (1916-1922)

Yet another system was introduced some time in 1916, under which the eastern end of the branch, from a newly-installed Home signal at $29^1/_4$m (just west of the LATHOL Western connection) was put under the control of a 'Pilot Guard' (in practice, the Thames Haven Station Foreman). This enabled all the existing sidings to be shunted as required by whatever loco was at Thames Haven at the time, without reference to the Thames Haven Junction signalman and the 'single line working'.

The ground frames at the LATHOL Western and Eastern connections were now released by an Annett's Key (known as the 'Sidings' or 'Oil Wharves' key) held by the Pilot Guard (instead of by Key on the Train Staff; no traincrew could work these sidings now unless the Pilot Guard was present). When a train was coming from Thames Haven Junction, the Station Foreman would don his 'Pilot Guard' badge (a metal plate lettered 'Thames Haven') on his left arm, and walk out to the LATHOL West End ground frame, which worked the new Home signal. He pulled off the signal, and the train then drew forward the 200 yards from the signal and picked him up at the ground frame. The Appendix continues

'Drivers and Guards must carry out the instructions given by the Pilot Guard respecting the working of the traffic, and no train or engine must stop anywhere between the London and Thames Haven Oil Co's siding and Thames Haven for traffic purposes unless special instructions for it to do so are given by the Pilot Guard. All points in the running line between the London and Thames Haven Oil Co's siding and the end of the branch at Thames Haven must either be padlocked or securely held for the safe passage of trains'.

(The last sentence was only a piece of common sense, rather than a particular part of the new arrangements; all points at Thames Haven station were unlocked hand points again by this date).

It is not wholly clear whether the Pilot Guard had to be physically present with any moving train or whether he could simply give instructions and then go away, enabling more than one train to be active at the same time within his area. It may be that in 1916 he did have to be present, but if so this was relaxed later (see next section).

The Train Staff and Ticket working of the branch continued as before, save for the fact that the 'block section' from the Junction now ended at the new Home signal. The Pilot Guard collected the Staff (or Ticket) from the driver at the Home signal, and took it to the office at Thames Haven station, where the telegraph instrument for communication with the Junction was still located. A departing train could be given the Staff (or Ticket) by the Pilot Guard either at the station or at the LATHOL sidings, as appropriate (provided, of

course, that the station office had first obtained 'Line Clear' from the Junction signalman). There was still no signal for departing trains, the Staff (or Ticket) alone constituting the driver's authority to proceed to the Junction.

It will be understood that this 'Pilot Guard' system, as used 1916-1961 at the eastern end of the line, was in no way related to the temporary 'Branch Pilotman' system of 1914/15, which was effectively adopting Pilotman working for the branch as a whole.

The new Miners' Safety siding of 1916 was outside the Pilot Guard's area and the ground frame was therefore released by Annett's Key on the Staff and worked by the traincrew.

ELECTRIC TABLET PLUS 'PILOT GUARD' (1922-c1950)

When the resumption of a passenger service, in the form of the Workmen's train, was authorised in 1921, it was also decided to introduce Tyer's Tablet working of the single line, in place of the Train Staff and Ticket working. There was no absolute need to do this merely because a passenger service was to be run, but the Midland had been putting in Tablet on its busier single lines since the 1880s. It gave more flexibility in the operating - with TS&T it had been necessary to know/guess which direction the next train was coming from before deciding whether to issue a driver with the Staff or a Ticket - and meant also that any train could shunt at the in-section Miners Safety siding ground frame.

The Tablet working was brought into use at 12 noon on 8.12.1922, three weeks before the passenger train started.

The single line section remained Thames Haven Junction to the Home signal at $29^1/_4$m (but the Tablet instrument at Thames Haven was located in the station office, as the telegraph instrument had been).

Although the service was only a 'Workmen's', this resumption of 'passenger' working was seen as requiring the locking of all points over which the train would pass. The Miners' Safety, West End, and East End ground frames were satisfactory, but with the branch having become clearly seen as goods-only by the 1900s, the more recently-installed connections to the Reedham Sidings (1918), the CLR/Shell Sidings (crossover, 1916), and the LATHOL fourth connection (c1920), all near the Dock House level crossing, had been given unlocked hand points only. Accordingly an additional ground frame (Manor Way GF) was provided in 1922 to work these. It was released by a key held by the 'Pilot Guard' (a different key to that for the LATHOL West End and East End GFs, in order that shunting could be carried out in both areas at the same time). No additional signals were deemed necessary for the start of the Workmen's service, and the points at Thames Haven station did not need to be interlocked again, as the Workmen's train did not carry passengers beyond Thames Haven Halt.

ELECTRIC TRAIN STAFF PLUS 'PILOT GUARD' (c1950-1961)

Some time around 1950 (3) the Tyer's Tablet was replaced by Miniature Electric Train Staff (Type M, Configuration A, Red). This was largely a piece of Eastern Region policy but it did enable 'shutting in' facilities to be more readily provided subsequently (see later).

In 1953, when the old station buildings at Thames Haven were abandoned, the instrument was transferred to the new Yard Inspector's Office at Dock House level crossing.

The new Shell Curry Marsh Sidings of 1949, and the new Fisons Siding of 1959, were both 'in section' and the ground frames were released by the ETS.

ELECTRIC TRAIN STAFF PLUS YARD INSPECTOR'S SHUNTING AREA (1961-1973)

When oil traffic began to increase more rapidly in the late 1950s, it became clear that significant changes would have to be made to the infrastructure, or the method of working, or both. In January 1958 the LT&S Line Traffic Manager sought the views of the District Engineer and District S&T Engineer on the possibilities of (a) lengthening the double line section at Thames Haven Junction (for the benefits of which, see next section) and (b) converting the existing running line between West End crossing and Dock House crossing into a dead-end 'headshunt' from the Thames Haven end, and laying a new running line alongside (on the north side), so that the LATHOL sidings could be shunted from Thames Haven Yard wholly independently of the 'branch' itself. However the first idea was to take 15 years to come to fruition, and the second was rejected immediately because of the £12,000 cost, and never came to pass.

SINGLE LINE WORKING METHODS
since 1916

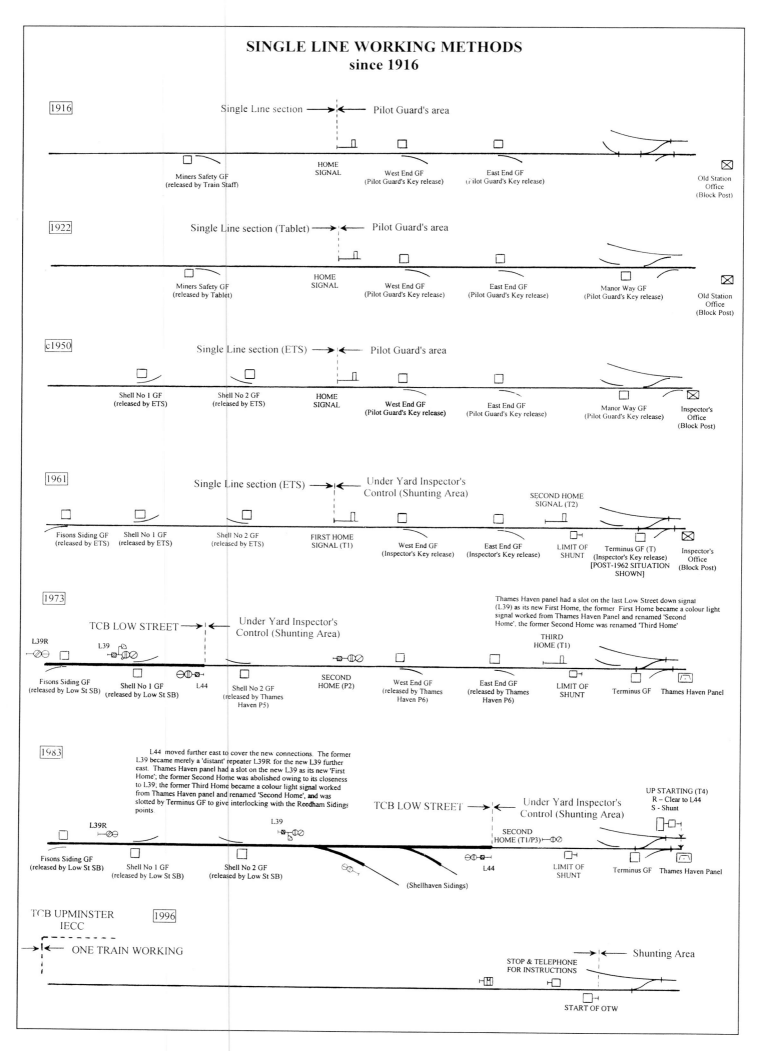

In 1959 attention became focused instead on the possibility of replacing 'Pilot Guard' working with something less time-consuming. It had worked well enough with three or four trains a day but was now inadequate. The Yard Inspector (ex Station Foreman) was being ferried out to the Home signal by the Yard shunting locomotive to perform his 'Pilot Guard' duties, as the walking time would have been too much, but this in turn was diverting the loco from its proper job. After initial thoughts of replacing the Home signal with a Stop Board and telephone (so that the Inspector would no longer need to go out in person but could give permission from his office), in 1960 the plan was changed to retaining the Home signal and having it worked by motor from Thames Haven. The revised scheme was brought into use in November 1961 (after a 'collision between an arriving empty tank train and the shunting engine' in September!) and Pilot Guard working was withdrawn, the branch east of the Home signal now being simply part of Yard limits. The ETS working was not affected save insofar as drivers would now always deliver and pick up the Staff at the Inspector's office. The LATHOL West End and East End GF connections remained released by a Key held by the Inspector (now, as previously, these sidings were never shunted by arriving trains because of the connections being facing to down trains; all arriving trains ran through to Thames Haven Yard and wagons for LATHOL were taken back as a shunt move later). An additional ground frame (Terminus GF) was brought into use by the Inspector's office, working the existing Home signal (now 'First Home') by motor, plus a new 'Second Home' signal which had been deemed necessary to protect shunting at Thames Haven Yard itself.

At the end of the first month's revised working, Yard Inspector Lennox was reported to be 'full of praise for the abolition of Pilot Guard working', but he was not impressed by the additional Second Home signal and he felt that trains could best wait at the First Home until they had a clear run into the Thames Haven Yard sidings.

TRACK CIRCUIT BLOCK FROM LOW STREET TO CURRY MARSH PLUS YARD INSPECTOR'S (EXTENDED) SHUNTING AREA (1973-1983)

With oil traffic still increasing through the 1960s, thoughts soon had to be turned to a new round of improvements. The changes of 1973 were :-

(1) the implementation of the 1958 scheme for layout alterations at Thames Haven Junction. The operating problems here had got worse since 1958. Firstly the branch Up Home signal was, unavoidably, situated on the rising (1/116) gradient approaching the junction. Even back in the 1910s it had been found that goods trains stopped at this signal were too often having trouble in restarting on the gradient, and a rule had been imposed (*vide* all Appendices from 1922 to 1969) that 'heavy goods trains' were to stop at the Branch Up Distant signal if it was at caution. A 'Train Waiting Treadle Bar' was provided which, when depressed by a train, rang a bell and worked an indicator in the Junction box to inform the signalman that a train had arrived at the Distant. This piece of non-standard operating had cured the restarting problem and provided a satisfactory solution until the 1950s, but it had done nothing for line capacity, (a) because an up train waiting here prevented any down train from proceeding on to the branch, and (b) because when the signalman eventually got Line Clear from Low Street after the previous up train had passed there, and pulled off for the waiting Up Branch train, it took 3-4 minutes longer to pass the junction than it would have done had it started from the Home signal. Pathing had been made the more difficult after 1961 as the Tilbury line passenger service had been increased to a 30-minute frequency on electrification.

Secondly, the short length of double track on the branch beyond the junction (which was really only there because of 1850s notions of junction design) was insufficient for other than an unusually-short down branch train to be held there, clear of the main lines at the junction, if it was not able to proceed immediately to Thames Haven (which, because of the first problem just discussed, was more often the case than it ought to have been!).

The idea evolved in 1958 (but then cast aside until implemented in 1973) was to move the junction south to Mucking Crossing, something which could easily be done by laying two extra tracks on the east side without any need for earthworks. At one stroke this both gave a new Branch Up Home signal on a down gradient, and a much longer section of double track for up and down branch trains to wait clear of both each other and of the main lines

(see Trackplans pp 62/3).

Had the work been done in 1958/9 there is no doubt that altered mechanical signalling would have been provided, but remote control technology had much advanced in the meantime and it was now decided in 1973 to abolish Thames Haven Junction box and work the junction from a panel in Low Street box. This both reduced the number of signalmen's jobs needed and improved operating on the main line, as the previous Absolute Block working (retained in 1961 on the sections Low Street - Thames Haven Junction - Stanford-le-Hope, despite objections from the operating side) was now replaced by Track Circuit Bock working Low Street to Stanford-le-Hope.

(2) replacement of the ETS working on the branch with Track Circuit Block Signalling controlled from Low Street as far as Curry Marsh, thence Yard Inspector's shunting area working (as since 1961 in principle but now commencing further west at Shell No. 2 GF).

(3) provision of electrical releases for all the intermediate ground frames (variously from Low Street and a new panel in Thames Haven Inspector's office). This gave more flexibility than the previous use of key release for the LATHOL connections, and also gave 'shutting in' facilities at all ground frames.

The new arrangements were all brought into use on 19th August 1973 (the date when the new Thames Haven Junction layout was commissioned and the box there abolished).

EXTENSION OF LOW STREET PANEL TCB AREA TO NEW SHELLHAVEN SIDINGS (1983-1996)

The changes made in 1983 were brought about purely by the opening of the new Shell 'Shellhaven' sidings (already mentioned in Chapter 10). It was decided to control the two main connections to these sidings - one new, the other the old LATHOL Western connection - from Low Street panel directly. Shell No.2 GF now became released by Low Street, and the old LATHOL Eastern connection was lifted. (In consequence, Thames Haven panel no longer released any ground frames).

The signals controlled from Low Street and Thames Haven panel/Terminus GF were altered (see sketch diagram here); the most notable change was the provision, for the first time in many decades, of a Thames Haven up starting signal, controlled from a second panel here; not a full running signal but a stop board and stencil indicator showing either 'R' (clear through to the first Low Street up signal L44) or 'S' (shunt only).

This provided a decidedly 'better' signalling and operating system overall, but (just as had happened after full interlocking had been installed in 1889!) the traffic to justify this collapsed only a few years later. Fisons and Curry Marsh sidings were unused by the early '90s, and the new Shellhaven sidings saw no traffic after 1993. These connections were secured out of use (4) (but were all left in situ, both in case any new traffic might materialise and to avoid the costs of physical removal).

ONE TRAIN WORKING (1996-)

The 1996 changes were set in course by the overall resignalling of the LT&S section, which meant the abolition of Low Street box. With traffic reduced to such low levels post-1993, and all intermediate connections now out of use, there was clearly no need to install full signalling from the new Upminster IECC on the branch. Instead 'One Train Working Without Staff' was introduced, with Upminster signals at the junction only (where the '1973' track layout was retained). This was effected on 8th April 1996 (when the whole Purfleet to Pitsea section was resignalled).

However some aspects did not go as originally planned. It was at first intended to retain the existing Thames Haven panels and signals T3 (down) and T4(up), thus avoiding any expenditure at the terminus (5). But when the resignalling team visited Thames Haven in late 1995 they found that the panels were in such poor condition that they could not be retained under current standards. In consequence the panels and the signals, plus Terminus GF, were abolished in April 1996 and replaced by a simple 'Stop-Telephone for Instructions' Board (plus Distant Board) for down trains, and a 'Start of One Train Working' Board for up trains. There were also 'problems' with the level crossings. Hydrocracker LC, a wholly-new AHB installation of 1983, could not be retained as such; it ended up being worked as a temporary manned (by a Railtrack mobile supervisor) crossing until made an AOCL in May 1997. In contrast No. 43 gate crossing, thanks to reduced usage, was downgraded in May 1997 from AOCL to ordinary open crossing.

The One Train Working on the branch is enforced by the

above The junction on 22nd October 1957 with the 12.20pm Thames Haven-Tilbury passenger approaching, and the signalman waiting to collect the staff. In 1961 the signalmen here made protests about the excessive speeds of freight trains coming off the branch - having built up speed on the 1/116 up from the Distant, there was not much incentive for drivers to slow down again merely to comply with the staff exchange regulations for the signalman's benefit! The signalmen claimed many 'nasty knocks', and often could not actually catch the Staff at all. The S&T kindly conceded a staff catcher (set down post) at an estimate of £50, and this was erected in April 1961 (followed by a delayed commissioning as there was no electric lighting!). (Frank Church)

left A closer view of the 1927 box, one of the many Midland Type 4d boxes on the LT&S.

(Frank Church)

left On 16th February 1958 the junction was relaid, in its existing form (just before the scheme to alter everything was drawn up!). 42501 rests with an engineer's train by the Down Home signals; note the replacement Midland arms on the main post. The nearest tree marks the site of the 1855 signal box. The iron 'viaduct' at right was part of the arrangements for tipping sand (etc) from the narrow gauge tramway wagons to standard gauge wagons in the Ballast Siding, which terminated very close to the main line here (and was seemingly lifted just prior to the date of this photograph).

(Frank Church)

right The converse view, from the branch. The Railway Signal Co lattice post signals dated from 1900 (see also title page view). Note also the RSCo/LT&SR ground arms for the crossover (which was little used save for running round the Ballast siding trains) and the manner in which the telegraph wires are crossed from the 'junction' pole by the signal box to the branch pole route on the up side.
(Bob Cogger)

correct sequential operation of the track circuits at the junction, and by the operation of transducers there (equivalent to axle-counters, but worked by magnetic eddy currents disturbed by the train wheels). A train passing the junction for Thames Haven must return to the junction before another train can go down, and if a train goes down double-headed it must return with both locos as well. The Upminster signalman is required to telephone the Thames Haven Yard Supervisor before signalling a train down the branch, but this is not a strictly 'signalling' function, merely a check that there is no reason to prevent the train being received.

In the privatisation break-up, responsibility for the staffing and working of Thames Haven Yard passed to Mainline Freight (now EWS). The resident Supervisor's post was abolished and a Mobile Supervisor (who also covers other locations in the South Essex area) now drives to Thames Haven as necessary to be present when a train is due.

THAMES HAVEN JUNCTION SIGNAL BOXES

There were three consecutive signal boxes here (or, possibly, four). The first, almost certainly dating back to the opening of the junction in 1855 (though there is no specific reference to it then) was on the up side immediately by the junction points, and is shown on the 1863 OS extract at page 23. Although no illustrations are known it was most likely a 'platform' with a hipped-roof timber hut on it, like the 1854 Tilbury boxes. There was no interlocking of signals and points.

In July 1875 the LT&SR Board gave Stevens & Sons a contract for interlocking this junction. No details are known but the low price (£150) suggests that a 'Stevens' hut may have been added to the 'platform' as was done with the Tibury boxes (Part 2, p.140), rather than a wholly new box being built.

The location was often referred to as 'Stanford Junction' or 'Stanford-le-Hope Junction' up to the 1870s.

The second (third?) box was built in 1880 after the destruction by fire of the 1855 (1875?) box on the evening of 4th September 1880, the dry grass having been set alight by sparks from a passing locomotive. The new box was on the same site as the old and was almost certainly built by Easterbrook's (there is no actual reference and, again, no photographs are known). It had about 15 levers.

The last box opened on 30th January 1927 and was situated in the fork. There were no track or signal alterations and the building of the box was simply part of a general LT&S section policy at this time of replacing the old Easterbrook boxes and frames with standard Midland boxes and frames. It had a 20-lever REC frame.

On 5.6.1961 colour light signalling was introduced on the main line, but the semaphores on the branch were retained.

The layout alterations of 1973, which led to the abolition of this box on 19.8.1973 and control of the junction passing to Low Street panel, were described earlier in this chapter.

THAMES HAVEN JUNCTION BALLAST SIDING SIGNAL BOX / GROUND FRAME

The LT&SR ballast siding was brought into use around January 1885 (see page 44). The points were 467 yards from the Junction box and thus could not be worked from it. In later years a simple ground frame would have sufficed but because of the very demanding attitude of the Board of Trade at this period, the LT&SR felt obliged to build a 'small dwarf cabin' (6 levers) with full signalling. The work was probably done by Easterbrook's (no known reference or photographs).

The precise status of the box, and its relationship to the Junction box, is unclear. If it did actually work the double/single line points as well it would have had to be open for any train proceeding on to the branch (not just for those wishing to use the ballast siding), although it could probably have been left with the points normal and up signals off. Probably the box was worked as an 'outpost' of the Junction box, under the orders of the signalman there (and perhaps by himself, walking out there as necessary). The block working on the branch almost certainly remained with the Junction box. It is a moot point whether trains proceeding only to the siding and back would have needed the branch Staff.

The box outlasted the shortlived ballast siding, probably because of its function in controlling the double/single line points, but was then abolished at an unknown date (6) and these points made spring points (sprung for up trains, run through by down trains). When the new junction box opened in 1927 these points were made wire-worked.

When the ballast siding reopened in 1931 a 2-lever open ground frame was provided, released by Annett's Key on the Tablet (later ETS). It was taken out of use c1956.

The double/single line points, with the Sewage Farm occupation crossing beyond, c1980.
(Chris Turner)

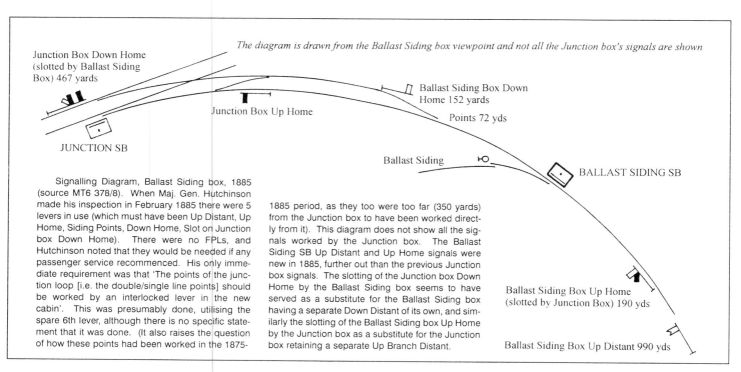

Junction Box Down Home
(slotted by Ballast Siding
Box) 467 yards

The diagram is drawn from the Ballast Siding box viewpoint and not all the Junction box's signals are shown

Ballast Siding Box Down
Home 152 yards

Points 72 yds

Junction Box Up Home

JUNCTION SB

Ballast Siding

BALLAST SIDING SB

Ballast Siding Box Up Home
(slotted by Junction Box) 190 yds

Ballast Siding Box Up Distant 990 yds

Signalling Diagram, Ballast Siding box, 1885 (source MT6 378/8). When Maj. Gen. Hutchinson made his inspection in February 1885 there were 5 levers in use (which must have been Up Distant, Up Home, Siding Points, Down Home, Slot on Junction box Down Home). There were no FPLs, and Hutchinson noted that they would be needed if any passenger service recommenced. His only immediate requirement was that 'The points of the junction loop [i.e. the double/single line points] should be worked by an interlocked lever in the new cabin'. This was presumably done, utilising the spare 6th lever, although there is no specific statement that it was done. (It also raises the question of how these points had been worked in the 1875-

1885 period, as they too were too far (350 yards) from the Junction box to have been worked directly from it). This diagram does not show all the signals worked by the Junction box. The Ballast Siding SB Up Distant and Up Home signals were new in 1885, further out than the previous Junction box signals. The slotting of the Junction box Down Home by the Ballast Siding box seems to have served as a substitute for the Ballast Siding box having a separate Down Distant of its own, and similarly the slotting of the Ballast Siding box Up Home by the Junction box as a substitute for the Junction box retaining a separate Up Branch Distant.

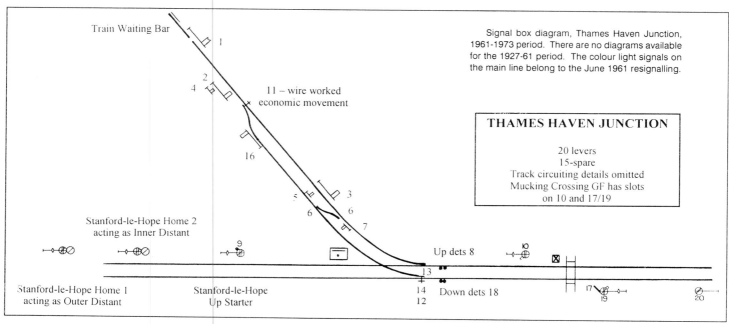

Train Waiting Bar

Signal box diagram, Thames Haven Junction, 1961-1973 period. There are no diagrams available for the 1927-61 period. The colour light signals on the main line belong to the June 1961 resignalling.

11 – wire worked
economic movement

THAMES HAVEN JUNCTION

20 levers
15-spare
Track circuiting details omitted
Mucking Crossing GF has slots
on 10 and 17/19

Stanford-le-Hope Home 2
acting as Inner Distant

Up dets 8

Stanford-le-Hope Home 1
acting as Outer Distant

Stanford-le-Hope
Up Starter

Down dets 18

left and right No accident worthy of a Board of Trade report has ever occurred on the branch, but one did make for local interest on 16th July 1926 when a down goods collided with a lorry belonging to Mr J. Richards on the occupation crossing at 27m 27ch. By chance this gives us a view of Thames Haven Junction Up Distant signal, a timber post Railway Signal Co product of c1900, with the straight stripe on the arm favoured by the LT&SR.

(The late Harry Hearn, courtesy Bill Hearn)

top Fisons Sidings Ground Frame, looking west c1980, when it was still seeing good use. It was renamed 'British Dredging GF' about this time, but the 'Fisons' name stuck in practice! Originally released by the ETS, with an auxiliary instrument and 'shut-in' facilities provided, this GF was from 1973 released instead by Low Street panel (switch 71). Lever 1 worked the FPL (and release), 2 the points, and 3 an elevated miniature semaphore signal for trains leaving the sidings (hidden by the bushes). Although the connection was secured out of use by 1995, the GF and pointwork are still in situ, unusable, in 1998.

second The western end of Curry Marsh sidings, also looking west c1980. When these sidings opened in 1949 there were two 3-lever ground frames, Shell No. 1 and Shell No. 2, both on the north side, released by the ETS. Shutting in facilities were not provided until 1966. On the 19.8.1973 resignalling of the branch, replacement GFs were provided (both on the south side). The new No.1 GF had four levers as it also worked a new position light signal under signal L39, for entry to the sidings. It was released by Low Street panel. The bogie tanker wagons are in the western end of the BR sidings. Introduced in the mid 1960s, these 100-ton bogie tankers became the mainstay of oil traffic in the 1970s and '80s, but 4-wheel tankers remained in use also.

third The eastern end of Curry Marsh, also looking west. In the foreground is Pump House level crossing, an additional occupation crossing installed c1950 in connection with the development of the Shell 'West Site'. It was a manned crossing and the attendant's hut (right) was almost certainly one of the 1922 huts from the branch Halts, moved here for reuse. This crossing closed in 1983 when the new Hydrocracker LC 9 chains further east opened. At left beyond the crossing is the 1973 replacement Shell No. 2 GF. This was released by Thames Haven panel at first, and by Low Street panel post-1983. Like Fisons Sidings GF, the two Shell GFs had been secured out of use prior to the 1996 branch resignalling, but remain in situ.

bottom The LATHOL 'Western connection' and West End level crossing, looking west c1980. The level crossing was new around 1901 when the European Petroleum Co site was being built up. It was a manned crossing, with iron gates worked by a LATHOL 'patrolman', on 24 hour duty. A 1936 LMS survey reported 100 vehicles a day but the patrolman had no communication with the signalling system, and worked 'on sight'. Lifting barriers replaced the gates in 1960 but on 30.6.1967 it became an early Automatic Open Crossing, with twin red flashing traffic lights and rail white indicator lights, and a 10mph speed restriction. The crossing closed in 1983 when Hydrocracker Crossing opened.

The siding connection was, when opened in 1902, worked by a 1-lever open GF released by Annett's Key on the Train Staff. At first named European Petroleum Co GF, it became known as West End GF after the LATHOL takeover. In 1916 it was replaced by a 3-lever Midland 'stage', released by Annett's Key held by the 'Pilot Guard' (lever 1 spare, lever 2 combined FPL and points, lever 3 'Home Signal' - spare from 1961 when Terminus GF took over this signal). This in turn was replaced on 19.8.1973 by the 2-lever open GF seen here (lever 1 FPL & release, lever 2 points), released by Thames Haven panel. The GF was abolished on 27.3.1983 when this connection, now adapted to access the new 'Shellhaven Sidings' terminal, was put on to Low Street panel direct.

(All - Chris Turner)

PETROLEUM STORAGE CO'S SIDING SIGNAL BOX

This siding was brought into use about April 1878 (see Chapter 7). As with the case of the Junction Ballast Siding, the LT&SR felt obliged to build a signal box here because of the demanding attitude of the Board of Trade at this period. Hutchinson describes it as a 'raised cabin'. There are no known photographs of it, and no known references to the contract for the work, though it is most likely that Easterbrook's were responsible. It is doubtful if it was ever a regularly-manned location (it is not included in the list of signal boxes produced by the LT&SR from 1897 on for signalmen's grading purposes) and it did not participate in block working (which continued to be between Thames Haven Junction and Thames Haven station). Effectively, therefore, it was just a glorified ground frame by function, released by Annett's Key on the Train Staff.

In 1901 when the European Petroleum Co Siding was about to be installed only 17 chains to the west, there were notions of replacing this box with a new box in between which could work both connections. But this did not come to pass, probably because of a recognition that there was no need for such boxes on what had become a quiet goods-only branch.

The box (which was really an anachronism) was replaced by a 1-lever Midland 'stage' known as LATHOL East End GF in (probably) 1916 (7), released by Annett's Key held by the Pilot Guard.

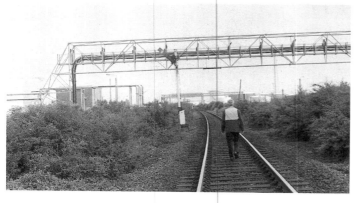

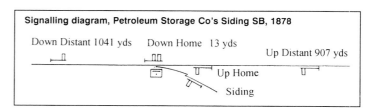
THAMES HAVEN STATION BLOCK POST AND SIGNAL BOX

In order to discuss the signalling arrangements at Thames Haven Station/Yard, we must depart from a strict 'line order' approach as the earlier signalling locations were at the old station whereas the later installations (discussed in the next section) were in the Dock House level crossing vicinity.

As mentioned previously, the Thames Haven station office acted as telegraph 'Block Post' from the start. There were Distant (8) and Home signals (the latter, which may have been Home plus Starting on one post, is shown on the 1863 OS at p.30). These signals, and the points, would have been worked by individual levers. Had the passenger service not ended in 1880 the station would almost certainly have been interlocked in 1880/1 when all the other LT&SR stations not yet interlocked were dealt with. As things were, it was left until c1889, when a signal box was built and full interlocked signalling installed as part of the improvement works of that time (9). The signals are shown on the 1895 OS at p.30 but there is insufficient information to attempt a signal box diagram. It is not known whether the block working was transferred from the station office to the box; there was probably a full-time signalman initially so it may have been (for a few years).

With the enormous reduction in train and shunting moves after the cattle traffic ended in 1895, this signal box became a white elephant. There was already no signalman as such by 1897 (10) but the box remained in use to work the signals and points, presumably staffed by one of the porters as necessary. In 1908 it was still seeing some sort of use, as the WTT of that year states

'Drivers of all Engines and Trains running to Thames Haven are to pull up at the Station signal box and wait Hand Signal before proceeding into the station yard'

which rather implies that the signals had passed out of use.

After that there is silence; the box seems to have finally fallen out of all use and been demolished around 1914 (11).

The station office remained (or resumed being!) the Block Post until 1953.

(The 1908 WTT also tells us that Shunting Horns were in use at Thames Haven for shunting on the pier and in the station yard).

THAMES HAVEN INSPECTOR'S OFFICE BLOCK POST AND PANELS, AND MANOR WAY AND TERMINUS GROUND FRAMES

As explained earlier in this chapter, the new Inspector's Office building at the Dock House level crossing served as the 'Block Post', with Miniature Electric Train Staff instrument, from its opening in 1953 to the end of block working as such in 1973.

The 1922 Manor Way Ground Frame stage (also referred to earlier) was close by and worked the running line points in the immediate proximity. The Inspector had direct charge of this GF (the key being held by him in his 'Pilot Guard' role).

In November 1961 the additional 2-lever open Terminus Ground Frame was provided to work the First and Second Home signals, but it was then realised that there was no real purpose in having two ground frames so close, so around 1962 Manor Way GF was abolished, a third lever added to Terminus GF to work the Reedham Sidings points, and the other two connections reduced to hand points (which was acceptable now that the Workmen's service had ended).

With the end of ETS working in 1973, Thames Haven could no longer properly be called a 'Block Post', but the Inspector's (Supervisor's) Office remained in charge of operations. As in 1961/2, there was a 'change of mind' over the 1973 changes here. A new 7-lever Terminus GF was installed in lieu of the 1961 GF, but it was then decided to install a panel in the office instead (or as well). In the event the functions were shared between the two (and, with only two GF levers in use, the whole purpose of having replaced the previous GF evaporated!).

In 1983 there was a further change. A second panel was added to work the new Up Starting signal and the new Down Second

p72 upper Where it all began - the 1878 Petroleum Storage Co private siding connection, which was never altered until removed altogether in 1983. The 1878 signal box was on the south side where the cabinet is here. The 1916 East End GF 'stage' was on the north side; it was replaced in 1973 by a 2-lever open GF released by Thames Haven panel which is however hidden by bushes in this view! The Advanced Warning Board is for West End LC. At left is the ex-LATHOL tanker loading area.

p72 middle The Down Second Home signal of 1961, known as the Down Third Home after 1973. The Sighting Committee had decided on a 15ft post and 3ft 9in arm. This signal was normally left off except when the Reedham Sidings connection was being shunted. Replaced by a colour light in the 1983 resignalling, this was the last semaphore running signal on the branch.

p72 bottom No. 43 Gate Level Crossing, a LATHOL occupation crossing, was opened c1910 and had a similar history to West End Crossing, being originally a manned crossing worked by a LATHOL Patrolman without the benefit of any communication. 130 lorries a day were recorded in 1936. Lifting barriers replaced the 'large iron gates' in 1960, and the conversion to Automatic Open crossing took place on 23.4.1969. Note the striped poles for the train driver's white indicator lights. In this c1980 eastward view the stops of Reedham Sidings are seen beyond the crossing. The area at left foreground had been 'LATHOL Halt' in the 1923-58 period, and prior to that had been the site of one of the c1910 LATHOL coal-unloading platforms.

(3 photos Chris Turner)

upper Looking west from Dock House LC in March 1952, with the 1916 crossover in the foreground, the CLR heading off at right, and the branch running line curving away to the left (with Reedham Sidings points). The 1922 Manor Way GF 'stage' (open hut) had taken a lean by this date!
(Frank Church)

middle In this c1980 eastward view, the Reedham Sidings points are in the foreground with the rodding run from Terminus GF at right. The photographer's minder is just passing the site of Manor Way GF. The CLR (left) had acquired a rounding loop by this date, and this 'Stop Board', brought into use in 1961 after a two-year grinding of the organisational wheels (and some pondering over whether a signal might be desirable).
(Chris Turner)

The second storey added to the 1953 office building in 1964 is seen to good effect in this June 1982 westward shot towards Dock House LC. The Shell (East Site) sidings connections appear at bottom right. Terminus GF is by the lamp post beyond the crossing. The panels were in the ground floor room at the west end of the 1953 building.

(Peter Kay)

An eastward shot from the same spot, c1980. The original 1916 Shell siding passes through the 'arch' at centre left, the additional connection of c1955 through the gate at centre. One of the Shell Thomas Hill locos is seen beyond. At right there are bogie tankers in Nos. 15, 16, and 17 sidings. The 'Halt' area at right foreground has now lost all signs of its former use.

(Chris Turner)

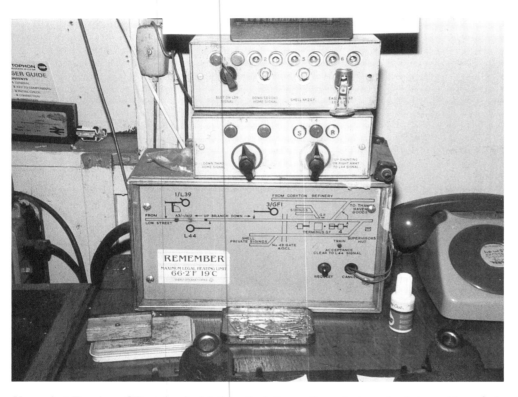

The Thames Haven Supervisor's (ex Inspector's) Office panels, in December 1989. The '1973' panel is at top, with only switch 1 in use; 2, 5, and 6 having been out of use since 1983. It will be seen that this switch panel was actually made without any switch 3 or 4, it having been decided that Terminus GF would, after all, work these functions. The '1983' panel (next beneath) had two switches numbered 3 and 4 for the new signals (but 3 is wrongly labelled 'Down Third Home Signal' instead of 'Down Second Home Signal'!). The diagram (bottom) dated from 1973 as such, but was wholly refaced for the revised layout in 1983 as seen here. Telephone to Low Street box at right.

(John Talbot)

Home, but Terminus GF retained a 'slot' on the latter as the easiest way of securing interlocking between the signal and the Reedham sidings points.

Finally in April 1996 the panels and Terminus GF were abolished and all signalling removed save for Stop Boards.

The level crossing here, referred to as 'Dock House' in this book to avoid confusion, but also often called 'Manor Way' in official railway parlance (and 'Pig' or 'Pig Gate' by some unofficially), was originally an unstaffed occupation crossing but after 1953 there were staff on site to mitigate against accidents, and lifting barriers were installed by 1960.

(1) Cf the fact that the 1885 works at the Junction Ballast Siding were put up for BoT inspection, but subsequent new works in 1901, 1916 and 1918 were not (works on goods-only lines not being inspectable).

2) LT&SR Board 25.6.1875 was told by Stride that he had 'arranged' to introduce Train Staff working, and Board 2.7.1875 that 'the Train Staff system on the branch works well'; the bringing into use date therefore falls in between.

3) Exact date not known; it must have been after the transfer of the LT&S section to the ER in 1949, but it was before the 1954 SOI. It may have been coincident with the transfer of staff to the new Inspector's office in 1953.

4) No specific dates are known for this but it was done prior to the April 1996 resignalling, which however reinforced the situation as none of these connections could be restored to use under the post-1996 signalling system, whereas prior to April 1996 any of them could have been brought back into use readily if any need had arisen. The securing out of use of the two Shellhaven sidings connections was clearly only effected some time in c1994/5 (after the 1993 end of traffic).

5) In the main resignalling notice EA-1 of February 1996, this was wrongly stated to still be the intention. The correct information for the revised scheme was given in Weekly Notice No. 2 of 6th - 12th April 1996.

6) Still there on 1895 OS, gone by 1917 2 chain survey, no other information.

7) The box is still included (as 'Petroleum Co's siding') in the fogging lists in the 1908 LT&SR WTT. The 1915 plan in RAIL 491/788/1 does not show how the connections are worked. The box is gone by the 1919 OS and 1920 2 chain survey.

8) Confirmed by the 'fogging' list in the 1884 WTT.

9) No reference has been found to the provision of this box. The work would most likely have been done by the Railway Signal Co, and the box was most likely a RSCo timber box, but no photographs are known.

10) LT&SR lists of signalmen's posts, first produced 1897, do not include Thames Haven.

11) Still shown on the '1913' plan in RAIL 491/788/1, but absent on the 1915 plan in RAIL 491/788/2, the 1919 OS, and the 1920 Midland 2 chain survey. The post-1908 WTTs do not contain any instructions at all and so do not help us.

APPENDIX

LONDON & THAMES HAVEN OIL WHARVES LTD LOCOMOTIVES

NAME/NUMBER	TYPE	BUILDER	ACQUIRED	DISPOSED OF
—	0-4-0 PM	Baguley 566 (1916)	new 1916	Scrapped 1917
(2)	0-6-0 fireless	Andrew Barclay 1553 (1917)	2h 19xx	Scrapped 1966
(3)	0-4-0 fireless	Andrew Barclay 1472 (1916)	2h 19xx	Sold 1955
(4)	0-6-0 fireless	Andrew Barclay 1551 (1917)	2h 19xx	Scrapped 1966
— (LMS 7051, WD 70027)	0-6-0 diesel-mech.	Hunslet 1697 (1932)	2h 1949	Sold 1951
—	0-4-0 diesel-mech.	Hunslet 4250 (1951)	new 1951	Sold 1972
—	0-4-0 diesel-mech.	Hunslet 4525 (1953)	new 1953	Sold 1972
—	0-6-0 diesel-hydr.	John Fowler 4240016 (1964)	new 1964	to Shell 1972
—	4 wheel diesel-hydr.	Thomas Hill 187v (1967)	new 1967	to Shell 1972

The Baguley proved useless and although new was scrapped. The second, third and fourth locos were probably acquired c1919. Effectively there was a requirement for three locos from then until 1949, and four from 1949 until 1972 when the LATHOL operations were integrated with Shell's and the last two locos renumbered into the Shell fleet.

SHELL (Shell Haven) LOCOMOTIVES

NAME/NUMBER	TYPE	BUILDER	ACQUIRED	DISPOSED OF
Starhaven Refineries No. 1	0-4-0 fireless	Andrew Barclay 1471 (1916)	2/h 19xx	Sold 1968
Starhaven Refineries No. 3	0-4-0 fireless	Andrew Barclay 1437 (1916)	2/h 19xx	Sold 1964
19	0-4-0 diesel-mech.	John Fowler 4210005 (1949)	new 1949	Sold 1966
20	0-4-0 diesel-mech.	John Fowler 4210007 (1949)	new 1949	Sold 1963
21	0-4-0 diesel-mech.	John Fowler 4210130 (1957)	new 1957	Sold 1979 (preserved)
22	0-4-0 diesel-hydr.	John Fowler 4220031 (1964)	new 1964	Sold 1980 (preserved)
23	0-4-0 diesel-hydr.	John Fowler 4220039 (1965)	new 1965	Sold 1980 (preserved)
—	4 wheel road/rail	Strachan & Henshaw 7509 (1968)	new 1968	c1971 (disposal nk)
(D9538)	0-6-0 diesel-hydr.	BR Swindon (1965)	2/h 1970	Sold 1970
19	0-6-0 diesel-hydr.	John Fowler 4240016 (1964)	ex LATHOL 1972	Sold 1979 (preserved)
20	4 wheel diesel-hydr.	Thomas Hill 187v (1967)	ex LATHOL 1972	Sold 1980
24	0-4-0 diesel-hydr.	Thomas Hill 239v (1972)	new 1972	Sold 1981 (to Mobil, Coryton)
25	4 wheel diesel-hydr.	Thomas Hill 279v (1978)	new 1978	Transferred 1993 to Stanlow
26	4 wheel diesel-hydr.	Thomas Hill 280v (1978)	new 1978	Transferred 1993 to Stanlow
27	4 wheel diesel-hydr.	Thomas Hill 281v (1978)	new 1979	Transferred 1995 to Stanlow
28	4 wheel diesel-hydr.	Thomas Hill 282v (1978)	new 1979	Transferred 1995 to Stanlow

The first two locos were probably acquired c1919. Effectively there was a requirement for two locos from then until 1949; four from 1949; six from 1972 when the LATHOL site operations were integrated; then a run-down to five in 1980, four in 1981, two in 1993, and none from 1995 after regular rail operations ceased.

Information provided by Industrial Railway Society. © Industrial Railway Society 1999.

FURTHER READING

The following secondary sources may be of interest to those wishing to pursue the local or industrial history beyond the immediate railway-related subjects:-

The Thameshaven Saga - Thesis by A. M. Crowe, Brentwood Training College, 1963. (Copy at Essex CRO T/Z 38/10).

Fobbing, Life and Landscape - R. Bingley, Lejins Publishing, Stanford-le-Hope (in association with Thurrock Museum), 1997.

History of The Royal Dutch/Shell Group of Companies (Shell).

35 Years of Oil Transport - J. D. Henry, 1907 (BM copy at 8805ff39).

History of The Second World War: Oil - D. J. Payton-Smith, HMSO, 1971.

The 'East Anglian branch' face of the line is highlighted in this 2nd March 1959 photograph of the 4.25pm Thames Haven - Ripple Lane near Fison's sidings.

(Frank Church)

H. C. Casserley was another participant in the 3rd April 1954 SLS Railtour, and captured this further view of 41985 shunting at Thames Haven on that date. The Pumping House for the water tank features at left.

(H. C. Casserley)